Biology of Spiders

Biology of Spiders

Rainer F. Foelix

Harvard University Press
Cambridge, Massachusetts, and London, England

Translated from the original German edition, *Biologie der Spinnen*
  (copyright © 1979 by Georg Thieme Verlag, Stuttgart)

Library of Congress Cataloging in Publication Data

Foelix, Rainer F., 1943–
    Biology of spiders.

        Translation of: Biologie der Spinnen.
        Bibliography: p.
        Includes index.
        1. Spiders.   I.   Title.
QL458.4.F6313   595.4′4   81-13269
ISBN 0-674-07431-9 (cloth)   AACR2
ISBN 0-674-07432-7 (paper)

Preface

Not long ago the spiders were the most neglected of the most interesting animals . . .

T. H. Savory, 1962

SPIDERS have always been treated as a minority group. Oddly enough, spiders have been largely ignored by most biologists, although quite a few people are fascinated by them. Many universities have large entomology departments, but few have an arachnology section. One objective of this book is to demonstrate that the achievements of spiders can well compete with those of crustaceans and insects; in fact, their evolutionary success has been attained largely at the expense of the insects.

The most recent books on the biology of spiders were published by T. H. Savory in 1928 and by E. Nielsen in 1932. Needless to say, arachnology has progressed immensely since then. Although there exist some newer and quite excellent books on the natural history of spiders, such as W. S. Bristowe's *The World of Spiders* (1958) or W. J. Gertsch's *American Spiders* (1949, 1979), no recent author has really attempted to pull together the various biological facets of a spider's life. The present book tries to fill this gap. Nevertheless, its aim is not to serve as a condensed handbook or as a review for the already knowledgeable arachnologist. It is meant instead for anybody interested in biology, especially for those who already find spiders particularly intriguing creatures. Those who wish to probe more deeply into specific subjects will be guided by the extensive bibliography.

The original version of this book appeared in German (*Biologie der Spinnen*, Stuttgart, Georg Thieme Verlag, 1979). The present book is a fairly close translation of that edition, although a few new paragraphs and pictures have been added and some findings reported in more recent literature have been incorporated into some chapters.

Many colleagues helped with the original edition and I want to give them credit here once again: F. G. Barth, L. Beck, R. R. Forster, W. W. Gettmann, P. Görner, M. Grasshoff, Å. Holm, H. Homann, J. S. Rovner, W.-D. Schröer, R. Wehner, and P. N. Witt. For reviewing chapters of the English translation I am grateful to D. J. Harris, H. W. Levi, P. J. Peters, N. I. Platnick, J. S. Rovner, and A. C. Whittle. Particular thanks go to my friend and colleague David Troyer, who critically checked the entire manuscript and eliminated most of my "Germanisms" as well as some inconsistencies. Rose M. Udics of Harvard University Press substantially improved the final draft, for which I am grateful. Chapter 5 was largely illustrated by Vernessa Riley; for all other drawings and diagrams I am responsible myself.

Finally, I would like to thank all those people who pointed out flaws in the original German edition. I have tried to make the appropriate corrections, but quite probably other shortcomings will come to light, for which I am, of course, fully responsible; I hope that these will not distract the reader.

Fall 1981   Rainer F. Foelix

Contents

Biology of Spiders

1

An Introduction
to Spiders

SPIDERS are distributed all over the world and have conquered all
ecological environments, with perhaps the single exception of the
air. Most spiders are relatively small (2–10 mm body length), yet
some large "tarantulas" may reach a body length of 80–90 mm.
Male spiders are almost always smaller and have a shorter life
span than females.

All spiders are carnivorous. Many are specialized as solitary
snare builders (web spiders), whereas others hunt their victims
(ground spiders or wandering spiders). Insects constitute the
major source of prey for spiders, but certain other arthropods are
often consumed as well.

A spider's body consists of two main parts, an anterior portion,
the *prosoma* (or cephalothorax) and a posterior part, the *opisthosoma* (or abdomen). These are connected by a narrow stalk, the
pedicel (Fig. 1). With respect to functions the prosoma serves
mainly for locomotion, for food uptake, and for nervous integration (as the site of the central nervous system). In contrast, the
opisthosoma fulfills chiefly vegetative tasks: digestion, circulation,
respiration, excretion, reproduction, and silk production.

The prosoma is covered by a dorsal and a ventral plate, the cara-

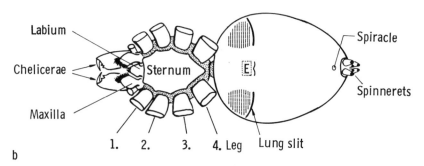

Fig. 1. External appearance of a spider's body: (*a*) Lateral view; (*b*) Ventral view; E = epigynum.

pace and the sternum, respectively. It serves as the place of attachment for six pairs of extremities: one pair of biting chelicerae and one pair of leglike pedipalps are situated in front of four pairs of walking legs. In mature male spiders the pedipalps are modified into copulatory organs—a quite extraordinary feature, not found in any other arthropod. The opisthosoma is usually unsegmented, except in some spiders considered to have evolved from ancient species (Mesothelae). In contrast to the firm prosoma, the abdomen is rather soft and sacklike; it carries the spinnerets on its posterior end.

A Sketch of Spider Systematics

At present taxonomists recognize more than 30,000 spider species, which they group into approximately 60 families. How this diversity should be arranged into a "natural" system of classification is still very much a matter of controversy. This is best illustrated by the fact that more than 18 different spider classifications have been proposed since 1900.

The order of spiders (Araneae) can be divided broadly into two suborders, the Orthognatha and the Labidognatha, on the basis of the different position of the chelicerae. Whereas all Orthognatha (for example, "tarantulas") possess horizontally directed chelicerae, which work approximately parallel to each other, the Labidognatha ("modern" spiders, considered to be more recently evolved) have vertical chelicerae, which oppose each other (Fig. 2).

Another group, the Mesothelae, although orthognath, is often regarded as a distinct suborder of its own. They constitute only the single family Liphistiidae, which represents the phylogenetically oldest spiders. In contrast to all other spiders the Mesothelae exhibit a clearly segmented abdomen, as well as several other "primitive" characters.

A division of the Labidognatha into higher taxa is somewhat problematical. The common division of this suborder into *Cribellatae* and *Ecribellatae* is based on the presence of a spinning plate (cribellum) situated in front of the spinnerets as the distinguishing character of the Cribellatae. All labidognath spiders without such a cribellum are grouped together as Ecribellatae. However, there now seems to be general consensus that Ecribellatae have evolved

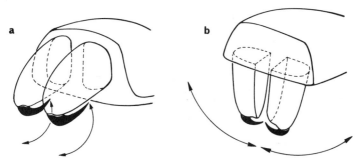

Fig. 2.   Movement of the chelicerae in (*a*) orthognath and (*b*) labidognath spiders. (After Kaestner, 1969.)

independently several times from Cribellatae and that a clear-cut phyletic division can no longer be maintained. The cribellate-ecribellate problem will be discussed in more detail in chapter 10.

Among the Ecribellatae, some spider families with simple genital structures, the so-called *Haplogynae*, can be separated from those which have complex genital structures, the *Entelegynae*. This classification dates back to Eugène Simon's *Histoire Naturelle des Araignèes* (1892–1903). Recently, however, some have voiced the opinion that the Haplogynae are not really a uniform group (Brignoli, 1975; Lehtinen, 1975; Platnick, 1975). If one accepts Simon's classification, the Entelegynae could be divided into *Dionycha* and *Trionycha*, depending on whether the walking legs have two or three tarsal claws.

Since the following text will often refer to certain spider families, the main families and their systematic position are listed here:

Order Araneae
1. Suborder Mesothelae   9 species
2. Suborder Orthognatha
    Family Theraphosidae   800
           Ctenizidae   700
           Atypidae   20
3. Suborder Labidognatha
    a. Infraorder Ecribellatae
        Haplogynae
               Scytotidae   200
               Dysderidae   250
               Pholcidae   500
        Entelegynae
            Dionycha (2 tarsal claws)
               Clubionidae   2,000
               Thomisidae   3,000
               Salticidae   4,000
            Trionycha (3 tarsal claws)
               Lycosidae   2,500
               Oxyopidae   500
               Theridiidae   2,500
               Linyphiidae   3,500
               Agelenidae   1,000
               Araneidae   2,500

b. Infraorder Cribellatae

Amaurobiidae	350
Dictynidae	500
Eresidae	100
Uloboridae	200

In order to familiarize the uniniated reader with this seemingly abstract system, the following natural history of some selected spider families will serve as an introduction.

Funnel-Web Spiders (Agelenidae)

Funnel-web spiders are familiar to most of us. In European houses, for example, we find *Tegenaria* usually in the bathroom, often trapped in the tub, where it cannot scale the smooth walls. Aside from its considerable size (10 mm body length), *Tegenaria* is quite conspicuous because of its long, hairy legs (12–18 mm) and the two long spinnerets protruding from its abdomen (Fig. 3). Outdoors we can readily find the somewhat smaller *Agelena* in short grass or low bushes. The sheet webs of agelenids usually cover vegetation, or bridge the corners of buildings. The flat web narrows like a funnel on one end, forming a small silken tube. This retreat is open on both ends, and most of the time the spider sits there in ambush, its outstretched front legs poised to receive vibrations from the web. When an insect blunders onto the web, the spider quickly darts out from its hideout, bites the victim, and carries it back. The actual feeding process always takes place inside the retreat. During the return to the tube the spider shows remarkably good orientation. For this reason funnel-web spiders have been a favorite subject for sensory physiologists (see chapter 4).

The water spider *Argyroneta aquatica* is also considered to be a member of the agelenid family. It is the only spider that lives constantly under water. Rather than build a web, she attaches an air bubble to a water plant and uses it as a residence. She hunts mostly fly larvae or small crustaceans which she catches as she swims about freely under water. To eat the prey the spider must return to her diving bell. The abdomen of the water spider is always encased in a shiny air bubble, and this silvery reflection has earned her the scientific name *Argyroneta* (Greek, *argyros* = silver). From time to time the air bag is replenished at the water surface. Thus the respiration of a water spider does not differ in principle from that of her land-living relatives.

Orb-Web Spiders (Araneidae)

The most impressive web design belongs to the orb weavers. The orb web of the common garden spider certainly represents the best-known type of all webs (Fig. 98). The spider either sits right in the center of the web or hides in a retreat outside it. Insects flying into the web become stuck to the sticky threads long enough for the spider to rush out from the hub to bite or wrap its victim.

Araneids are among the most successful spider families, as the enormous diversity of their species (>2,500) testifies. Thus it comes as no surprise to find as well hundreds of structural variations on the orb-web design. Some examples will be given in chapter 5. The body structures of araneids may also vary considerably; most notable are the tropical orb weavers, which can be very colorful and exotically shaped (Fig. 4).

An orb web is typical not only for the Araneidae but also for two other spider families, the Tetragnathidae and the Uloboridae. Uloborids build an orb web that is very similar to the webs of the araneids but that differs from them in one important aspect: the catching threads are not studded with glue droplets but are decorated instead with an extremely fine mesh of "cribellate" silk ("hackle band").

Wolf Spiders (Lycosidae)

Wolf spiders are vagabonds which lie in ambush or freely hunt their prey. They are best recognized by their characteristic eye arrangement of four uniformly small eyes in the anterior row of eyes and two large median eyes in the posterior row (Figs. 5, 9). About 2,500 different species occur all over the world, and they may vary quite a bit in size. Smaller wolf spiders (4–10 mm body length) roam freely among stones or low vegetation; only the larger representatives (*Arctosa, Trochosa, Alopecosa;* 10–20 mm) dig burrows. Certain species live close to the water and can even walk on its surface (Fig. 116). Members of the aptly named genus *Pirata* hunt insects on the water surface, or even dive after tadpoles or small fish

---

Fig. 3. (*a*) Juvenile female house spider (*Tegenaria*) sitting at the entrance of her retreat. (*b*) Typical agelenid sheet web, covered with early morning dew. (Photo *b*: Paas.)

Fig. 4. (*a*) The best known of all orb weavers, the garden spider *Araneus diadematus*. (Photo: Grocki and Foelix.) (*b*) This *Gasteracantha versicolor* from Madagascar bears long spines on its abdomen, as exotic araneids often do. (Photo: Emerit, 1969.) (*c*) A North American orb weaver, *Micrathena gracilis*, hanging on a horizontal thread. Note the position of the spinnerets (arrow).

(Gettmann, 1978). A few species of wolf spiders (*Aulonia, Hippasa*), thought to be more primitive varieties, actually build webs reminiscent of the sheet webs of agelenids.

The most famous wolf spider is certainly the Mediterranean tarantula (the name being derived from the Italian town of Taranto). True tarantulas (*Lycosa, Hogna*) can reach an impressive 30 mm of body length, but they are not related to the big tropical "tarantulas," the mygalomorphs, also known as bird spiders. Although tarantulas have long had a bad reputation as dangerous spiders, the ancient fear of their poisonous bite has been proven to be quite

Fig. 5. A female wolf spider (*Lycosa rabida*) in an attentive posture.

wrong; probably any bites alleged to be from a tarantula were in fact inflicted by black widow spiders. Tarantulas live in silk-lined burrows in the soil. Some species even construct a sort of lid to close the tube, creating a burrow quite similar to that of the trap-door spiders. At night tarantulas leave their burrows to prowl in search of insects. However, wolf spiders generally do not actively run down their prey, as their name might suggest, but sit quietly and wait until a victim happens to come by (Ford, 1978).

Wolf spiders react mainly to vibrations caused by the wing beat or by the characteristic walking pattern of the prey. Visual cues also play a role in detecting prey, but the eyes of wolf spiders perceive only a coarse image, and thus only objects very close by can serve as visual stimuli. This becomes apparent during courtship, when the dark palps or front legs of the male are waved in a species-specific manner to attract the attention of the female.

Female wolf spiders are well known for their brood care. After laying their eggs they attach the egg case to their spinnerets and carry it around wherever they go. Some weeks later, just before the young spiderlings are ready to leave the cocoon, the mother rips the cocoon wall so that the young can emerge. As soon as the spiderlings have crawled out, they clamber onto their mother's back (Fig. 151). Since they may number more than one hundred, they huddle there in several layers. They ride their mother's abdomen for about a week, then gradually disperse and take in food for the first time.

Another group of spiders, the Ctenidae, was formerly considered a separate family, but recently has been reclassified as a subfamily of the Lycosidae (Homann, 1971). The most notorious ctenid spider is the extremely poisonous and aggressive *Phoneutria fera* (Fig. 38d). A less ferocious ctenid spider, which will be mentioned in many of the following chapters, is *Cupiennius salei* from Central America (Fig. 118).

Crab Spiders (Thomisidae)

Crab spiders lie quietly in ambush and do not build webs (Fig. 6). They sit motionless on leaves or in blossoms where with attentively outstretched legs they await landing insects. Their small eyes can produce sharp images only at very short distances, yet they perceive motions as far as 20 cm away (Homann, 1934). If prey comes within reach (0.5– 1 cm), it gets seized by the spider's strong front legs and then paralyzed by its poisonous bite. The victim is sucked out through the tiny bite holes. Since its exoskeleton remains intact, the victim appears practically unharmed when the spider has finished its meal.

Crab spiders may be very colorful—they are often white or bright yellow, and some are green. To some degree adult females can adapt their coloration to the background on which they sit. Even the less colorful species are usually well camouflaged and are hard to detect among the vegetation. The name crab spider comes from their ability to walk sideways very adroitly. The family Philodromidae is often grouped together with the Thomisidae, although they bear only a superficial resemblance to crab spiders (Homann, 1975). Most notably, their legs are all of equal length, a feature typical of wandering spiders.

Jumping Spiders (Salticidae)

At least for an arachnologist the "jumpers" are among the most attractive, if not congenial, spiders. They are all rather small (3– 10 mm), with short stout legs and a square prosoma. Most con-

Fig. 6. (*a*) The crab spider *Misumenoides formosipes* is eye-catching be-cause of its bright yellow abdomen. Note the strong front legs, which are used to seize prey. (*b*) Portrait of the crab spider *Xysticus.* (Photo *b*: Bein-brech.)

spicuous are the anterior eyes, which occupy the entire front of the carapace (Fig. 7). Jumping spiders react very definitely to visual stimuli like passing insects or the approaching finger of an ob-server: first they turn to face the object, then they walk closer. They can distinguish different shapes at a distance of less than

Fig. 7. (*a*) Jumping spider about to leap off an edge. The front legs are raised; only the hind legs provide the thrust for the jump. (*b*) Portrait of the jumping spider *Heliophanus*. (Photo *b*: Chu-Wang and Foelix.)

10 cm; this limit can be observed while the spider stalks prey, and also during courtship. Males often possess conspicuously marked legs, which they use for display toward the females. The hunting behavior of jumping spiders reminds one of cats, for they stalk and pursue their prey until it is close enough for a final pounce. Long jumps up to 16 cm can be seen when a jumping spider flees. Before it jumps, the spider always attaches a safety thread to the ground, so that if it falls off an edge it will simply be held back by the thread and can quickly climb back the few centimeters to the point of takeoff.

Jumping spiders are most active during the day. They prefer sunshine; in cloudy or rainy weather they withdraw inside small silken nests. These shelters not only protect them from the environment but also permit them to molt safely, to build egg cases, and to hibernate.

2

Functional Anatomy

Prosoma

The dorsal plate of the prosoma is called the carapace. It often bears a distinct indentation along its midline (Fig. 8). This indented area extends on the inside of the carapace as a solid cuticular ridge, which serves as the attachment site for the dorsal muscles of the sucking stomach. Several furrows radiate from the dorsal groove: two shallow, diverging lines separate an anterior, cephalic part from a posterior, thoracic part. Even fainter subdivisions may be recognized laterally, pointing from the center of the carapace toward the coxae of the legs. It seems doubtful whether these furrows correspond to the original segmentation of the prosoma, although embryological studies indicate that the prosoma is formed by six fused segments.

The "head" part of the prosoma bears the eyes and the chelicerae. Most spiders have eight eyes, which are arranged in specific patterns in the various families. Usually the eyes lie in two rows (sometimes in three), and accordingly they are referred to as anterior lateral eyes (ALE), anterior median eyes (AME), posterior lateral eyes (PLE), and posterior median eyes (PME) (Fig. 9). The rela-

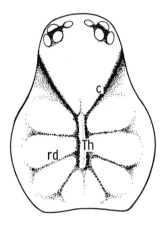

Fig. 8. Carapace of the "primitive" spider *Hypochilus,* dorsal view. Two grooves (c) extend from the thoracic furrow (Th); they separate the carapace into a "head" and a "thoracic" portion. The latter is further subdivided by radial furrows (rd).

tive position of the eyes is very important for the systematic classification of spiders. Just by looking at the arrangement and relative size of the different eyes one can often immediately determine the family of a particular spider. For example, all jumping spiders (Salticidae) possess one row of large frontal eyes, with the AME being the largest; wolf spiders have four uniformly small frontal eyes but rather large PLE and PME (Figs. 5, 9). The area between the anterior row of eyes and the edge of the carapace is called the *clypeus.*

Often the eyes stand close together in pairs, sometimes clearly raised above the surrounding cuticle, as in the Theraphosidae and Filistatidae. In their most extreme arrangement we find them perched on the ends of eye stalks, as in some midget spiders (Micryphantidae; Fig. 10). Some spiders have fewer than the usual

a   b

Fig. 9. Eye pattern in (*a*) the wolf spider *Lycosa* and (*b*) the orb weaver *Tetragnatha.* AR = anterior row of eyes, PR = posterior row of eyes. (*a* after Kaston, 1972; *b* after Bristowe, 1958.)

Fig. 10.   Aberrant position of the eyes in a male midget spider, *Walcken-aera acuminata*, and a daddy longleg spider, *Pholcus podophthalmus.* (*a* after Crome, 1957; *b* after Millot, 1949.)

eight eyes. The so-called six-eyed spiders (Dysderidae), the spitting spiders (Scytodidae), and some daddy longleg spiders (Pholcidae), have only six. In some species we find a reduction to four (*Tetrablemma,* Theridiidae) or even to two eyes (*Nops,* Caponiidae), and some cave-dwelling spiders have lost their eyes altogether (Millot, 1949).

Sternum

An undivided sternal plate (*sternum*) lies on the ventral side of the prosoma (Fig. 1). Developmentally it is derived from four fused *sternites;* the partition lines can sometimes just be discerned in very young spiders. Anteriorly, a small medial plate, the *labium,* is attached to the sternum. In most spiders the labium and sternum are hinged together by a cuticular membrane (Fig. 11). Both ster-

Fig. 11.   Mouth parts of a wolf spider (*Lycosa*) as seen ventrally. Ch = chelicerae, Lab = labium,   Mx = maxilla   (endite), St = sternum. (After Kaston, 1972.)

num and carapace are rather stiff parts of the prosomal exoskeleton. They are, however, connected by a soft pliable area, the *pleurae* (stippled area of Fig. 1), which enables them to move in relation to each other.

Chelicerae

The chelicerae are the first appendages of the prosoma. In the spider embryo they lie behind the mouth opening, but during subsequent development they migrate to an anterior position, as do the antennae of other arthropods. Each chelicera consists of two parts, a stout basal part and a movable articulated fang. Normally the fang rests in a groove of the basal segment like the blade of a pocket knife. When the spider bites, the fangs move out of their groove and penetrate the prey. At the same time poison is injected through a tiny opening at the tip of the fang (Fig. 12).

Both sides of the cheliceral groove are often armed with cuticular teeth. These act as a buttress for the movable fang. Spiders

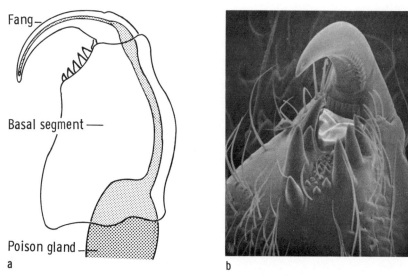

a   b

Fig. 12. (*a*) Schematic drawing of a chelicera with fang, basal segment, and poison gland. (After Millot, 1949.) (*b*) Articulation of the cheliceral fang. Note the opening of the poison gland near the tip of the fang. 90×. (Photo: Foelix and Axtell.)

Fig. 13. Comparison of the cheliceral span in orthognath (white) and labidognath spiders (black). (After Kaestner, 1969.)

whose chelicerae are equipped with such teeth mash their prey into an unrecognizable mass. Spiders without such teeth can only suck out their victims through the small bite holes. The number and size of the cheliceral teeth are important diagnostic characteristics for the taxonomist.

The chelicerae are used not only for subduing prey or for defense, but also serve as "pliers" for all kinds of grasping; therefore they have been referred to as the spider's "hands." The versatility of the chelicerae is best demonstrated when we look at their main tasks in various spider families. Trap-door spiders (Ctenizidae) use their chelicerae to dig burrows, nursery-web spiders (Pisauridae) for carrying egg cocoons, and orb weavers (Araneidae) to transport small prey. In the long-jawed orb weavers (Tetragnathidae) and the cribellate Dictynidae, the males and females interlock their chelicerae during mating. Finally, some money spiders (Linyphiidae) possess chelicerae with stridulatory organs for producing sounds (see chapter 9).

It has already been noted that Orthognatha and Labidognatha move their chelicerae in quite different manners (Fig. 2). The opposed chelicerae of Labidognatha have the advantage of a much larger span (Fig. 13), so that even rather large prey can be overpowered. Some spiders, such as the Archaeidae from Madagascar, possess extremely large chelicerae (Fig. 14a), and they literally spear their prey with these enormous tools. Often male spiders have larger chelicerae than the females (Fig. 14b). The common zebra spider, *Salticus scenicus* (Fig. 120), is a typical example of such sexual dimorphism.

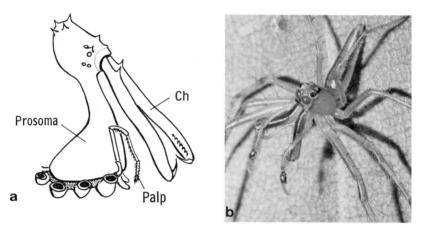

Fig. 14. Extreme development of the chelicerae (*a*) in *Archaea workmani* (after Legendre, 1972) and (*b*) in the male spider *Lyssomanes viridis* (Photo: Hill).

Pedipalps and Mouth Parts

The second pair of appendages are the pedipalps. Their segmentation corresponds to that of the legs, except that one segment, the metatarsus, is lacking (Fig. 16). Despite their general resemblance to legs, the palps are usually not used for locomotion. Instead, they often play a role during prey catching, when they constantly touch and manipulate the prey.

The most notable modification of the palps is found in male spiders. Male palps act as copulatory devices. The coxae of the pedipalps represent another specialization, for these have been transformed into chewing mouth parts (*maxillae,* or *endites*). In "primitive" spiders, such as Mesothelae and "tarantulas," the maxillae are only slightly modified, whereas in the Labidognatha they are broadened laterally. In most Labidognatha the anterior rim of each maxilla is clearly serrated; this rim, the *serrula* (Fig. 15), is used as a saw for cutting into the prey. The inner sides of the maxillae are fringed by a dense cover of hair that acts as a filter while the spider is sucking in the liquefied food.

The mouth opening is bordered laterally by the maxillae, in front by the rostrum, and in the back by the labium. These four mouth parts form the mouth proper, which leads into a flattened *pharynx*. The pharynx consists of a movable, hinged front (rostrum) and a back wall (labium) and is lined by cuticular platelets. These contain very fine grooves covered by small teeth which to-

Fig. 15. The serrula, a sawlike cuticular ridge on the palpal coxae (*Cupiennius*). 230×.

gether function as a microfilter. The pharyngeal lumen can be widened by the action of several muscle bands (Fig. 39). Thus the pharynx acts as a suction pump.

Walking Legs

Four pairs of legs fan out radially from the pliable connection between carapace and sternum. Each leg has seven segments: a *coxa* and a *trochanter*, which are both short; a long *femur* and a kneelike *patella;* a slender *tibia* and *metatarsus;* and finally a *tarsus* with two or three claws (Fig. 16). Usually the front legs (1 and 2) are relatively long, and the first pair of legs in particular is often used as feelers to probe the environment. The sensory capacity of the legs stems from a variety of sensory hairs that densely cover the distal leg segments.

Tarsal claws. The tip of the tarsus bears two bent claws which are generally serrated like a comb (Figs. 17, 18). Some spiders

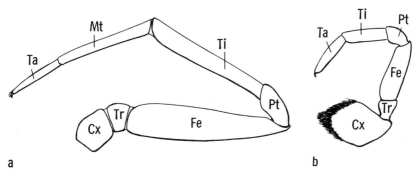

Fig. 16. Segmentation of (*a*) a walking leg and (*b*) a pedipalp. Ta = tarsus, Mt = metatarsus, Ti = tibia, Pt = patella, Fe = femur, Tr = trochanter, Cx = coxa. (After Kaston, 1972.)

(Trionycha) have an additional middle claw. All claws arise from a single cuticular platelet. They can be lifted or lowered as a unit by the action of two antagonistic muscles, the musculus levator praetarsi and the musculus depressor praetarsi (Fig. 24). The middle claw is quite important for web spiders, because they use it to catch hold of the silk threads of their webs—in fact, only the middle hook and not the big main claws grasps the thread. The thread is pushed by the middle claw against serrated bristles situated opposite the claws (Fig. 18b). There it is held, snagged in the little notches of these bristles. To release the thread, the middle claw is lifted by the musculus levator praetarsi; the inherent elasticity of the thread simply causes it to spring back out of the clasp of the claw (Wilson, 1962b).

Scopulae. Many hunting spiders possess dense tufts of hair, the scopulae, directly under the claws (Fig. 19a). In some spiders, especially in "tarantulas" (mygalomorphs), the entire ventral side of the tarsus and metatarsus may be covered by such scopula hairs. All spiders that have scopulae on their feet can easily walk on

Fig. 17.   Tip of the tarsus of the fourth leg in *Araneus diadematus*, viewed from the side. C = main claw, M = middle hook, B = serrated bristle. 1,150×.

smooth vertical walls, or even on window panes. This remarkable ability can be explained if we look at the fine structure of the scopula hairs. The ventral surface of each hair splits into thousands of fine cuticular extensions ("end feet"), giving the hair the appearance of a hand broom (*scopa* means broom in Latin). A crab spider, with only about 30 scopula hairs on each foot, can nevertheless achieve 160,000 contact points with the substrate, because each scopula hair has 500–1,000 end feet (Foelix and Chu-Wang, 1975). Thus, the actual contact between the foot and the substrate is mediated by the thousands of microscopic "end feet" (Figs. 19b–d).

The commonly held belief that the scopulae function like suction cups is erroneous. Electrostatic forces are not involved either. The spider's sure-footed grip is achieved merely by the forces of physical adhesion. Adhesion is enhanced by the capillary forces of an extremely thin water film on the substrate (Homann, 1957). If the water film is absent, as in Teflon foil, then even scopulae-equipped spiders begin to slide or fall off, although normally they can easily walk upside down on glass plates. It has been calculated that a spider weighing 3 grams would have 70 ponds of capillary force available, provided that all possible contact points are estab-

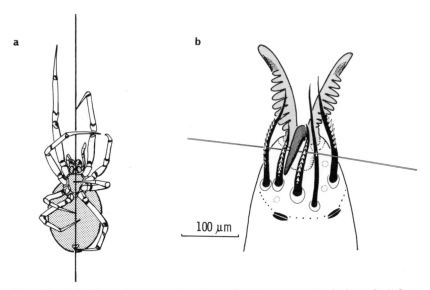

100 μm

Fig. 18. (*a*) The orb weaver *Zygiella* climbing a vertical thread. (After Frank, 1957.) (*b*) Grasping a thread: interaction of the middle hook and serrated bristles. (After Foelix, 1970a.)

Fig. 19.   Scopula hairs. (*a*) Tip of the tarsus of the jumping spider *Salticus scenicus.* The claw tuft is formed by many scopula hairs (Sc). 160×. (*b*) Part of a claw (C) and a scopula hair of a *Philodromus aureolus.* 3,600×. (Photo: Gnatzy and Foelix.) At higher magnification (*inset*) the triangular "end feet" of the scopula hair are clearly visible. 6300×. (*c*) Cross section of a scopula hair from the wolf spider *Lycosa punctulata.* The ventral side bears hundreds of cuticular extensions, but typical "end feet" are lacking. 2,850×; *inset:* 13,000×. (*d*) Horizontal section of a scopula hair (of *Lycosa*) illustrating the "footprint" that a single scopula hair produces when in contact with the substrate. 4,800×. (Photos *c, d*: Chu-Wang and Foelix.)

lished (Homann, 1957). This explains why a spider can still hold
fast when some legs are lifted during walking. Incidentally, the
same phenomenon of highly efficient adhesion forces is known in
some reptiles, such as in the skinks, which can walk sure-footedly
on walls and ceilings (Hiller, 1968). One problem that is not quite
resolved is how such a grip is loosened again. Recently it has been
suggested that a spider can, by degrees, detach its scopula hairs
hydraulically by gradually increasing the hemolymph pressure
(Rovner, 1978).

In their natural surroundings spiders with scopulae certainly
have the advantage of being able to climb securely on overhanging
rocks or leaves. Thus certain environments that normally would be
inaccessible become available. If one looks at the scopulae of various ground-living spiders, one notices that they differ structurally
and functionally. Wolf spiders, for instance, do not possess true
scopulae, but have scopulate hairs on their tarsi. Nevertheless they
cannot climb smooth walls, because their scopulate hairs have
only rudimentary "end feet" (Fig. 19c). However, the scopulate
hairs of wolf spiders are apparently used for other purposes, such
as holding down a struggling prey (Rovner and Knost, 1974;
Rovner, 1978).

Leg Joints and Musculature. The movability of the seven leg segments is determined not only by the extensive musculature but
also by the different types of joints. Most joints are dicondylous,

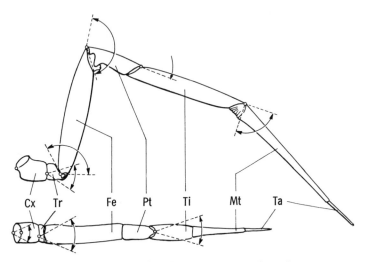

Fig. 20. Range of movement for the leg joints in the orb weaver *Zygiella.*
Top: Lateral view of leg 1. *Bottom:* Dorsal view of leg 3. For abbreviations
see Fig. 15. (After Frank, 1957.)

that is, they can move only in one plane (vertical movements; Fig. 20). In contrast, the coxa-trochanter joint represents a kind of "saddle joint" and thus can be moved forward and backward. This lateral movability is absolutely necessary for locomotion and is most important for legs 2 and 3 (see chapter 6). The joint between patella and tibia also moves laterally and assists in positioning the leg tip precisely (Frank, 1957). A so-called passive joint lies between the tarsus and metatarsus; although a hinge is present, the muscles are not involved in the movement between the two segments (Figs. 21, 24).

There is little variation in the leg musculature of different spider families. For instance, 33 different leg muscles have been described for the orb weaver *Zygiella* (Frank, 1957); the "tarantula" *Eurypelma* (synonym *Dugesiella*), with 30, has just about as many (Dillon, 1952; Ruhland, 1976). Most joints are equipped with several muscles (Fig. 21) that either bend the joint (the flexors) or stretch it (the extensors). Two remarkable exceptions are the femur-patella joint and the tibia-metatarsal joint, both of which lack extensors (Petrunkevitch, 1909). How these joints can be stretched at all has puzzled arachnologists for a long time. It has been shown only recently that the extension is caused by a hydraulic mechanism, that is, an increase in the hemolymph pressure (Ellis, 1944; Parry and Brown, 1959; R. S. Wilson, 1970, 1973; Anderson and Prestwich, 1975).

The hydraulically mediated extension of these joints can be elicited by gingerly squeezing a leg with forceps. In contrast, no such movement occurs if the leg is squeezed after its tip has been cut off. An important question is where the "pressure pump" is located within the living spider. It turns out that a contraction of the musculi laterales, which traverse the carapace vertically on both sides, leads to a reduction in the volume of the prosoma and thus to increased pressure there (Fig. 22). This hemolymph pressure has been measured directly in several spiders (Homann, 1949; Parry and Brown, 1959). In a "tarantula," pressures of 40–60 mm of mercury (Hg) were measured during rest and 100 mm Hg during walking. At maximal activity (struggling), values of 480 mm Hg were observed (Stewart and Martin, 1974). These values are generally comparable to human systolic and diastolic blood pressures, which for a twenty-year-old are normally 120 and 80 mm Hg respectively.

Histologically, all spider leg muscles are typical striated skeletal muscles. Each cell consists of many myofibrils, with light I-

Fig. 21.   Diagram of the leg musculature and its innervation in the "tarantula" *Dugesiella;* N_A, N_B = motor nerves A and B. (After Ruhland and
Rathmayer, 1978.)

bands (isotropic) and darker A-bands (anisotropic). The Z-disks,
which define the functional unit of a myofibril (the sarcomere) can
be seen clearly under the light microscope. The ultrastructure of
the contractile elements (actin and myosin) is very similar to that
of skeletal muscles of other arthropods (Fig. 23) (Zebe and Rathmayer, 1968; Sherman and Luff, 1971; Fourtner, 1973). However,

spider muscles contain only few mitochondria (Linzen and Gallowitz, 1975), and since mitochondria ultimately provide the energy for the cell, it is not surprising that spider muscles fatigue rapidly. It has been known for many years that although spiders can achieve high levels of momentary activity, they usually become exhausted after a few seconds of exertion (Bristowe and Millot, 1933).

Fig. 22. Synchronous recording of blood pressure in the prosoma and leg 2 of the "tarantula" *Dugesiella.* In the resting state the blood pressure is about 30 mm Hg. The onset of activity is marked by a concomitant increase of blood pressure in the prosoma and in the leg. (After Stewart and Martin, 1974.)

Fig. 23. (*a*) Leg musculature in the tibia of *Pholcus phalangioides,* longitudinal section. The muscle fiber pictured in the upper half is in the relaxed state. The micrograph clearly shows dark A-bands and light I-bands with distinct Z-lines. The lower muscle fiber is contracted, hence the light I-bands have almost disappeared. Mitochondria (Mit) are rare. 6,800×. *Inset:* motor nerve endings branch on the surface of the muscle and form multiple synapses (Golgi preparation). 340×. (*b*) Leg musculature in the patella of *Zygiella x-notata*, cross section. The muscle cell is subdivided into myofibrils (Mf), which radiate from the nucleus (N). Each myofibril consists of a hexagonal array of myosin filaments and of less regularly distributed thin actin filaments (*inset*, 92,000×). Two neuromuscular contacts (S) are seen on the surface of the muscle cell. 13,600×.

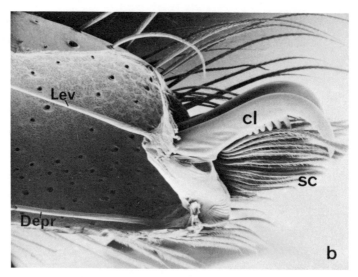

Fig. 24. Musculature of the tarsal claws. (*a*) The m. levator praetarsi (Lev) lifts the claws; the m. depressor praetarsi (Depr) lowers them. The long tendons of both muscles pass through a collar near the metatarsal joint. (*b*) Exuvium of the tarsus of *Phidippus*, opened longitudinally. Note the attachment of the cuticular tendons (Lev, Depr); cl = claws, sc = scopula. (*a* after Sherman and Luff, 1971; *b* from Hill, 1977a. Copyright © Linnaean Society of London.)

   Some muscles are elongated at one end into long "tendons." These tendons consist of fine cuticular tubes covered by a thin epithelium (hypodermis). Every time a spider molts, the cuticular part of the tendon is discarded along with the shed skin (exuvium). A typical example for such tendons is provided by the claw muscles located in the metatarsus and tibia. Their long tendons operate the claws as reins manipulate a bridle (Fig. 24).

   Innervation. The innervation of spider muscles is polyneuronal; that is, each muscle cell is supplied by several (usually three) motor nerve fibers (Rathmayer, 1965b). The nerve endings are dis-

Fig. 25.   (*a*) Cross section of the three leg nerves (A, B, C) in the femur of *Zygiella*. Nerve C is purely sensory and contains about 5,000 small fibers. Nerve B is a motor nerve consisting of about 120 large fibers. 2,400×. (*b*) The small nerve A is made up of two motor axons (Ax) and about 50 sensory axons. Peripherally the nerve fibers are enveloped by a glial cell (G1). 14,500×.

tributed over the entire length of a muscle fiber where they form numerous neuromuscular contacts (synapses; Fig. 23b).

Each spider leg is traversed by three main nerves (A, B, C). Nerve A is the smallest and contains sensory as well as motor fibers (Rathmayer, 1965a). The many thousands of nerve fibers (axons) that form the large nerve C (Fig. 25) arise from the numerous receptors on the spider leg and is thus purely sensory. Nerve B consists of rather few but large motor fibers. Physiologically, spiders have both fast and slow contracting muscle fibers, and it has recently been reported (Brenner, 1972) that slow muscle fibers have an inhibitory innervation similar to that of insect and crustacean muscles.

Leg Receptors. All leg segments are covered with various sensory hairs, discussed here only briefly (for details see chapter 4). Most of these *sensilla* are movable, articulated setae, or bristles, which function as mechanoreceptors (touch, vibration). Each leg receptor is associated with several primary sensory cells, and consequently, sensory nerves are built up by thousands of separate sensory fibers (Fig. 25; Foelix, Müller-Vorholt, and Jung, 1980).

A particularly interesting type of sensillum is the *trichobothrium*, a very thin hair set almost at a right angle to the leg axis (Figs. 26, 55). Originally the trichobothria were thought to represent hearing organs (Dahl, 1883), but nowadays they are considered "touch-at-a-distance" receptors, because they react to air currents and low-frequency air vibrations (Görner and Andrews, 1969).

Less conspicuous mechanoreceptors are the slit sensilla, which occur on all leg segments, singly or in groups (*lyriform organs;* Figs. 26, 59). The slits of the lyriform organs are usually located near the leg joints, where they measure the stress in the surrounding cuticle (Barth, 1972a, b). Inside the joints lie groups of proprioreceptors, which gather information on the position of a particular leg joint (Rathmayer, 1967; Rathmayer and Koopmann, 1970).

In addition to the mechanosensitive sensilla we also find chemosensitive hairs on all distal leg segments (Foelix, 1970b; Foelix and Chu-Wang, 1973b). These hairs are characterized by an open tip in which several nerve fibers are exposed directly to the environment. It has been known for a long time that spiders can test the chemical quality of a substrate merely by probing it with the tips of their legs. (Bristowe and Locket, 1926; Kaston, 1936; Bristowe, 1941). Another chemoreceptor, and possibly also a humidity receptor, is the so-called tarsal organ, which usually forms a spherical pit on the dorsal surface of each tarsus (Figs. 26, 65).

Fig. 26. Leg receptors. (*a*) Lateral view of a tarsus in *Agelena*. Most sensilla are simple tactile hairs (T), but a few slender trichobothria (Tr) and chemosensitive hairs (Ch) can also be seen. TO = tarsal organ, C = main claws, M = middle hook. 250×. (*b*) Dorsal view of the tarsus-metatarsus joint in *Araneus*. The metatarsal lyriform organ (Ly) lies close to the joint; the tarsal organ (TO) superficially resembles an empty hair socket. 230×.

Internal Organs of the Prosoma: An Overview

Inside the prosoma lie the central nervous system (CNS), part of the intestinal tract, a pair of poison glands, and an extensive mus-

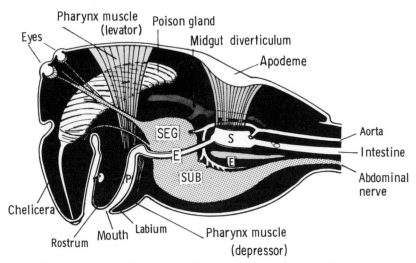

Fig. 27. Longitudinal section of the prosoma. E = endosternite, E = esophagus, P = pharynx, SEG = supraesophageal ganglion, S = sucking stomach, SUB = subesophageal ganglion.

culature (Palmgren, 1978) for the extremities, the pharynx, and the sucking stomach. Figure 27 provides a simplified picture of the spatial relationships of the various organs. A special feature is the narrow esophagus, which traverses the CNS horizontally, dividing it into a supra- and a subesophageal ganglion. Another peculiarity of spiders is the branching of the midgut. These branches (diverticula) extend into the entire prosoma and may even enter the leg coxae (Fig. 41). Similar gut diverticula fill the abdomen, but there they are further subdivided into many lobules. A more detailed description of the prosomal organ systems follows in chapters 3 and 4.

Opisthosoma

An Overview of the Internal Organs

The midgut enters the opisthosoma through the narrow stalk of the pedicel. Many lobed diverticula branch off the main tract before it widens into the large stercoral pocket (Figs. 28, 30). From there a short hindgut connects to the anus. Embedded between the many branched gut diverticula are: the heart and the abdominal

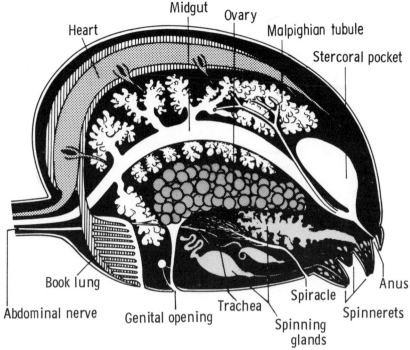

Fig. 28. Longitudinal section of the opisthosoma of a female spider.

arteries; the excretory organs (Malpighian tubules), which empty into the stercoral pocket; the respiratory organs (book lungs and tubular tracheae); the reproductive organs (ovaries and testes); and the various spinning glands, which are connected to the spinnerets via long ducts.

Segmentation

In most spiders the opisthosoma is soft and expansible. It usually shows no trace of segmentation. Only the Mesothelae, believed to represent an ancient form from which present day spiders are derived, possess a clearly segmented abdomen. A close look at the opisthosoma in this suborder provides an idea of its basic organization for all spiders.

Twelve abdominal segments can be distinguished in all. Each consists of a dorsal *tergite* and a ventral *sternite*. Both parts are connected by the pliable pleurae (Fig. 1), which are not segmented, but form a continuous band on each side (Fig. 29). The first abdom-

inal segment is merely a small stalk (pedicel) that unites the prosoma and the opisthosoma. The next segments (2–6, or body segments 8–12) are the largest, and in these the tergites are most
easily recognizable. The posterior segments (7–12) become gradually smaller and terminate in the anal tubercle (segment 12).

Looking at the ventral side, the second sternite is by far the largest. Its posterior margin forms the entrance to the respiratory
organs (book lungs) and to the reproductive organs (epigastric furrow). In the Mesothelae a second pair of book lungs lies underneath the sternite of the third segment. This second pair is, however, lacking in most other spiders. The fourth and fifth sternites
each carry a pair of spinnerets. The next sternites (6–12) are not as
clearly marked and are recognizable only as a series of ventral furrows. As can be seen from Figure 29, the spinnerets of the Mesothelae lie approximately in the midregion of the abdomen, but in all
other spiders they are always situated caudally. The terminal position of the spinnerets is the result of a longitudinal expansion of
the third sternite during phylogeny such that the spinnerets became displaced posteriorly. Immediately in front of the spinnerets,
at the borderline between the third and the fourth sternite, another respiratory opening (*spiracle*) can be seen in many spiders.
This is the entrance to the tubular tracheae.

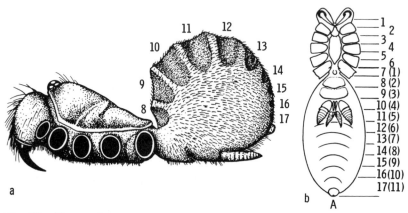

Fig. 29.   External segmentation of the opisthosoma of *Liphistius*. (After
Millot, 1949.) (*a*) Lateral view: the platelike tergites are marked with the
numbers of the respective body segments. (*b*) Ventral view: two pairs of
book lungs are illustrated on segments 8 and 9; segments 10 and 11 bear
two pairs of spinnerets each. A = anus. Numbers in parentheses refer to
the *abdominal* segments.

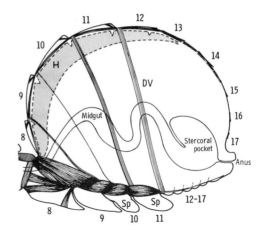

Fig. 30. Internal segmentation of the opisthosoma in *Liphistius.* Well-developed longitudinal muscles connect the segments ventrally, whereas the dorsal longitudinal muscles are inconspicuous. Dorsoventral muscles (DV) connect tergite and sternite of the same segment. H = heart, Sp = spinnerets. (After Millot, 1949.)

The segmentation of the opisthosoma is visible not only externally but also in the internal organization of the abdomen. This becomes obvious when one considers the abdominal musculature (Fig. 30). On the one hand, a segmentally arranged longitudinal musculature traverses the abdomen dorsally from tergite to tergite and ventrally from sternite to sternite. On the other hand, some muscles run intrasegmentally (that is, within a single segment) in a dorsoventral direction, connecting the corresponding tergites and sternites. The heart is also segmentally organized. In spiders with a transparent cuticle the heart tube is visible from the outside along the dorsal midline of the opisthosoma. On either side of this line are several small indentations of the cuticle (*apodemes*) that serve as insertion sites for the dorsoventral musculature. The serial arrangement of apodemes is further evidence of segmentation.

Exoskeleton

As members of the arthropods, spiders possess a hard external body shell, the exoskeleton. The exoskeleton is made of a stiff material called the *cuticle.* The function of the cuticle is manifold: it is the building material of the entire body surface, the joint membranes, tendons, apodemes, sensory hairs, and even the lining of the respiratory and reproductive organs. Apart from its purely structural function, the cuticle also serves to protect the spider and prevents dessication of its body (Nemenz, 1954; 1955). Spider cuticle is quite similar in composition to insect cuticle (Barth, 1969;

Fig. 31. Cuticle (C) of a wolf spider after Mallory staining. In the prosoma (*a*) three layers (exo-, meso- and endocuticle) are apparent, whereas the opisthosoma (*b*) is made up mainly of endocuticle. 670×. (*c*) Electron microscopical view of the leg cuticle in *Zygiella*. Endo- and mesocuticle exhibit the typical lamellar structure. P = pigment granules of hypodermis cells, Pc = pore canals. 32,000×.

1970), and accordingly, various layers of epi-, exo-, meso-, and endocuticle can be distinguished (Fig. 31). In contrast to most insects, however, spiders possess a mesocuticle even in the adult stage.

The epicuticle is extremely thin, and because it forms the outermost layer, it determines the permeability properties of the entire cuticle. Mechanically abraded epicuticle is replaced by material supplied by the pore canals, which traverse the cuticle layers vertically and terminate at the surface. The exocuticle, lying just beneath the epicuticle, is much thicker. It consists of many stacked

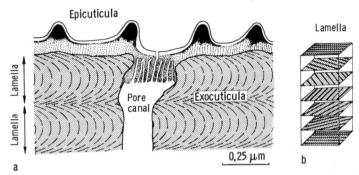

Fig. 32. Epicuticle and part of the exocuticle of *Cupiennius*. (After Barth, 1969.) (*a*) The lamellae of the exocuticle are traversed by a pore canal that splits into delicate channels shortly before reaching the epicuticle. (*b*) Each cuticular lamella consists of many parallel layers of differently oriented microfibers; in sections this gives the impression of arcuate structures as pictured in (*a*). (After Barth, 1973a.)

lamellae (Figs. 31, 32), which are structures also characteristic of the meso- and endocuticle.

Each lamella is composed of microfibers that are ostensibly arranged in a paraboloid fashion. After careful analysis, however, it becomes apparent that each lamella is made up of many thin

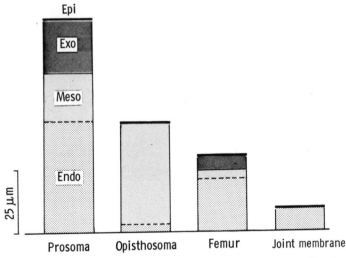

Fig. 33. Composition of the cuticle in different body regions (*Cupiennius*). The hard exocuticle is well developed in the prosoma and the legs (femur), but is lacking in the opisthosoma and the joint membranes. (After Barth, 1973a.)

layers of microfibers (Barth, 1973a); these microfibers are oriented in the same direction within any given layer but change their direction by increments from layer to layer so that a complete rotation (180°) of the fiber direction takes place within one lamella (Fig. 32b).

From a technological viewpoint the cuticle is thus a kind of laminated composite material. Its basic component is a protein into which the microfibers, made of chitin, a polysaccharide, are incorporated. This construction confers great strength and, at the same time, high elasticity to the cuticle. Most likely, it is the exocuticle that is toughest, and hence this layer is most responsible for the overall qualities of the cuticle. This becomes evident in the soft cuticle of the opisthosoma or of the joint membranes: there an exocuticle is lacking altogether (Fig. 33). In contrast, the stiff sensory hairs consist almost entirely of exocuticle, as do the shed skins (exuvia) after a molt. Although endo- and mesocuticle do not differ in their structure, they react differently to certain dyes (for example, Mallory stain; Fig. 31a). Since the endocuticle is the last cuticular layer to be secreted by the epithelial cells, it seems that the meso-

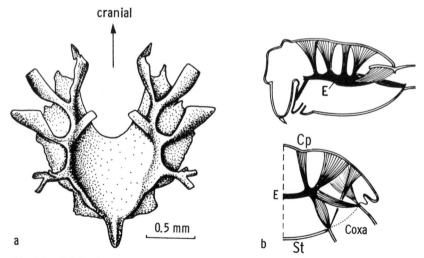

Fig. 34. (*a*) Endosternite from the prosoma of *Araneus*, dorsal aspect. The lateral processes serve as insertion sites for muscles. (After Gerhardt and Kaestner, 1938.) (*b*) Endosternite (E) with attached muscles: (*top*) longitudinal section; (*bottom*) corresponding cross section of one-half of the prosoma. Cp = carapace, St = sternum. (After Whitehead and Rempel, 1959.)

Fig. 35. (a) Endosternite of the house spider *Tegenaria,* longitudinal section. The endosternite (Es) consists of a fibrous matrix which is secreted by connective tissue cells (CT). The muscle cells (M) interdigitate directly with the endosternite. 4,400×. (b) The attachment of a muscle cell (M) to the leg cuticle (Cu) is always mediated by an intercalated tendon cell (T). Note the conspicuous desmosomal connections between tendon cell and muscle cell. The tendon cells are tightly packed with microtubules, which probably transmit tension from the muscle to the cuticle. 21,000×. (Photo *b*: Choms and Foelix.)

cuticle is simply an already more sclerotized form of cuticle. The pore canals mentioned earlier constitute the direct connection between epithelial cells and the cuticular surface. They measure 1–2 μm in width and spiral through the cuticular lamellae. Only near the epicuticle do they begin to fan out into finer canals (Figs. 31c, 32).

In addition to the exoskeleton, the underlying epithelium (hypodermis), which secretes the cuticle, also belongs to the integument. It has often been claimed, from light microscopical observations, that the hypodermis is syncytial, because cell borders are usually unrecognizable. All electron-microscopic investigations, however, have shown convincingly that the epithelial cells are separated by cell membranes. The epithelial cells normally form a single layer, yet other cells, for example sensory and gland cells, may be interspersed among them. Each epithelial cell may contain inclusions such as pigment granules or guanine crystals.

Endoskeleton

It is a little-known fact that spiders also possess an internal skeleton. Parts of the exoskeleton invaginate into the body. Such invaginations are termed *apodemes* or entapophyses, and they serve as attachment points for muscles. A typical example is the tergal apodeme (Fig. 27), which projects from the thoracic groove of the carapace into the prosoma and provides the attachment site for the dorsal muscles of the sucking stomach. Besides this ectodermal endoskeleton, spiders also have mesodermal skeletal elements, called *entosterna*. The mesodermal endoskeleton is quite different from the ectodermal exoskeleton. Chitin fibers, which are typical for the exoskeleton, are completely lacking in the endoskeleton (Cutler and Richards, 1974).

Histologically, the entosterna resemble the cartilage of vertebrates. Connective tissue cells secrete a homogeneous substance into which collagen fibers are incorporated (Baschwitz, 1973). The largest of these entosterna is the *endosternite*, a bowl-like platelet that lies in the middle of the prosoma (Figs. 34, 35). The many lateral projections of the endosternite serve for the attachment of the lateral stomach muscles and also for muscles of the limbs. Additional but smaller entosterna lie between various muscle strands in the opisthosoma (Fig. 30). It is noteworthy that the muscle cells are inserted *directly* into the entosterna. In contrast, the muscles attached to the exoskeleton always possess a specialized intercalated epidermal cell, the tendon cell (Smith, Järlsfors, and Russell, 1969; Baschwitz, 1974). During molting the muscles do not really detach from their insertion points; they always maintain their connection with the tendon cells.

3

Metabolism

SPIDERS have developed an unusual mode of food intake: digestion
is initiated outside the body. After the prey has been subdued by a
poisonous bite or wrapped with silk, the spider vomits some digestive fluid from the intestinal tract onto the victim. After a few seconds a drop of the predigested liquid prey is sucked in and this process is then repeated many times.

Feeding behavior differs markedly among the various spider
families and depends on whether cheliceral teeth are present or
not. Theridiids and thomisids, which lack cheliceral teeth, inflict
only a small wound on their prey. The digestive fluid is pumped in
and out through this hole, and the dissolving tissue is gradually
sucked out. After the meal the prey remains as an empty shell that
appears externally unharmed. Spiders with cheliceral teeth mash
up their prey so that it can hardly be identified afterwards. For instance, when an orb weaver has finished with a fly, it leaves only a
small ball of conglomerated cuticular parts. Similarly, after a
large "tarantula" has captured a frog, the combined action of the
digestive fluid and the continuous mashing of the chelicerae soon
produces an unrecognizable mass of tissue with only a few protruding bones (Gerhardt and Kaestner, 1938).

Although spider poison may contain some proteolytic enzymes (Kaiser and Raab, 1967), it plays an insignificant role in actual digestion. Only a little is known about the glands situated inside the maxillae and the rostrum. Probably their secretions serve mainly as saliva to soften the food.

Poison Glands and Toxicity

All spiders except for the family Uloboridae possess a pair of poison glands located in the prosoma (Figs. 27, 36). Each poison gland consists of a long cylindrical part and an adjoining duct, which terminates at the tip of the cheliceral fang (Fig. 12). A conspicuous muscle layer spirals around the body of the gland and serves to expel the venom rapidly as the muscle contracts. The muscle fibers are cross-striated and have their own motor nerves, which facilitates the rapid triggering of venom release. The glandular epithelium itself is also innervated (Järlfors, Smith, and Russell, 1971); possibly this nervous supply stimulates or regulates the synthesis of poison.

In the large "tarantulas" (mygalomorphs) the poison glands are quite small and lie inside the chelicerae. In contrast, most labidognath spiders have relatively large poison glands that may extend out of the chelicerae and reach far into the cephalothorax (Fig. 36). In some extreme cases (*Filistata*, for example) the glands may be even larger and subdivided into lobules. The most curious specialization is found in the spitting spider, *Scytodes* (Fig. 37). There the gland consists of an anterior part that produces the venom and of a posterior part that produces a gluey substance (Kovoor and Zylberberg, 1972). *Scytodes* catches its prey by quickly spitting glue on it, thereby fixing it to the ground before it is poisoned (Monterosso, 1928; Dabelow, 1958).

Chemically, spider venom is heterogeneous in that it may contain many different substances. It is a mixture mostly of neurotoxic polypeptides (molecular weight 5,000–13,000), but biogenic amines and proteolytic enzymes are also present (Habermehl, 1975; Kaiser and Raab, 1967; Bachmann, 1976). Since practically all spiders have poison glands, they are all potentially poisonous — at least with regard to their normal prey. Dangerously poisonous for man, however, are only about 20–30 of the 30,000 species of spiders (Schmidt, 1973).

The prime example is certainly the black widow spider, *Latrodectus mactans*, from the family Theridiidae. The bite is extremely

Fig. 36. (*a*) Prosoma of a theridiid spider, longitudinal section. The large poison glands (Gl) extend up to the carapace. Ch = chelicerae, Cly = clypeus, SEG = supraesophageal ganglion. 100×. (*b*) The wall of a poison gland (*Tegenaria*) consists of a (spiraled) muscle layer (M) that is connected via a basal lamina (BM) to the glandular cells (Gl). Secretory droplets (S) containing poison accumulate toward the center of the lumen. 2,700×.

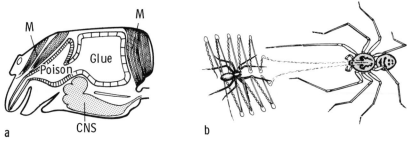

Fig. 37. (*a*) Longitudinal section of the prosoma of the spitting spider *Scytodes*. The enormous poison glands consist of an anterior portion that produces venom and a posterior part that synthesizes a glue substance. Rapid contraction of the prosomal muscles (M) squirts out a mixture of poison and glue from the chelicerae. CNS = central nervous system. (After Millot, 1949.) (*b*) Prey capture method of *Scytodes*. Prey passing within a distance of 1–2 cm is quickly (140 msec) squirted with poisonous glue and becomes paralyzed and stuck to the substrate. (After several authors.)

painful—less so at the actual site of the bite than in the lower abdomen and the limbs. Physiological effects are an accelerated heart beat, increased blood pressure, breathing difficulties, and paralysis. If death does occur, it is usually because the breathing muscles are paralyzed and the victim suffocates. Antidotes are now commercially available (for example, *Lyovac;* McCrone and Netzloff, 1965), but often an intensive clinical treatment of the heart and circulatory system is still necessary. The poison is a neurotoxin that affects the neuromuscular synapses (see Fig. 23). The synaptic vesicles become completely depleted, causing a permanent blockage of the synapse (Clark, Hurlbut, and Mauro, 1972; Griffiths and Smyth, 1973; Ceccarelli et al., 1979).

The highly effective *Latrodectus* venom consists of seven different proteins (McCrone and Hatla, 1967). As a measure for the toxicity of a given substance, the lethal dose 50 (LD_{50}) is usually given. This term refers to the dosage of venom that will kill 50% of injected experimental animals. For the venom of *Latrodectus mactans* the LD_{50} for a mouse equals 0.0009 mg per gram of body weight. As can be seen in Table 1, however, susceptibility to the venom varies greatly among different animals (Maroli, Bettini, and Panfili, 1973).

"Tarantulas" (mygalomorphs), despite their large size, are much less dangerous than is commonly thought. A tarantula bite, it is true, is deadly for mice or insects, but for a man it is hardly

Table 1. LD_{50} of venom from *Lactrodectus mactans* for various animals.

| Animal | Lethal dose 50 | |
	mg/animal	mg/g body weight
Frog	2.18	0.145
Chicken	0.19	0.002
Mouse	0.013	0.0009
Cockroach	0.015	0.0027
Fly	0.000013	0.0006

worse than a wasp sting (Schanbacher et al., 1973). The European tarantulas (Lycosidae) have never deserved their bad reputation, which has stuck to them since the Middle Ages (Crome, 1956). The symptoms of tarantism were probably related to many other causes, ranging from other spider bites, notably those of the black widow, to epilepsy. However, some tropical lycosid spiders may well be dangerous, for example, *Lycosa erythrognatha* of Brazil. After sustaining a bite the skin surrounding the injured area becomes necrotic, and secondary bacterial infections are likely to occur (Bücherl, 1956).

Another well-known spider whose bite is much feared is the American brown recluse, *Loxosceles reclusa* (Sicariidae; Fig. 38c). The bite causes local swelling as well as necrosis of the skin. In Australia, the funnel-web spider *Atrax robustus* (Dipluridae) is dangerous. Effects of the bite are severe pains, shivering, muscle cramps, loss of eyesight, and paralysis of the breathing center. In Europe, there are two other spiders one should handle cautiously, although neither is really dangerous: *Cheiracanthium* (Clubionidae) and the water spider *Argyroneta* (Agelenidae). Their bites are painful, but the symptoms (itching, shivering, vomiting, slight fever) disappear within 2–3 days (Habermehl, 1974). Most of the smaller spiders, however, cannot even pierce the human skin. In those rare cases where the skin is broken (as may happen from our garden spider), the effects, local swelling, blisters, and a slightly raised body temperature, are negligible (Maretić, 1971).

Most poisonous of all are certain ctenid spiders (Fig. 38d) of South America (Bücherl, 1953). In contrast to most other dangerous spiders mentioned above, these ctenid spiders are extremely aggressive. One representative, *Phoneutria fera*, injects about 8 mg (dry weight) of venom per bite. This amount would theoretically suffice to kill 300 mice (LD_{50} = 0.013 mg/animal).

Fig. 38.   Dangerous poisonous spiders. *Top:* (*left*) The American black widow, *Latrodectus mactans,* with the typical (red) hourglass mark on the ventral side of the abdomen. (Photo: Cooke.) (*right*) Another *Latrodectus* species from South America, dorsal aspect. The black abdomen has contrasting white and red chevron markings. *Bottom:* (*left*) A brown recluse spider (*Loxosceles*) capturing a cricket. (*right*) The ctenid *Phoneutria fera* from South America, in its typical threat posture. (Photo: Tretzel.)

Internal Digestion

The liquefied food is sucked through the narrow mouth opening by the action of the muscles of the pharynx and the stomach. An initial filtering effect is brought about by the many bristles bordering the mouth opening. A second filtration occurs in the flattened pharynx, as the food passes the rostral cuticular lining. This "palate plate" possesses a median furrow and thousands of laterally situated cuticular platelets arranged like shingles (Fig. 39). Only very small particles (< 1 μm) can pass through this filter, whereas all larger ones get caught. This can be nicely demonstrated by feeding a spider a suspension of india ink in a neutral red solution. The entire gut content will turn red but will contain only a very few grains of india ink; the ink particles become lodged in the lamellae of the palate plate (Bartels, 1930). Obviously, the spider needs to clean this filter device, and this is done with an antiperistaltic stream of digestive fluid. When a carmine dye solution was fed to a spider, it took only 30 minutes until the dye particles appeared at the mouth parts in the form of a solidified pellet. Shortly thereafter the pellet was brushed off with the palps (Zimmermann, 1934).

In the lateral walls of the pharynx lie cells which are ostensibly connected with the sense of taste (Millot, 1936). However, this con-

Fig. 39. Rostral plate in *Cupiennius*. (*a*) Inside view near the mouth opening. The liquefied food is sucked into the mouth in the direction of the arrow and is filtered at the lateral ridges. MG = median groove. 80×. (*b*) Each lateral ridge consists of cuticular platelets arranged like shingles. 200×. (*c*) Horizontal section through the pharynx of *Zygiella*. G = median groove with inserting muscles (M); these muscles expand the pharynx. 150×.

Fig. 40.   Diagram of the sucking stomach. Dilation muscles connect dorsally to the carapace and laterally to the endosternite. Smaller circular muscles can constrict the lumen of the sucking stomach. (After Kaestner, 1969.)

clusion is based on histological observations and still needs confirmation (see chapter 4). The fact that spiders readily accept a drop of water but quickly reject a weak quinine solution proves that they are capable of tasting. However, the seat of taste reception need not be located only beyond the mouth, but could also be accounted for by the contact chemoreceptors (taste hairs) on the maxillae and the palps.

The sucking stomach serves as the main pump for food intake. In contrast to the narrow esophagus, the stomach is of large diameter. In cross section it typically exhibits the shape of a collapsed square (Fig. 40). This shape is due to the pliable cuticular walls, which are closely apposed in the resting state. Several strong muscle bands connect the upper stomach wall with the dorsal apodeme and the lateral walls with the endosternite. When all these muscles contract, the stomach lumen increases greatly and the stomach thus functions as a suction pump. Several thin annular muscles, which lie between the expanding muscles, act antagonistically; that is, they act to diminish the stomach lumen (Schimkewitsch, 1884). A precise coordination of both sets of muscles causes wavelike contractions of the sucking stomach. Thus despite an extremely small mouth opening, the food is taken in rather quickly.

Fig. 41. Position of the midgut diverticula in the prosoma of *Tegenaria*, dorsal view. SM = sucking stomach. (After Plateau, 1877, and Zimmermann, 1934.)

Regulatory valves, which are present at the entrance and exit of the sucking stomach, assure that the food passes in a caudal direction as the annular muscles contract (Legendre, 1961a).

The midgut has its origin directly behind the sucking stomach. Its proximal part is still situated in the prosoma, while its median and posterior portions are in the opisthosoma. The proximal part gives off two lateral extensions, each of which splits into several fingerlike processes (Fig. 27, 41). The arrangement and shape of these diverticula may vary considerably among different spider families; in most cases the diverticula extend into the coxae of the walking legs.

The branches of the midgut fill out most of the opisthosoma and surround many organs, such as the spinning glands and the reproductive tracts. Gut diverticula are also present in the prosoma and may be numerous there. For instance, in jumping spiders the midgut extensions even penetrate between the eyes (Fig. 67b). Such an extensively developed intestinal system explains in part why spiders can survive for a long time without eating. In one experiment with black widows, adult spiders were not fed at all, yet continued to live for 200 days (Kaston, 1970). Well-nourished "tarantulas" often do not feed for several months.

The entire pharynx, as well as the sucking stomach, is covered by a thin cuticular lining. The midgut lacks such a lining and is therefore the only part suitable for digestion, that is, the breakdown of food and the absorption of nutrients. It has been known for a long time that spiders possess two different kinds of cells in the intestinal epithelium: *secretory cells* and *resorptive cells* (Bertkau, 1885; Millot, 1926) (Fig. 42). The secretory cells contain diges-

Fig. 42.   Midgut diverticula of *Tegenaria.* *(a)* The secretory cells (S) are characterized by many densely stained enzyme granules, whereas the resorptive cells (Rs) possess irregular food vacuoles. Lu = gut lumen, M = Malpighian tubule, IS = interstitial tissue. 2,900×. *(b)* Secretory cell with zymogen granules (Z) and extensive endoplasmic reticulum; resorptive cell with tubular indentations (*pinocytosis*, arrow) and large food vacuoles (Vc). 9,000×.

tive enzymes, which can be seen as dark cytoplasmic granules under the microscope. Most of the intestinal cells are of the resorptive type. They can be recognized by their many inclusions (the "food vacuoles"). The resorptive cells process the nutrients further and then pass them on to the underlying interstitial tissue or into the hemolymph.

After prey has been captured, the following cellular events take place in the intestinal epithelium (Nawabi, 1974). Within a few minutes the secretory cells empty their enzymatic granules into the gut lumen. After about an hour, while the prey may still be in the process of being sucked out, the first food vacuoles appear inside the resorptive cells. Initially the food vacuoles are seen only at the cell's apex, but soon they become distributed throughout the entire cell. Eight hours after food intake has begun, most of the secretory cells have become void of enzymatic granules. At the same time, the first excretory products can be detected basally in the resorptive cells. After 24 hours the secretory cells have resynthesized their enzymatic granules and the resorptive cells contain only a few food vacuoles. Excretory products are often concentrated apically in the resorptive cells, or they may be deposited as crystals in the underlying interstitial tissue. This tissue also serves as a reservoir for accumulated glycogen and lipids.

In addition to the secretory and resorptive cells, the intestinal epithelium contains two other cell types, *basal cells*, which eventually replace old secretory and resorptive cells, and *guanocytes*, in which guanine crystals become deposited (Millot, 1926; Seitz, 1975). The guanocytes can be thought of as specialized resorptive cells which take up metabolites (for example, purines) and store them temporarily in the form of crystals. Guanocytes may form a contiguous cell layer directly beneath the hypodermis (Fig. 43b). Since the guanine inclusions totally reflect the incoming light, they appear white and can be seen through transparent parts of the cuticle. The white cross pattern on the abdomen of the common garden spider *Araneus diadematus* (Fig. 43a) is a well-known example of such an accumulation of guanine.

Whereas the shape of the midgut appears rather confusing owing to its elaborate branching, the next section of the digestive system is structurally much simpler. The posterior end of the midgut widens to form the stercoral pocket, or cloacal chamber. It consists mainly of a large, blind sack into which the Malpighian tubules (see below) exit, and it connects to the anus via the short hindgut. The excrement stored in the stercoral pocket is periodically passed to the outside at the anus.

Fig. 43. (*a*) Abdomen of the garden spider *Araneus diadematus*, dorsal view. The markings in the form of a white cross are caused by guanine cells, which shine through the transparent cuticle. (Photo: Foelix and Grocki.) (*b*) Histological section of the abdomen showing guanine crystals deposited in specialized guanine cells (Gu) at the periphery of the gut diverticula (D). C = cuticle, H = hypodermis. 400×.

Excretion

That the intestinal cells themselves can accumulate guanine and thereby perform an excretory function has already been mentioned. The main excretory organs, however, are the *Malpighian tubules*. These originate from either side of the stercoral pocket as two thin evaginations and are thus entodermal derivatives, quite in contrast to insect Malpighian tubules, which are of ectodermal origin. Histologically, the Malpighian tubules do not differ much from the stercoral pocket or from the hindgut (Seitz, 1975). The excretory cells form a flat epithelium with a typical apical brush border (Figs. 42, 44). Below the excretory cell bases lie delicate muscle cells that probably assist in the transport of the excretion products. The excretory substances are first taken up at the base of the cell. There the cell membrane is highly infolded, a typical feature of cells with augmented transport activity. Inside the cytoplasm the metabolites are concentrated and stored before they are expelled into the lumen of the Malpighian tubule. The main excretory products are guanine, adenine, hypoxanthine, and uric acid. All these substances are nearly insoluble in water, a property reflected in their tendency to crystallize.

Less conspicuous excretory organs, the segmentally arranged

Fig. 44.   Excretory organs. (*a*) Malpighian tubule in longitudinal section (*Tegenaria*). The flat tubule cells possess typical brush borders (Mv). Empty spaces in the lumen (Lu) represent excretions that have dissolved during tissue preparation. IS = interstitial tissue. 8,000×. (*b*) Coxal gland (*Zygiella*). The interior of the gland cell is filled with excretions (Ex) that are transported toward the lumen (Lu). Muscle cells (M) and their processes (arrows) surround the base of the excretory cells and apparently aid in dispersing excretions. 4,400×. (*c*) Nephrocyte (*Zygiella*). The excretory products (Ex) are accumulated in intracellular compartments. N = nucleus. 4,700×.

coxal glands, lie in the prosoma (Fig. 44b). They open to the outside
at the coxae of the walking legs. In "primitive" spiders (Mesothelae, Orthognatha) two pairs of coxal glands open onto the posterior
side of the first and third coxae (Buxton, 1913). The Labidognatha
have retained only the anterior pair, and even these show gradual
stages of regression in the various families. The original type of
coxal gland consists of four parts: a saccule, a collecting duct, a
labyrinth, and an excretory duct. This type becomes substantially
reduced in orb-web spiders, in which a collecting duct is lacking
and the labyrinth apparently no longer has an excretory function.
Additional excretory "organs" are represented by the many
nephrocytes. These huge cells tend to accumulate at specific sites in
the prosoma, for instance, beneath the subesophageal ganglion.
With a diameter of 30–80 μm they are the largest cells of the spider's body. Presumably the nephrocytes take up metabolites from
the hemolymph and store them intracellularly (Fig. 44c).

Circulatory System

Spiders, like most invertebrates, have an open circulatory system.
This does not mean that they lack blood vessels. On the contrary,
they have quite distinct arteries that originate from the heart and
that branch through the entire body (Fig. 45). Some smaller vessels
even reach the tips of the legs. At the termination of such small arteries the blood (hemolymph) seeps freely between the tissues. It
collects in lacunae on the ventral side of the body. The flow of the
hemolymph back to the heart follows the gradient of decreasing

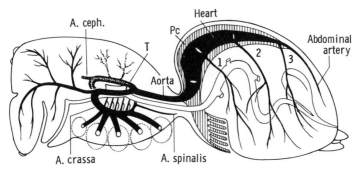

Fig. 45. Diagram of the arterial circulatory system. A = arteria, A.
ceph. = arteria cephalica, Pc = pericardial sinus; 1, 2, 3 = lateral opistho-
somal arteries; T = trunci peristomacales. (After various authors.)

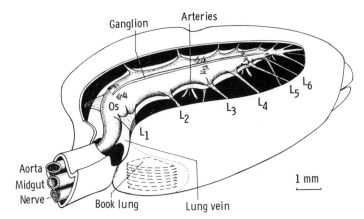

Fig. 46.   Position of the heart in the opisthosoma of the banana spider *Heteropoda*. L_{1-6} = lateral ligaments, Os = ostium. (After R. S. Wilson, 1967.)

pressure. Since not all of the hemolymph passes the respiratory
organs before returning to the heart, one cannot clearly differentiate between an arterial and a venous system.

Heart and Blood Vessels

The heart lies dorsally in the anterior part of the opisthosoma
(Figs. 28, 46). It is formed by a muscular tube suspended in a wide
chamber (the *pericardial sinus*) by dorsal, ventral, and lateral ligaments. The heart tube itself has two or three pairs of buttonhole-
shaped slits (*ostia*), which open to the pericardial sinus. This sinus
is covered by a thin layer of smooth musculature. When the heart
tube contracts (systole), the ostia, acting as passive valves, close
automatically (Fig. 47a). During this contraction the heart elon-
gates and the hemolymph is pushed forward into the anterior
aorta in the prosoma and backward into the posterior aorta in the
opisthosoma. Special valvelike structures at either end of the heart
tube (in addition to the closed ostia) prevent a backflow of the hemolymph (Figs. 47b, c).

   The course of the various arteries through the body can be followed after carefully injecting a spider's heart with carmine or
india ink (Petrunkevitch, 1910; Crome, 1953). The anterior aorta
passes through the pedicel and then, close to the sucking stomach,
splits into two lateral branches (trunci peristomacales; Fig. 45).
Each of these branches divides again, into the arteria cephalica,

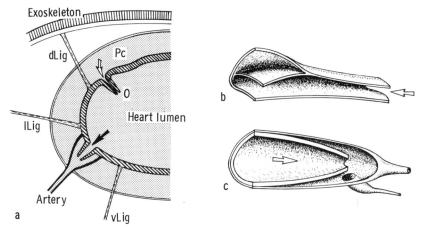

Fig. 47.   Diagrammatic cross section of the heart tube. Arrows indicate direction of hemolymph flow. dLig, lLig, vLig = dorsal, lateral, and ventral ligaments; O = ostium; Pc = pericardial sinus. (*b* and *c*): Heart valves: the valve leading into the aorta (*b*) is a flapvalve, whereas the one at the caudal end of the heart (*c*) is funnel-shaped. (*a, b, c* after Crome, 1953.)

which supplies the supraesophageal ganglion, the chelicerae, and the mouth parts, and the arteria crassa, which sends off one artery per extremity. The two arteriae crassae are cross-connected horizontally by means of six rami transversales; from these vessels smaller arteries branch off ventrally and penetrate the subesophageal ganglion. From the last ramus transversalis emerges horizontally the arteria spinalis, which proceeds along the upper side of the subesophageal ganglion. Most of the arterial hemolymph is directed to the central nervous system and to the skeletal muscles (Millot, 1949). In most spiders the organs of the opisthosoma receive a direct tracheal supply and thus are less dependent on oxygen carried by the hemolymph. Still, the opisthosoma has two or three arteries of its own that originate laterally from the heart tube (Fig. 45).

The expansion of the heart (diastole) is caused by the ligaments that connect the heart tube with the exoskeleton. When the heart tube is in the contracted state (systole), these ligaments are stretched and under tension. When the contraction subsides, the ligaments shorten passively due to their inherent elasticity. This in turn causes the ostia to open, and hemolymph enters the heart lumen from the pericardial sinus (R. S. Wilson, 1967; Figs. 47a, 51b).

Structure and Function of the Heart

The heart tube consists of a thin outer layer (*adventitia*) composed of connective tissue and of the actual muscle layer (*myocardium*) that forms the circular heart lumen (Seitz, 1972a). An inner layer (*intima*) seems to be lacking in spiders; instead, the muscle cells are in direct contact with the hemolymph (Sherman, 1973a). As in vertebrates, the heart muscle cells are cross-striated, branched, and multinucleate. In contrast to regular skeletal muscles (Fig. 23), they contain many mitochondria (Fig. 49; Midttun, 1977), which provide for the continuous energy demand of the heart.

In spiders, as in most other arthropods, the heartbeat is controlled neurogenically. A threadlike ganglion on the dorsal side of the heart tube (Fig. 46) gives off axons that innervate the heart muscle cells (R. S. Wilson, 1967; Legendre, 1968; Sherman et al., 1969; Ude and Richter, 1974). This ganglion probably contains pacemaker neurons that control the heartbeat via intercalated motoneurons. The heartbeat itself is the result of the synchronous contraction of the entire heart tube.

Heartbeat frequency has been investigated in many spiders (Bristowe, 1932; Sherman and Pax, 1970; Carrel and Heathcote, 1976). In general, the heart rate decreases with increasing body size. Large "tarantulas" have a heartbeat frequency of 30–40 beats per minute, whereas small spiders show a resting frequency of over 100. During running, the heartbeat accelerates rapidly. A wolf spider, for which a resting frequency of 48 beats/min was measured, increased its heart rate to 176 beats/min after only 30 seconds of activity (Sherman and Pax, 1968).

In many spiders the heartbeat frequency can be determined simply by counting the pulsations of the abdomen under a binocular microscope. By applying a fine wire electrode to the body, directly over the heart, one can also record an electrocardiogram (EKG). This method not only automatically yields the heart rate but also proves its neurogenic origin by registering oscillatory bursts.

EKGs have been obtained even from extirpated spider hearts. The resting frequency is about the same as in the living animal and is apparently determined by the heart ganglion (Sherman and Pax, 1968; 1970a). Adding L-glutamate causes the heart to contract. L-glutamate is perhaps the natural neurotransmitter in the spider heart, for other known neurotransmitters, such as acetylcholine or gamma-aminobutyric acid (GABA), have no effect on heart action (Sherman and Pax, 1970b, c).

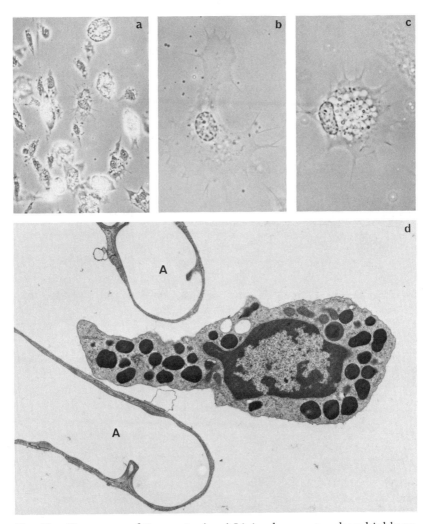

Fig. 48.   Hemocytes of *Tegenaria*. (*a–c*) Living hemocytes show highly re-
fractive granules when viewed in a phase contrast microscope; pseudopodia are the first sign of blood clotting (*a* = 260×; *b* and *c* = 650×.) (*d*) A
granular hemocyte just entering the hemolymph space between two air
spaces (A) of a book lung. 7,000×.

The central nervous system (CNS) can also exert an excitatory
or an inhibitory effect on the heartbeat (R. S. Wilson, 1967); this is
obvious because even minor sensory input influences the heart
rate: spiders that are physically restrained for observation show a
markedly faster heartbeat than normal. Cardioregulatory neurons

Fig. 49.   Two prehemocytes (PHc) in the process of being pinched off from the heart wall (HW). Lu = heart lumen. 3,050×.

in the CNS have recently been demonstrated by electrophysiological methods (Gonzalez-Fernandez and Sherman, 1979).

Blood Cells and Hemolymph

The spider's hemolymph exhibits a large variety of blood cells (*hemocytes*). Although very little is known about the function of specific hemocytes, it seems likely that they play a role in blood clotting, wound healing, and the fighting off of infections. Structurally, at least four different types can be distinguished (Seitz, 1972a, b; Sherman, 1973b). Most common are the granular hemocytes, which have many dense granules concentrated in the cytoplasm (Fig. 48); it has been suggested that the granular hemocytes contribute to the sclerotization of the exocuticle (Browning, 1942). Some hemocytes, called leberidiocytes, enclose a single secretory vacuole. Other blood cell types are believed to act as phagocytes or as storage cells. During molting the relative percentage of the different hemocyte types changes drastically.

The curious origin of the hemocytes should be mentioned here: they derive directly from myocardium cells of the heart wall

(Franz, 1904; Millot, 1926). This is easily seen in young spiders, where immature "pre-hemocytes," or hemoblasts, sit on the luminal side of the heart tube, where they undergo mitotic divisions (Fig. 49). These hemoblasts develop into the different types of hemocytes by acquiring specific cell organelles (Seitz, 1972a).

Fresh spider hemolymph appears bluish because it contains the copper-containing respiratory pigment *hemocyanin*. Apparently, hemocyanin is synthesized in special blood cells, the cyanocytes (Fig. 50). Initially the hemocyanin is stored in crystalline form, but mature cyanocytes may deliver it to the hemolymph (see Fahrenbach, 1970). The hemocyanin content of spiders is relatively high, 1.4% of the body weight; in humans the corresponding value for hemoglobin is 1.2% (Martin, 1974). Since hemocyanin has a strong affinity for oxygen, this element can be given off to the surrounding tissue only if the local oxygen pressure is low there ($p_{O_2} < 10$ torr). Values of 1–10 torr were recorded in muscle tissue of *Eurypelma helluo*, whereas the "arterial" hemolymph inside the heart lumen measured 31 torr (Angersbach, 1975). However, hemocyanin may be more of a storage site for oxygen than a carrier of oxygen.

Only a few studies have concentrated on the composition of spi-

Fig. 50. Cyanocytes (Cy) from the lung sinus of *Tegenaria*. The cytoplasm is packed with bundles of hemocyanin crystals (Cy). A = air space, N = nucleus. 3,000×. *Inset:* Hemocyanin bundles at higher magnification. 35,000×.

der hemolymph. For the "tarantula" *Dugesiella* (*Eurypelma*) the following ions have been determined (Rathmayer, 1965c): 220 Na$^+$, 5 K$^+$, 4 Ca^{2+}, 1.1 Mg^{2+}, 3 HCO$_3^-$ (mM/l). A synthetic solution of these substances can be used as a spider "Ringer's solution" for physiological experiments. Its pH lies around 7.3 and the osmolarity is between 400 and 600 mosm (Pinkston and Frick, 1973). A more detailed analysis of spider hemolymph is available for *Cupiennius* (Loewe, Linzen, and v. Stackelberg, 1970). The inorganic ion distribution is similar to that of the "tarantula," but the pH is 8.1–8.3. Most of the soluble substances in the hemolymph are proteins (7%), and of these hemocyanin is the most common. Furthermore, there is a lipoid fraction (2%) that is considered to be a circulating store of fatty acid. The major carbohydrate of hemolymph is glucose.

Outside the body the hemolymph coagulates quickly; coagulation is initiated by many fine pseudopodia that grow out from the hemocyte (Fig. 48; Deevey, 1941; Grégoire, 1952). The hemolymph

Fig. 51. Structure of a book lung. (After Kaestner, 1929.) (*a*) Three-dimensional representation of the lower part of a book lung. The white arrow indicates the air entering the atrium of the book lung; the black arrows show the direction of hemolymph flow. (*b*) Cross section of the opisthosoma at the level of the book lungs. The arrows show the hemolymph coming from the lung sinus (Ls), passing through the book lung, and then entering the heart (H). Lv = lung vein, M = abdominal muscles, Md = midgut diverticula, Mg = midgut, N = abdominal nerves, Pc = pericardial sinus.

accounts for about 20% of the body weight of a spider (Stewart and Martin, 1970). It is surely imperative for a spider to maintain a certain hemolymph volume, since the hydraulics of the leg joints depend on the pressure, and thus on the quantity, of the hemolymph. Under normal conditions the exoskeleton protects the spider from desiccation. If extremely dry spells occur, or if the spider suffers direct blood loss through injury or autotomy, the animal attempts to replace lost fluid by drinking.

Respiratory Organs

Most spiders possess two entirely different kinds of respiratory systems: one pair of strictly localized *book lungs* and one or two pairs of *tubular tracheae,* which can branch throughout the body. The "primitive" spiders (Mesothelae, Orthognatha, Hypochilidae) have only book lungs, but always *two* pairs. These are situated on the second and third abdominal segments. In the majority of labidognath spiders only the first pair of book lungs has been retained, while the second pair has been modified into tubular tracheae. The book lungs are structurally very uniform in all spiders, but the tubular tracheae vary considerably in relative size and pattern of distribution (Kaestner, 1929).

Book Lungs

The book lungs lie ventrally in the anterior opisthosoma (Fig. 28). Their location is often visible from the outside as a hairless patch of cuticle that borders posteriorly on a narrow slit, the lung slit (Fig. 1), which leads to the interior of the abdomen. There a small atrium enlarges and then extends into many horizontal air pockets that are in contact with blood-filled lamellae (Figs. 51, 52). In other words, stacks of air-filled spaces alternate with leaflets of hemolymph spaces—hence the descriptive term *book lung.* The leaflets as well as the atrium are covered by a very thin cuticle. Short vertical extensions of this cuticle form minute columns that act like struts to prevent collapse of the narrow air pockets (Figs. 53b, c). Each leaflet is formed by a doubling of the thin hypodermis, leaving an open space in between, where the hemolymph can circulate freely. In regular histological preparations the acidophilic hemolymph stains distinctly, yet the thin hypodermis extensions are hardly visible (Fig. 52). Only the nuclei of the hypodermis cells

Fig. 52. Microscopic structure of a book lung. (*a*) Longitudinal section (wolf spider). At = atrium, LS = lung sinus with stained hemolymph, S = lung slit. 80×. (*b*) Cross section (*Tegenaria*). The hemolymph is unstained in this preparation, but hemocytes (Hc) are clearly recognizable in the lung sinus (LS). Note the extremely thin walls of the air pockets (Air). 1,000×.

are apparent; they become more conspicuous if they lie exactly opposite each other within one leaflet. In such cases the two hypodermis cells seem to form a pillar between two air spaces (Fig. 53a).

Almost all the hemolymph that returns from the lacunae to the heart has to pass through the book lungs. The hemolymph coming from the prosoma flows along two lateral lacunae in the pedicel and enters the "lung sinus" in the anterior part of the abdomen. Lacunae are also present in the posterior opisthosoma, and the flow of hemolymph there is directed forward toward the lung sinus. Streaming along the midline of the abdomen, the flow of the hemolymph divides to enter the leaflets of each book lung laterally (Fig. 51b). Oxygen from the air spaces must penetrate the thin cuticular lining and the hypodermis cells of the book lung in order to reach the hemolymph. Since both the cuticle and hypodermis are extremely thin (Fig. 53b), they pose no significant barrier to the process of diffusion. After the hemolymph has become oxygenated, it

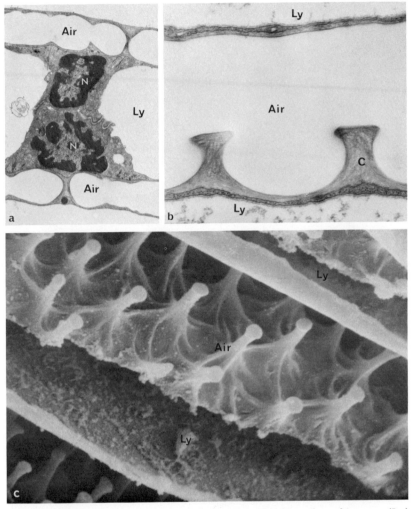

Fig. 53.   Ultrastructure of a book lung. (*a*) The hemolymph space (Ly) often contains two cells stacked on each other and thus forming a minute supporting column between neighboring air pockets (Air) (*Tegenaria*). N = nucleus. 5,000×. (*b*) To reach the hemolymph (Ly), oxygen must diffuse through the cuticular lamella (C) lining the air pocket and through the underlying cellular layer (*Zygiella*). 22,000×. (*c*) Cryofracture of the book lung of *Phidippus* showing the cuticular struts projecting into the air pockets (Air). 9,000×. (Photo *c*: Hill.)

leaves the book lungs laterally and continues upward into another sinus, the lung vein, which then connects with the pericardial sinus. During diastole the oxygenated hemolymph is sucked into the heart tube via the opened ostia.

The lung slits can be enlarged by the action of specific muscles. Usually, however, such "ventilation" movements do not occur. It has been claimed that, because no actual movement between the leaflets of the book lung is detectable, diffusion alone accounts for the uptake of oxygen. Nevertheless, some observers have noticed a distinct pulsating of the lamellae in synchrony with the heartbeat (Willem, 1918; Hill, 1977b). This, of course, implies a mechanical facilitation of gas exchange within the book lung. How important the book lungs are becomes clear after one closes the lung slits with vaseline; after only two minutes the animals become severely paralyzed, and after several hours most of them are dead (Kaestner, 1929).

Tubular Tracheae

The tubular tracheae lie behind the book lungs in the third abdominal segment. Externally they are barely visible as one or two small openings, the *stigmata*, or *spiracles*. Most spiders have only a single stigma, which is located in front of the spinnerets (Figs. 1, 28). The tubular tracheae have developed quite differently among various spider families. Some families (for example, Filistatidae) possess only very short tubes; others, such as Salticidae and Thomisidae, have highly branched tubes that pervade the prosoma and even the extremities. I describe here only a few of the many variations.

Usually, a median stigma leads into a small atrium from which two lateral and two medial tubes arise. The two lateral tubes correspond to the second pair of book lungs of some "primitive" spiders, but the two median tubes are derived secondarily. They develop from muscular insertion points (entapophyses) in the third abdominal segment; presumably they became hollowed out and can now function as respiratory organs (Purcell, 1909, 1910). The lateral and median tubes of the tracheal system are hence of completely different origin. Furthermore, tracheal tubes can either split into many branches or be unbranched. If unbranched, they remain restricted to the opisthosoma; if highly branched (as they are, for example, in Dictynidae), they also enter the prosoma and supply the various organs there with oxygen. The tracheae in spiders, unlike those in insects, always terminate in an open end with-

Fig. 54.   Tube tracheae. (*a*) Tubular tracheae (tt) and adjacent book lung
of a water spider (*Argyroneta*). All soft tissue has been removed by treatment with potassium hydroxide, but the cuticular parts remain intact.
240×. (*b*) Similar preparation of tube tracheae from the opisthosoma of a
jumping spider (*Salticus*) 350×. (*c*) Longitudinal section of a tracheal tube
surrounded by muscle cells. Note the cuticular reinforcements on the inside of the tube (*Dysdera*). 300×. (*d*) Several tubular tracheae in cross section from a leg of *Dysdera*. 1,400×.

out contacting a cell (Fig. 54), so oxygen is not delivered directly.
Instead, it is always the hemolymph which is responsible for the
final transport of oxygen to its destination.

Comparison of the Two Respiratory Systems

The question of which of the two respiratory organs is the more
efficient one cannot be answered clearly, since comparative physiological studies are lacking. It is usually assumed, however, that a
highly branched system of tubular tracheae would provide the
better solution (Levi, 1967). In species with branched tubular tracheae the circulatory system is normally reduced: the heart is

shorter, and the number of ostia and arteries is smaller. Such is the case for the water spider *Argyroneta aquatica* (Crome, 1953). The small book lungs of a water spider cannot store much oxygen, compared to the extensively developed tubular tracheae (Braun, 1931). If both the lung slits and the stigma of a water spider are sealed, it takes days before any effects (disturbed motor behavior) become noticeable. In comparison, a relative of *Argyroneta*, the house spider *Tegenaria*, is paralyzed within a few minutes after such an operation. The question of relative efficiency is further complicated by the fact that the water spider can apparently also exchange gases through its integument. Carbon dioxide can pass directly through the abdominal cuticle and into the captive air bubble, thus preventing carbon dioxide poisoning (Crome, 1953). Some lesser-known spider families (Caponiidae, Symphythognathidae) have no book lungs at all. Instead these possess, in the second abdominal segment, special tubular tracheae called *sieve* tracheae. Sieve tracheae are delicately branched and arise immediately from the atrium.

The following simplified summary constitutes an overview of the types of respiratory organs and their respective development in different kinds of spiders (Kaestner, 1929):

1. one pair of book lungs only (for example, Pholcidae)
2. two pairs of book lungs only (Mesothelae, Orthognatha)
3. one pair of book lungs and one pair of tubular tracheae (Araneidae, Lycosidae)
4. one pair of sieve tracheae and one pair of tubular tracheae (Caponiidae)
5. one pair of sieve tracheae only (Symphytognathidae)

Phylogenetically, book lungs must be regarded as more ancient ("primitive") than tubular tracheae. This can be concluded from embryological studies (because book lungs are homologous to appendages) and also from the observation that all "primitive" spiders have only book lungs and no tracheae. Elaborate tubular tracheae occur only in small spiders, which are more prone to desiccation; perhaps tubular tracheae have evolved as an adaption to provide the necessary protection (Levi, 1967).

4

Neurobiology

THE behavior of spiders, like that of all animals, is controlled by the central nervous system. Of the various types of sensory organs that collect information about the environment—for example, mechanoreceptors, chemoreceptors, and visual receptors—the mechanoreceptors are the most important among spiders.

Mechanical Senses

Mechanoreceptors respond to external stimuli such as touch, substrate vibrations, and air currents and also keep the spider informed about leg and joint positions. Usually we find different receptor types for the various stimuli. On the other hand, structurally similar receptors may subserve quite different functions. The most common mechanoreceptor is the hair sensillum. It may appear as a simple tactile hair or as a more complex filiform hair (a *trichobothrium,* Fig. 55). Whereas tactile hairs are distributed over the entire body surface, the trichobothria occur only on the extremities. Other less conspicuous but nevertheless characteristic mechanoreceptors of spiders are the *slit sensilla* (Fig. 59).

Fig. 55. Mechanosensitive hair sensilla from a leg of the wolf spider *Lycosa gulosa.* The slender trichobothrium (Tr) arises vertically from a prominent socket; the stronger tactile hair (T) emerges obliquely from a less-developed socket. 1,250×. (Photo: Chu-Wang and Foelix.)

These small sensory organs are embedded in the exoskeleton at "strategic" points. Their function remained obscure for many years, but during the last decade their mechanosensitive capacity has been proved beyond doubt (Barth, 1976). In addition to these external mechanoreceptors there are also internal proprioreceptors inside the legs; these measure the relative positions of the joints.

Tactile Hairs

The hairiness of spiders is proverbial, and it is certainly this characteristic which contributes most to the general dislike many people have of spiders. For those interested in the biology of these animals, though, this hairiness sparks some scientific questions: Why are spiders hairy? Do the thousands of hairs merely decorate the exoskeleton, or do they fulfill some vital functions? The fact that most of these hairs are innervated proves their nature as sensory organs. This can also be demonstrated in a simple behavioral experiment: touching but a single hair triggers escape or aggressive reactions from the spider.

It is hard to imagine that the thousands of hairs on a spider's body are all innervated, yet examination of histological sections shows that indeed all large, movable, articulated hairs have a triple innervation. Only the short body hairs and most adhesive scopula hairs lack innervation. The regular tactile hair consists of a long, exocuticular hair shaft that is suspended in a slipper-shaped socket in which it can move (Figs. 55, 56). Three dendritic nerve endings are attached to the base of the hair shaft (Foelix and Chu-Wang, 1973a) and monitor movements of the shaft. Electrophysiological recordings show that the tactile hairs react like typical phasic receptors; that is, only changes from the resting position are answered with nerve impulses (Den Otter, 1974). Furthermore, the initial bending of the hair elicits more nerve impulses than its return to the resting position (Fig. 56b).

The large leg spines are also triply innervated (Harris and Mill,

Fig. 56. (*a*) Innervation of a tactile hair, longitudinal section. The dendritic terminals (T) attach to the base of the movable, suspended hair shaft (Hs). D = dendrites, Rlc = receptor lymph cavity, SH = sheath cell. (After Foelix and Chu-Wang, 1973a, and Harris, 1977.) (*b–d*) Electrophysiological recordings from tactile hairs. (*b*) Displacement of the hair shaft (lower tracing) elicits nervous impulses from two sensory cells (1, 2). (*c*) Stimulation with a 50 Hz vibration. (*d*) Responses from three sensory cells of a trichobothrium after lateral displacement of the hair shaft. (*b–d* after Harris and Mill, 1977a.)

Fig. 57.   Fine structure of various spider hairs. (*a*) Urticating hair from a "tarantula." The hair base (left) breaks off easily; the hair shaft exhibits spirally arranged barbs. 950×. (*b*) Surface structure of a calamistrum bristle of *Hypochilus*. The hair shaft bears multiple rows of cuticular teeth on one side. 5,700×. (*c*) Scale hair from the jumping spider *Salticus*. The leaflike hair shaft consists of a delicate cuticular meshwork. 1,000×.

1977a). These spines become erect when hemolymph pressure increases. Nerve impulses of leg spines, unlike those of simple tactile hairs, can be recorded only during the erection phase, but not during the return to the flat resting position; the spines are therefore considered to be hemolymph pressure receptors rather than touch receptors.

Aside from specific sensory functions many hairs also serve purely mechanical tasks (Fig. 57). The row of specialized bristles forming the *calamistrum* on the fourth leg of cribellate spiders is used to comb out fine catching threads. Actually, each bristle is serrated on one side and thus acts as a comb (Foelix and Jung, 1978). Theridiid spiders also have a row of serrated bristles on their fourth legs. These tarsal bristles comb out sticky silk threads from the spinnerets as the spider wraps its prey. Some spiders (for example, *Zelotes*, Gnaphosidae) have specialized brushlike hairs that are used as cleaning devices during grooming (Berland, 1932). Finally, the scopula hairs must be mentioned here, since they provide for increased adhesion to the substrate (see chapter 2).

The short hairs covering the opisthosoma of many spiders may have special functions. In the water spider *Argyroneta aquatica*, for instance, these abdominal hairs are necessary for establishing the air bubble that surrounds the opisthosoma (Braun, 1931). Some female wolf spiders have special "knobbed" abdominal hairs, used by the young spiderlings to hold on to their mother (Rovner, Higashi, and Foelix, 1973). A more impressive example of how a spider can use its abdominal hairs is found in the New World "tarantulas." When these animals feel threatened, they can quickly brush off clouds of abdominal (urticating) hairs (Fig. 57a) with their hind legs. Each hair is covered by hundreds of little hooks, which cause severe itching when in contact with the skin, especially in the nose and eye region. Experiments show that these urticating hairs can work themselves 2 mm deep into human skin (Cooke, Roth, and Miller, 1972; Cooke et al., 1973). Sometimes this happens quite inadvertently when one works with dead "tarantulas" (preserved in alcohol or as dry exuvia), as many museum curators can testify!

Trichobothria

The filiform hairs, or *trichobothria*, are extremely fine hairs within special sockets. They are much less numerous than the common tactile hairs and are usually arranged in regular rows on certain leg segments. In *Tegenaria*, for instance, they form one dorsal row on each tarsus and metatarsus, with the length of their respective hair shafts gradually increasing toward the tip of the leg. On the tibia, in contrast, we find four rows of trichobothria with hair shafts of different lengths (Görner, 1965; Christian, 1973). The ar-a

b

Fig. 58. (*a*) Innervation of a trichoboth-rium of the house spider *Tegenaria*, longi-tudinal section. When the hair shaft (Hs) is deflected (dashed line), the helmet struc-ture (He) pushes against the dendritic terminals (T), triggering the generation of nerve impulses. Rlc = receptor lymph cav-ity, Sh = sheath cells. Hy = hypodermis, M = articulating membrane. (After Chris-tian, 1973.) *inset:* the directional sensitivity of a trichobothrium as seen from above; displacements of the hair shaft within each of the three sectors indicated are pref-erentially answered by one of three sensory cells (1, 2, 3). (After Görner, 1965.) (*b*) Slightly oblique section of a trichobothrium in a young *Latrodectus*. This micrograph was taken just before the animal molted; thus the "outside" (exuvial space) is filled with hemolymph and hemocytes (Hc). 1,500×.

rangement of trichobothria is constant within a species and is hence often used by systematicists to characterize certain spider species and to clarify taxonomic relationships (termed *tricho-bothriotaxy;* Emerit and Bonaric, 1975; Lehtinen, 1980).

The most striking feature of the trichobothria is their extreme sensitivity. The long slender hair shaft is suspended in a very thin (0.5 µm) cuticular membrane (Fig. 58) so that the slightest air current will make it quiver. Four dendritic nerve endings attach to the specialized hair base (the "helmet"), and three of the four have been found to have a specific directional sensitivity (Fig. 58a, inset). Each sensory cell reacts to displacements within a defined sector, and there is little overlap between the three neurons (Görner, 1965; Harris and Mill, 1977a). In the field, normal stimuli are air currents and low frequency air vibrations (sound). The air vibrations that an insect produces with its wings suffice to trigger a directed capture response from the spider. Even a totally blinded spider can accurately locate a buzzing fly as much as several centimeters away (Görner and Andrews, 1969). For this reason trichobothria have also been called "touch-at-a-distance" receptors. Proof that the trichobothria are involved in eliciting prey capture behavior was obtained by plucking off all trichobothria with fine forceps; the reaction of the spider toward a source of vibration was greatly impaired.

Slit Sense Organs

The exoskeleton not only serves as a protective shield and as the insertion site for the muscles, but also transmits mechanical stress that may be caused by substrate vibrations, by gravity, or by the spider's own movements (Barth, 1976). The specific stress (strain) receptors are the *slit sense organs,* or sensilla, which are embedded in the exoskeleton. They are distributed over the entire body surface but are most numerous on the legs. An adult *Cupiennius,* for instance, has more than 3,000 slit sense organs. Of these, 86% lie in the hard exocuticle of the extremities, whereas only 3% are found in the soft abdominal cuticle (Barth and Libera, 1970).

Slit sense organs may occur either singly or in groups (Fig. 59). Most conspicuous are those groups where the slits run strictly parallel to each other. They are then called *lyriform organs,* because their shape is reminiscent of a lyre. Lyriform organs are found mostly on the extremities, particularly near the joints (Figs. 59, 60). Single slit sensilla can be found anywhere on the body surface, yet some specific localization and orientation of these organs

Fig. 59. (*a*) A single slit sensillum (*left*) and two hair sockets (*right*) from the sternum of the social spider *Mallos gregalis*. 1,500×. (*b*) Lyriform organ from a walking leg of *Zygiella x-notata*. The attachment sites of the dendrites are indicated by arrows. 1,800×. (Photo: Jung and Foelix.) (*c*) Metatarsal lyriform organ in *Araneus diadematus*. The slits are arranged perpendicular to the leg axis at the border of the metatarsus (Mt) and the tarsus (Ta). 1,200×. (From Foelix, 1970a.)

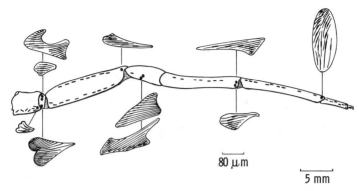

80 μm

5 mm

Fig. 60.   Distribution of lyriform sensilla on the back side of the first leg of *Cupiennius salei*. Single slit sensilla are indicated as dashes, lyriform organs as black dots; the latter are enlarged to show greater detail. (After Barth and Libera, 1970.)

is still noticeable. On the legs, for instance, the single slits are generally oriented parallel to the leg axis (Fig. 60).

There is no difference in the basic design of single slit sensilla and that of lyriform organs (Barth, 1971). Each slit is only 1–2 μm wide, yet may be from 8 to 200 μm long. The slit is bordered by a cuticular lip on either side (Fig. 59a), and the gap between these ridges is spanned by a thin cuticular membrane (Fig. 61). Beneath that covering membrane a trough extends downward and widens into a bell-shaped structure at the border of the exo- and mesocuticle. Each slit sensillum has two dendrites, but only one of these traverses the trough and attaches to the covering membrane. The dendritic tip contains a "tubular body," which is a microtubule assembly characteristic of arthropod mechanoreceptors.

The cuticular structures of the slit sensilla are quite important for transmitting the adequate stimuli to the nerve endings. Even very small loads or slight stresses on the cuticle lead to a deformation of the slit. Most effective are those forces that are oriented perpendicular to the slit (Barth, 1972a, b). In technical terms one could say that the slits function as mechanical filters. When the slit narrows, the covering membrane is indented and the tip of the dendrite becomes deformed. Only compression, not dilatation, of the slit elicits nerve impulses (Barth, 1973b). In the lyriform organ all the slits are of different lengths, and peripheral slits can be deformed more easily than central ones (Barth and Pickelmann, 1975); this implies that they are differentially sensitive. The site of maximal compression usually coincides with the attachment site of the dendrite, which means that the system works with maximum sensitivity.

The function of the slit sensilla cannot be generalized, since different slit sensilla are used for different tasks. Usually, the slit sensilla are categorized as proprioreceptive mechanoreceptors, but this is not entirely accurate since the stimuli need not be related to the spider's own movements. For a single tarsal slit sensillum, responses to airborne sound have been shown electrophysiologically (Barth, 1967); the highest sensitivity was noted between 300 and 700 Hz. Some slit sensilla on the pedicel may act as gravity receptors, since they probably register the relative movements between prosoma and opisthosoma (Barth and Libera, 1970).

The metatarsal lyriform organ (Fig. 59c) is a highly sensitive vibration receptor (Walcott and van der Kloot, 1959; Liesenfeld,

Fig. 61. (a) Diagram of a single slit sensillum from the tarsus of *Cupiennius*. Each slit is supplied by two dendrites (D), but only one of these extends to the covering membrane. Exo, Meso = exo-, mesocuticle, Rlc = receptor lymph cavity, Sh = sheath cells. (After Barth, 1971.) (b) Covering membrane (M) of slit sensillum with dendritic attachment. 14,000×.

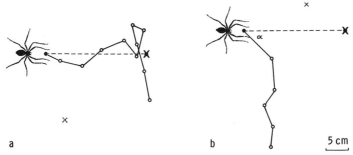

Fig. 62. Involvement of lyriform organs in kinesthetic orientation. The spider (*Cupiennius*) caught a fly at X and was then chased away from it; the dead fly was then moved to x. In (*a*), a normal spider returns in a direct course to the capture site. In (*b*), all tibial lyriform organs had been destroyed; the direction of the return run (indicated by the angle α) deviates markedly from the ideal course (dashed line). (*a* and *b* after Seyfarth and Barth, 1972.)

1961). In the web spiders *Zygiella* (Araneidae) and *Achaearanea* (Theridiidae) a displacement of the leg tip by 10 to 25 Å (at 2– 5 kHz) sufficed to elicit a response. However, if a vibrating needle is hooked to the web, the spider will only attack within a narrow frequency range (400–700 Hz). It has been known for more than a hundred years that spiders react to a vibrating tuning fork in the same manner as to a buzzing insect (Boys, 1881). Vibrations, incidentally, are important not only for capturing prey but also during courtship, when the male signals his presence to the female (see chapter 7). Tibial and femoral lyriform organs are used for kinesthetic orientation. Wandering spiders (*Cupiennius, Pardosa*) can normally orient themselves according to their previous motility pattern; that is, they can retrace the direction and distance of a previous run without the help of external stimuli (Fig. 62). This is no longer true if the tibial or femoral lyriform organs have been destroyed (Seyfarth and Barth, 1972; Görner and Zeppenfeld, 1980).

Slit sense organs are typical of all arachnids, but, in none of the arachnid orders (harvestmen, whip spiders, whip scorpions, and scorpions) are they as diversified as in the "true" spiders (Araneae). It is interesting that similar sense organs, the *campaniform sensilla*, are found in insects; these likewise measure stress-induced deformation of the cuticle.

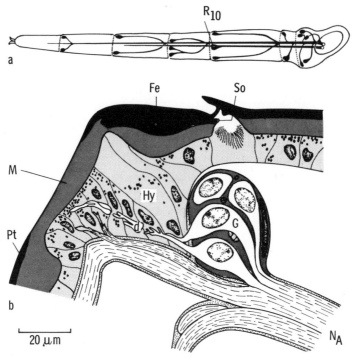

Fig. 63. Position and structure of proprioreceptors in a spider leg. (*a*) Each leg contains 18 receptor groups, which invariably lie near the joints. (After Rathmayer and Koopmann, 1970.) (*b*) Longitudinal section of R_{10}, a receptor group located at the femur-patella joint (Fe, Pt). Ten sensory cells form a compact ganglion (G), which gives off branched dendrites (d). The dendritic terminals fan out into the hypodermis cells (Hy) underlying the joint membrane (M). N_A = nerve A, So = socket. (After Foelix and Choms, 1979.)

Proprioreceptors

Several groups of sensory cells (ganglia) lying inside the palps and legs of spiders (Fig. 63) provide the animal with information about each joint (Rathmayer, 1967; Rathmayer and Koopmann, 1970). These *proprioreceptors* register not only the position but also the beginning, direction, and velocity of changes in position of a joint.

The more freedom of movement a joint has, the more propioreceptor ganglia are present. The coxa-trochanter joint, which can move in all directions, has five proprioceptive ganglia. All the other joints possess only two or three ganglia, which are located near the pivoting points of the joint. Within a given joint, one ganglion may be sensitive only to bending, while the other may respond only to stretching of the joint (Mill and Harris, 1977). The sensory cells of the ganglion are multipolar and lie directly below the joint membrane (Fig. 63b; Parry, 1960). Their dendrites fan out into the hypodermis beneath the joint membrane and terminate there as delicate free nerve endings. The shearing forces generated during leg movement are presumably transmitted to the dendritic terminals via the rigid hypodermis cells (Foelix and Choms, 1979). The situation is further complicated by small nerve fibers that make synaptic contacts with the sensory cells and their dendrites. These efferent nerve fibers possibly originate in the central nervous system and might control (inhibit) the activity of the proprioreceptor.

Chemical Senses

It has been known for a long time that spiders react to chemical stimuli. Just as humans can differentiate between the sense of smell (olfaction) and taste, so can spiders. *Taste* implies contact with a substance, usually at high concentration, whereas *olfaction* denotes that volatile substances affect receptors over relatively large distances, and often at very low concentrations. With many highly volatile substances (such as essential oils), one can easily elicit a behavioral reaction from the spider simply by putting the compound close to the animal. Strongly odoriferous substances usually cause the spider to run away, or at least to exhibit a local reaction like withdrawing a leg. Although such experiments prove the existence of an olfactory sense, they tell us little about the significance of olfaction under natural conditions.

   In the natural environment the spider most likely uses olfaction to find a mate during courtship and perhaps to recognize prey and enemies (see chapter 9). It has been shown that male orb-web spiders are apparently attracted by the "scent" given off by the female (Blanke, 1972; 1975b). A few days before her last molt, a male will not be attracted to a female; immediately after she molts, however, often several males will flock around her web. Presumably the mature female produces sex-specific substances (*sex pheromones*) that attract the male. Such pheromonal effects are, of course, well known from studies of insects (such as butterflies), and the pheromones involved have been chemically analyzed in great detail.

   Although there can be little doubt about the spider's ability to smell, the location of the actual olfactory organs has been under debate for a long time. The *tarsal organs* (Fig. 64) have remained likely candidates since they were first described in detail (Blumenthal, 1935). Usually the tarsal organs are small pits on the dorsal side of each tarsus, although in some spider families they may appear rod-shaped, like a hair (Forster, 1980). In either case they are multiply innervated and are connected to the external environment by several small pores (Foelix and Chu-Wang, 1973b). Recent electrophysiological investigations have shown that different volatile substances can excite the tarsal organs (Dumpert, 1978). Perhaps the best proof for the olfactory function of tarsal organs was attained by using the species-specific sex pheromone as a stimulus (Fig. 64b). The tarsal organ is also considered to be a sensor of humidity (Blumenthal, 1935), but further experiments are needed to

b   Pheromone   200 µV
1 sec

Fig. 64. (*a*) Tarsal organ of *Araneus diadematus.* The dendritic endings lie within the cuticular pit. The shafts of two tactile hairs can be seen on the left. 1,300×. (*b*) Electrophysiological registration of nerve impulses from the tarsal organ of a male *Cupiennius* after stimulation with female pheromone. (*b*) after Dumpert, 1978.)

clarify this function. The same is true for a putative olfactory receptor located between the rostrum and the palps (Legendre, 1956).

The most important chemoreceptors of spiders are the *contact chemoreceptors,* or taste hairs, which are found mainly on the distal segments of the legs and palps (Foelix, 1970b; Foelix and Chu-Wang, 1973b; Harris and Mill, 1973). At first glance these hair sensilla resemble the normal tactile hairs, yet they differ from them in three respects: (1) they arise at a steep angle (about 70°) from the leg surface, (2) the hair shaft is S-shaped, and (3) the hair tip is open to the outside. Each taste hair is usually innervated by 21 sensory cells: 2 nerve endings (mechanoreceptors) with tubular bodies terminate at the hair base, while the other 19 (chemosensitive) dendrites traverse the hair shaft to the opening near the hair tip (Fig. 65a).

An adult spider (*Araneus*) can possess over 1,000 chemosensitive hairs, most of which are concentrated on the tarsi of the first legs. This distribution helps explain many observations of spider behavior. For instance, spiders readily accept freshly killed flies after briefly touching them with their legs. Old dead flies, in contrast, are quickly discarded (Heil, 1936; Eberhard, 1969). Apparently spiders can determine the chemical properties of a substrate merely by probing it with their tarsi. Bristowe (1941, 1958) noted this ability in many different spiders and coined the term "taste-by-touch" sense. The observation that most spiders drop certain bugs or ticks after briefly touching them can be easily explained by the presence of chemicals detected by the taste hairs. In recent years the chemical sensitivity of these sensilla has also been proven directly by using electrophysiological methods (Drewes and Bernard, 1976; Harris and Mill, 1977b).

In addition to testing the quality of food, contact chemoreceptors are also used during courtship. Many male ground-living spiders follow the trail of a conspecific female and often begin their courtship rituals (such as palp drumming) when they encounter threads laid down by her (Bristowe and Locket, 1926; Kaston, 1936; Rovner, 1968a; Dijkstra, 1976). Most likely, some specific substances, perhaps sex pheromones, associated with the female's silk trigger the male's courtship behavior. If the female's spinnerets are sealed with wax so that no silk can be deposited on the ground, then the males fail to court (Dondale and Hedgekar, 1973). So far, very little is known about these pheromones, and it is not clear whether they are perceived by contact chemoreception alone or, eventually, also by olfaction (as in web spiders). The borderline

Fig. 65. (*a*) Diagram of a chemosensitive hair. Two mechanosensitive dendrites (arrow) terminate at the hair base, while the chemosensory dendrites traverse the hair shaft until they reach the terminal pore opening. (After Foelix and Chu-Wang, 1973b.) (*b* and *c*) Electrophysiological recording after stimulation of a single hair sensillum. (After Harris. 1974.) (*b*) Stimulation with a 1 M salt solution causes several neurons to respond with spikes. (*c*) Displacement of the hair shaft in a distal or proximal direction triggers the response of a mechanoreceptor at the hair base.

between olfaction and taste is not very distinct, and it may well be that the taste hairs also sense certain smells.

Contact chemoreception has been extensively studied in insects. The hair receptors of insects are very similar to those described for spiders, and they are similarly located on the legs and mouth parts. In flies, stimulation of a single tarsal hair with sugar will trigger the extension of the proboscis. A comparable behavior reaction was elicited from wolf spiders after a single chemosensitive hair on the palp was touched with a 0.2 M salt solution: the spider responded by flicking the entire palp in withdrawal (Drewes and Bernard, 1976).

Some chemosensitive hairs do occur on the mouth parts (on the maxillae and labium), but the presence of "taste cells" in the pharynx (Millot, 1936, 1946) remains questionable. My own electron-microscopic investigations of the gullet have shown that the supposed "taste cells" are in fact gland cells. On the other hand, it is known that spiders wipe their mouth parts extensively after having bitten into distasteful prey (Bristowe, 1941).

Vision

In most spiders the sense of vision plays only a minor role in behavior. Many spiders are active at night and are thus more dependent on tactile and chemical cues than on sight. For web spiders visual stimuli seem to be especially unnecessary, since these spiders can build their webs at night and can catch their prey in total darkness, but to conclude from these observations that vision is irrelevant for such spiders would be premature. For instance, the orb weaver *Araneus sexpunctatus* (synonym *Nuctenea umbratica*) can detect very subtle changes in light intensity (Homann, 1947); leaving its retreat in the evening is apparently closely related to the diminishing light at dusk. Other orb weavers drop very quickly out of the hubs of their webs when an observer approaches them, and this behavior is most likely a response to visual stimuli alone.

Vision is, however, important to some spiders other than orb weavers. Sheet-web spiders (Agelenidae) and wolf spiders (Lycosidae) can perceive polarized light and use it to orient themselves. For most "modern" hunting spiders (Lycosidae, Thomisidae, Salticidae), the sense of vision is vital, not only for capturing prey but also for recognizing the opposite sex during courtship. Jumping spiders kept in the dark (or under dark red light) cannot catch prey or notice a conspecific (Jackson, 1977). Even if a fly bumps into the spider, she will not attempt to seize it. In a later section we will look in more detail at the highly developed eyes of salticids.

Eye Structure and Function

Most spiders possess eight eyes arranged in two or three rows on the frontal carapace. According to their position, one can differentiate between anterior median eyes (AME), anterior lateral eyes (ALE), posterior median eyes (PME), and posterior lateral eyes (PLE) (see Fig. 9). All cells are ocelli, or so-called simple eyes: beneath a single cuticular lens lie a cellular *vitreous body* and the *visual cells*, which together with *pigment cells* compose the *retina*

(Fig. 66). Structurally the eyes are of two different types, *main eyes* and *secondary eyes*.

The *main eyes* are always the AME. The light-sensitive parts (rhabdomeres) of the visual cells lie distally; that is, they point toward the light, and are thus called everted eyes (Fig. 66a). Since the main eyes lack a reflecting layer (tapetum), they appear black. In some spiders the retina can be displaced sideways by the action

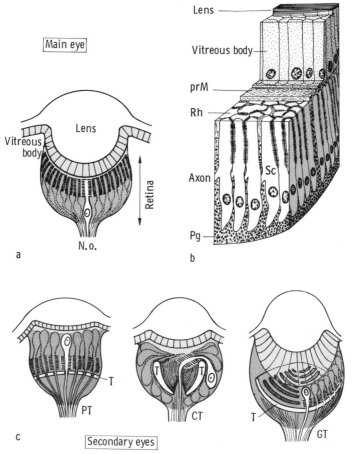

Fig. 66. (*a*) Diagrammatic sagittal section through a main eye. N.o. = nervus opticus. (After Homann, 1971.) (*b*) Fine structure of a main eye of *Agelena*. Pg = pigment cells, prM = preretinal membrane, Rh = rhabdome, Sc = sensory cell. (After Schröer, 1977.) (*c*) The three types of secondary eyes differ in the structure of their tapetum (T). PT = primitive type, CT = canoe-shaped type, GT = grate type. (After Homann, 1971.)

of 1–6 muscles, which leads to a considerable increase of the visual field. Actual focusing of the image does not occur; this is not really necessary, since the lenses are small and of short focal length, yielding a large depth of field for objects at close range. The optic nerve usually arises from the middle of the eye cup. In some spiders (such as Agelenidae), however, the optic nerve emanates from one side of the eye cup, because the axon of each visual cell originates laterally (Fig. 66b). The main eyes of most spiders are small and have rather few visual cells (Homann, 1971). Jumping spiders (Salticidae) and crab spiders (Thomisidae) are an exception; their specialized main eyes will be discussed below. Those spiders with only six eyes (Dysderidae, Sicariidae, Oonopidae) lack main eyes.

The *secondary eyes* are "inverted," that is, the light-sensitive rhabdomeres point away from the incoming light (Fig. 66c); this construction is similar in principle to that of the vertebrate retina. Most secondary eyes possess a light-reflecting *tapetum* of crystalline deposits and therefore appear light. It has been assumed that such eyes are especially suited for seeing at night or in dim light, but this has never been substantiated experimentally. Although the tapetum varies a great deal among the different spider families, we can distinguish three basic types (Fig. 66c): (1) a primitive tapetum (PT), which fills the entire eye cup and leaves holes only for nerve fibers; (2) a canoe-shaped tapetum (CT), which consists of two lateral walls and a medial gap to allow nerve fibers to exit; and (3) a grated tapetum (GT), which resembles the grill of an oven. In some spider families (for instance, Salticidae and Oxyopidae) a tapetum is altogether lacking.

Whereas the main eyes are structurally rather uniform in most spiders, the secondary eyes differ considerably among different spider families. Since these differences are small among members of one family, the anatomy of the secondary eyes has been used for the systematics of spiders (Homann, 1950, 1952).

PT-type secondary eyes are typical for the Mesothelae, Orthognatha, and haplogyne spiders (the "primitive" spiders). The CT-type is common among theridiids, agelenids, clubionids, amaurobiids, and many linyphiids and araneids. The GT-type is found in many hunting spiders: Lycosidae, Oxyopidae, Pisauridae, and in the cribellate Psechridae and Zoropsidae. Even within the same species different types of secondary eyes can occur together. *Araneus diadematus*, for instance, has anterior lateral eyes of the CT-type. Its posterior lateral eyes, however, are only laterally of the CT-type; medially, they lack a tapetum (Homann, 1971).

The most efficient secondary eyes are those with a grated tapetum. The spherical lens ensures an image of high quality, and the elongated vitreous body provides the necessary distance for a sharp focus. The resolution of the image depends on the number and density of rhabdomeres in the retina. The PME of the wolf spider *Pardosa* contain about 2,500 rhabdomeres, the ALE of *Araneus* only 80, and the secondary eyes of *Speocera* only 10–20. Obviously, with such a small number of visual cells in the retina a spider would not be expected to detect much more than movement (Homann, 1971).

Perception of Polarized Light

Although by human standards most spiders have poor vision, some spiders can "see" something we cannot: polarized light. Sunlight becomes polarized when light waves are scattered by molecules or other small particles in the earth's atmosphere. The light waves then vibrate in a specific direction at each point of the sky. This results in a specific polarization pattern that changes with the position of the sun. Whereas the human eye, or generally speaking any vertebrate eye, cannot register the polarization pattern of the sky, arthropod eyes can. Studies of bees and ants have shown that they use polarized light for orientation (von Frisch, 1967; Wehner, 1976). Very similar observations have been made for some wolf spiders and sheet-web spiders (Papi, 1955; Görner, 1958; Magni, 1966).

The wolf spider *Arctosa perita* dwells along the banks of rivers and the shores of lakes and can easily walk on the water's surface (see Fig. 116). If such a spider is thrown onto the water, it returns directly to shore (Papi, 1955). However, if *Arctosa* is transferred from its customary northern shore to the opposite southern shore of a lake and is then thrown onto the water, it will run out onto the lake, but only if the sky is clear. If the sky is overcast, the spider will return to the closest shore. Apparently, under a clear sky the spider orients itself by using the sun and the direction of the polarized light. It uses visual landmarks for its orientation if the sky is cloudy.

The sheet-web spider *Agelena labyrinthica* becomes disoriented during a return to its retreat if one changes the normal pattern of sky light by rotating a polarization filter above the spider (Görner, 1958). By covering specific eyes with opaque paint it has been shown that only the main eyes (AME) can analyze the plane of polarization. It has been found that the ventral visual cells have rhabdomeres with specifically aligned microvilli that are probably responsible for detecting polarized light (Schröer, 1974, 1976). The retina of the main eye seems to be divided into two functional parts: a ventral part for polarized light perception and a dorsal part for the perception of relatively coarse images.

The Visual Sense of Jumping Spiders

It is well known that the behavior of jumping spiders is strongly dependent on their visual sense; orientation, prey capture, courtship, and escape are all essentially controlled by visual stimuli. Indeed, among the most distinctive features of jumping spiders are their large eyes. Especially impressive is the anterior row of eyes, which consists of the large main eyes (AME) and the slightly smaller anterior lateral eyes (ALE) (Figs. 7, 67). The posterior median eyes (PME) are also of considerable size, whereas the posterior lateral eyes (PLE) are much reduced (some workers refer to the PME as PLE, and vice versa). Many elegant experiments (Homann, 1928; Crane, 1949) have demonstrated that the secondary eyes are primarily movement detectors, while the main eyes perceive detailed images (form perception). Before we discuss these experiments in any detail, we must get acquainted with the specialized anatomy of the jumping spider's eyes.

The efficiency of any eye is determined by the design of its optics and by the structure of the retina. Both are well developed in the eyes of jumping spiders. The main eyes are characterized by large lenses (Fig. 67), a large vitreous body with a focal length of 770 μm, and a retina with multiple layers of visual cells (Land, 1969a; Eakin and Brandenburger, 1971). The main eyes can be compared optically with a telephotographic lens, through which only a small area of an image can be seen, but at high resolution. The "movable" retinas of the main eyes partly compensate for the narrow angle of vision; several antagonistic muscles are attached to the main eye (Scheuring, 1914), and they can move the retina in all three dimensions (Fig. 68). This, of course, greatly increases the visual field.

The retina is composed of four different layers of visual cells (Fig. 69a). It is possible that each layer is preferentially sensitive to a certain wavelength of light. Devoe (1975) and Yamashita and Tateda (1976) have shown that the retina of a jumping spider indeed has different spectral sensitivities. Maximal sensitivities were found at wavelengths of 360, 480–500, and 580 nm, and it was concluded that each retinal layer contains a different visual pigment. In the most distal layer (layer 4) the rhabdomeres are aligned

Fig. 67. (*a*) Head-on view of the jumping spider *Phidippus*. Most of the frontal carapace is occupied by the anterior row of eyes. (Photo *a*: Troyer and Foelix.) (*b*) Horizontal section through the anterior row of eyes. AME = anterior median eyes, ALE = anterior lateral eyes, PME = posterior median eyes, ON = optic neuropil of the CNS, R = retina. 85×.

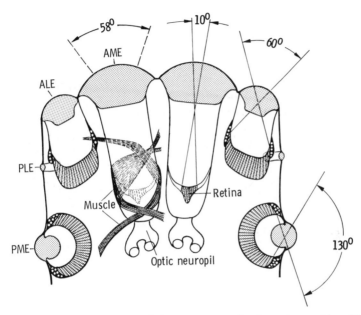

Fig. 68. Horizontal section of the prosoma of a jumping spider. Visual angles of the various eyes are indicated. The angle (58°) given for the left main eye refers to the maximum visual angle that the spider can attain by using its retinal muscles to shift the eye cup laterally. Abbreviations as in Fig. 67. (After Homann, 1928, and Land, 1969b.)

roughly perpendicular to the rhabdomeres of layers 1–3. Therefore, one might expect that layer 4 might detect polarized light. The specialization of layer 4 is underscored by the fact that, for optical reasons, it can no longer receive a truly focused image. This corresponds somewhat to the situation found in insect ocelli, where the focal plane of the lens also lies behind the retina.

Another interesting feature of the jumping spider's main eyes is the distribution of the 1,000 visual cells within the retina. The density of visual cells is ten times higher in the central region (the *fovea*) than in the periphery (Fig. 69b), and the angle of divergence between neighboring receptors is very small in the fovea—12′, compared to 40′ in the periphery. The spider's greatest visual acuity must therefore lie in the center of the retina (Homann, 1928; Land, 1969b). The back of the retina is covered by dark pigments, as in vertebrate eyes. The visual cells of the main eyes, however, lack the individual pigment screens found in cells of the secondary eyes.

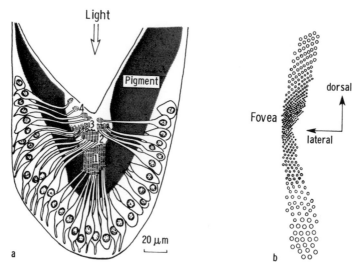

Fig. 69.   Retina from the main eye of a jumping spider. (*a*) Horizontal section showing four different receptor layers (1–4), surrounded by a pigment layer. (*b*) Schematic frontal view of layer 1 of the retina; each circle represents the terminal of a visual cell. Note that the density of receptors is highest in the central retina (fovea). (After Land, 1969a.)

The secondary eyes of jumping spiders are either elongated (the ALE have a focal length of 330 μm) or spherical (PME focal length of 240 μm) and possess relatively large visual fields (Figs. 68, 70). The extent of the entire visual field of a jumping spider is effectively the sum of the individual visual fields of the secondary eyes (Fig. 68). It is significant that the visual fields of the ALE overlap by 40° (Homann, 1928); the resulting binocular vision enables the spider to estimate distances. The very narrow visual fields of the main eyes, in contrast, do not overlap. Structural characteristics of the secondary eyes are the lack of a tapetum, the location of the visual cell bodies outside the eye cup (Fig. 70a), and the occurrence of pigmented and unpigmented supporting cells between the rhabdomeres (Figs. 70–72; Eakin and Brandenburger, 1971). The single-layered retina has only one cell type, which is maximally sensitive to wavelengths between 535–540 nm (Yamashita and Tateda, 1976). The number of visual cells in the secondary eyes is higher than in the main eyes, 3,000–6,000 cells in an ALE and 8,000–16,000 in a PME (Land, 1972b).

How does a jumping spider use its sophisticated eye structures? The exceptional visual abilities of jumping spiders become most

Fig. 70. (*a*) PME of a jumping spider. The bodies of the visual cells (S) are situated outside the eye cup and thus do not interfere with the incoming light. A tapetum is lacking. L = lens, R = retina, Vb = vitreous body. 150×. (*b*) ALE of a theridiid. The retina (R) is bordered by the canoe-shaped tapetum (T); a vitreous body is barely visible as a thin layer beneath the lens (L). The visual cells (S) are demarcated by pigment granules. 530×.

evident during prey capture (Homann, 1928; Land, 1969b). Moving prey is usually first detected by the wide-angle lenses of the secondary eyes. These eyes respond to small *movements* of an object, analogous to our peripheral vision. The maximum distance at which a spider can still see something is 30–40 cm. If the object (prey) moves closer than 20 cm, the spider turns to face it, and now the object becomes fixed with the movable retinas of the main eyes. The image of the prey is projected exactly onto the fovea, the central region of the retina. If the prey moves on, the eye muscles shift the retinas appropriately to maintain foveal vision. Behavioral experiments show that a true perception of images occurs at distances of less than 8–10 cm. In this range only about 100 visual cells are stimulated, yet even this may suffice to allow prey to be distinguished from conspecifics. At this distance the spider will pursue the prey, and at less than 3–4 cm it will stalk it.

During the "recognition" process the muscles of the retinas are in constant motion: the shape of the object is quickly scanned horizontally, and, at the same time, the main eye is rotated along its optical axis. This scanning procedure is apparently necessary to permit identification of an object; only thereafter follows the stalking of the prey. The final leap is performed at a distance of 1–2 cm.

Fig. 71. Fine structure of the retina. (*a*) Longitudinal section of a ALE of a jumping spider. The rhabdomeres (Rh) of the visual cells are surrounded by pigmented (P) and unpigmented supporting cells (Sc). Rf = axons of visual cells. 3,600×. (*b*) Cross section corresponding to (*a*). Note the pronounced isolation of the rhabdomeres by the interspersed pigment cells. 3,000×.

From the foregoing description a definite "division of labor" between the main eyes and the secondary eyes is thus apparent. Although most of the total retinal area belongs to the secondary eyes, it serves only for perceiving and locating *movement*. The small central region of the main eye's retina is the only area suitable for *form perception*. The importance of the main eyes becomes clear when one covers their lenses with opaque wax (Homann, 1928): stalking behavior is completely absent during prey capture, and the final leaps are too long and often unsuccessful. A male with his main eyes blinded will likewise leave out the typical courtship dances that he usually performs in front of the female (Fig. 142). In contrast, eliminating the visual input from the secondary eyes produces less drastic effects. Obviously, the total visual field becomes extremely narrow, and therefore the spider has difficulty in noticing the prey at all. If prey is located, the stalking behavior is iniated much earlier (at a distance of 10 cm) and the final jump is aimed too far.

The perception of images can be impressively demonstrated by setting up a mirror in front of a male jumping spider. The mirror image is then threatened like a real conspecific opponent (Fig. 73; Forster and Forster, 1973). Models of prey will also be attacked if they are moved in front of a jumping spider. It is interesting that

Fig. 72. (*a*) Rhabdomeres (Rh) in longitudinal section. The laterally projecting microvilli contain the visual pigment. 17,000×. (*b*) A cross section of the rhabdomeric microvilli shows the tight packing of these light sensitive structures. 20,000×.

Fig. 73. A male jumping spider (*Trite auricoma*) threatens his own mirror image. (Photo: *Forster.*)

three-dimensional models are definitely preferred to two-dimensional figures (Drees, 1952).

Whether or not jumping spiders can see colors remains an open question. That jumping spiders are often conspicuously colored has been noted repeatedly as an indirect argument for their color vision. This seems reasonable, since in fish and birds a colorful phenotype is often correlated with the ability to differentiate colors. Somewhat more convincing evidence comes from behavioral experiments in which jumping spiders could distinguish blue and orange paper strips from 26 shades of gray (Crane, 1949; Kaestner, 1950). The sensitivities of the main eyes to different parts of the visible spectrum further argue for color vision (De Voe, 1975; Yamashita and Tateda, 1976). Since we still lack rigorous proof, we should perhaps be reminded that it took several decades to demonstrate color vision in the domestic cat.

What use jumping spiders make of their ultraviolet (UV) receptors (maximum spectral sensitivity at 360 nm) also remains to be explained. Experiments dealing with prey capture under UV-light have given both positive (Young and Wanless, 1967) and negative results (Kaestner, 1950). Most spider eyes seem to be insensitive to red light, as are most insect eyes.

It should be emphasized that the visual acuity of jumping spider eyes can easily compete with that of the compound eyes of insects. (Homann, 1928). The main eyes of a jumping spider are even superior to the insect's compound eyes in optical resolution. The commonly used term *simple ocelli* does not apply here; on the contrary, the highly developed eyes of jumping spiders demonstrate just how sophisticated ocelli can be.

Central Nervous System

Compared with other arthropods, spiders have a highly condensed central nervous system (CNS). Instead of a chain of interconnected ganglia (a ventral nerve cord) extending throughout the body, spiders have only two compact ganglia: the *supra-* and the *subesophageal ganglia.* They are both located in the prosoma (Fig. 74). True abdominal ganglia exist only in the embryo. During development they migrate into the prosoma where they fuse with the ganglia of the appendages, giving rise to the large subesophageal ganglion. The much smaller supraesophageal ganglion sits in front and on top of the subesophageal ganglion; it consists of the cheliceral ganglia and the "brain" (the association centers). The boundary between supra- and subesophageal ganglion is marked by the esophagus, which divides the CNS horizontally (Figs. 74, 75b). Several nerves emanate from each ganglion and together constitute the *peripheral nervous system.*

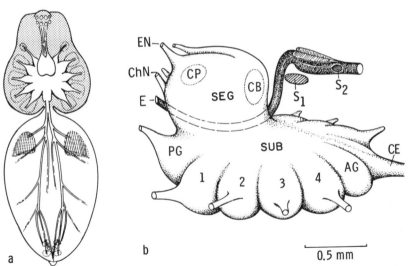

Fig. 74. (*a*) Nervous system of *Tegenaria*, dorsal view. The CNS lies in the prosoma and gives off nerve bundles to the extremities and to the organs of the opisthosoma. (After Gerhardt and Kaestner, 1938.) (*b*) CNS of *Tegenaria*, lateral view. The esophagus (E) divides the CNS into a supra- (SEG) and a subesophageal ganglion (SUB). EN = eye nerves, ChN = cheliceral nerves, PG = palpal ganglion, 1–4 = leg ganglia, AG = abdominal ganglion, CE = cauda equina, CB = central body, CP = corpora pedunculata, $S_{1,2}$ = Schneider's organs 1 and 2. (After Kühne, 1959.)

Fig. 75. Prosoma of a young *Tegenaria*, longitudinal section. (*a*) The CNS is clearly divided into separate ganglia (cf. Fig. 74b). Cb = central body, Ch = chelicera, Chg = cheliceral ganglion, E = eye, ES = endosternite, Gl = poison gland, MX = maxilla, Pg = palpal ganglion. (*b*) This sagittal section demonstrates the subdivision of the CNS into a central neuropil (Np) and a peripheral cortex (Ctx). E = esophagus, Ph = pharynx, Ro = rostrum, St = sucking stomach. 230×.

General Structure

That the compact CNS of spiders is composed of individual ganglia can clearly be seen in young spiderlings, where septa of connective tissue, which also contain blood vessels and sometimes tracheoles, delineate the borders of adjacent ganglia (Fig. 75a). In the "ancient" Mesothelae, segmentation of the CNS is still apparent in the adult (Millot, 1949).

The star-shaped subesophageal ganglion consists mainly of the fused ganglia of the ten appendages (Fig. 74). The different ganglia are interconnected by many interneurons. Motor nerves for the palps and legs are given off laterally from these ganglia. Caudally, the abdominal ganglia are attached to the subesophageal ganglion, and from them arises a tapered nerve bundle, the *cauda equina*, which innervates the entire opisthosoma. The cheliceral ganglia stem originally from the subesophageal ganglion, but during embryonic development they migrate forward and come to rest on either side *above* the esophagus. Topographically then, they belong to the supraesophageal ganglion, though remarkably, the fibers that connect these ganglia remain behind the esophagus (the *postoral commissures*). The cheliceral ganglia give off the nerves for the musculature of the chelicerae, the pharynx, and the poison glands (St. Rémy, 1887). The "brain" itself receives only the optic nerves and thus contains only visual and association centers. The combination of the cheliceral ganglia and the brain is called the syncerebrum, or *supraesophageal ganglion*.

Cellular Structure

Histological sections show a distinct division of the CNS into a marginal layer of neurons (the *cortex*) and a central mass of nerve fibers (the *neuropil*). The surface of the CNS is covered by a connective tissue layer, which is rather thick in Orthognatha (Babu, 1965; Legendre, 1958, 1961b). The cell bodies of the neurons are found mostly on the ventral side of the CNS, and most of them give off only a single axon (that is, they are pseudo-unipolar; see Fig. 76). Several different types of neurons can be distinguished, the largest of which are thought to be motoneurons; others are interneurons, which connect different ganglia, and some can be identified as neurosecretory cells (Babu, 1965, 1969). The total number of motoneurons has been counted as 900 for a female orb-web spider (*Argiope*) but only 60 for the male (Babu, 1975). The entire CNS ap-

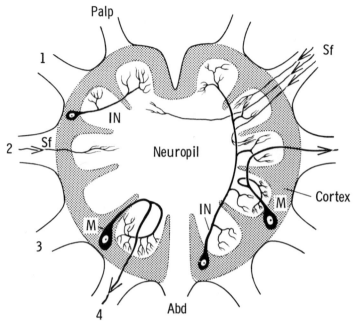

Fig. 76. Subesophageal ganglion of a "tarantula" (*Poecilotheria*), horizontal section. Simple connections are pictured on the left: an interneuron (IN) connecting the pedipalp ganglion with the ganglion of leg 1; an afferent fiber (Sf) coming from leg 2; a motoneuron (M) exiting into leg 4. Connections of greater complexity are shown on the right: an interneuron (IN) sending branches to all extremities; a motoneuron (M) of the third leg ganglion, the axon of which exits into the second leg; three sensory fibers (Sf) from the first leg, which either remain ipsilateral (near leg 2) or continue contralaterally to the palpal ganglion. Abd = abdominal nerve. (After Babu, 1969.)

parently contains 30,000 neurons, 13,000 of which belong to the supraesophageal ganglion.

The neuropil is a dense network of nerve fibers, and most of the synaptic connections occur there (Fig. 77b). During postembryonic development the number of nerve fibers forming the neuropil increases markedly (Meier, 1967), because of the repeated branching of the dendritic processes (Fig. 77b, inset). The number of neurons within the cortex remains constant, however (Babu, 1975). Thus the apparent growth of the CNS is caused mostly by an increase of the neuropil. In very young spiderlings the CNS takes up almost 50% of the volume of the prosoma; in adult spiders the volume has

Fig. 77. The complexity of the CNS is apparent in electron micrographs. (*a*) Border region of cortex (CTX) and neuropil (NP) of the central body, 3,000×. (*b*) Detail from the neuropil. Innumerable small nerve fibers intertwine and make synaptic contacts (S). 12,600×. *Inset:* The delicate ramifications result from repeated branching of one dendrite (Golgi preparation, 430×.)

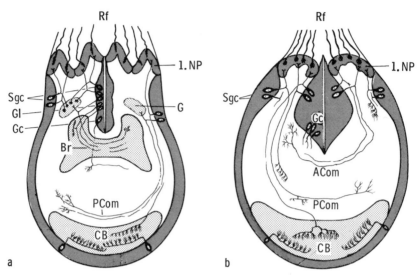

Fig. 78. Comparison of the supraesophageal ganglion in (*a*) wandering spiders and (*b*) web spiders, horizontal section. Rf = receptor fibers, Sgc = visual ganglia cells, Gl = globuli cells, Gc = simple ganglia cells, G = glomerulus, Br = bridge, Acom = anterior commissure, PCom = posterior commissure, CB = central body, 1.NP = first optical neuropil. (After Hanström, 1928.)

dropped to 5–10%, even though the adult CNS is 10–20 times larger than it is in early nymphal stages (Babu, 1975).

The dorsal part of the brain, the *lobus opticus*, is a particularly complex part of the CNS and is quite different in web spiders and wandering spiders (Hanström, 1921, 1928, 1935). The brain of wandering spiders has two different visual centers: an anterior association center (the *corpora pedunculata*), which receives information only from the secondary eyes, and a posterior association center (the *central body*), which integrates input from the main and secondary eyes (Fig. 78a). Immediately after entering the brain the axons of the visual cells form an optic neuropil, where each axon makes multiple synapses with visual ganglion cells (Trujillo-Cenóz, 1965). These cells relay information to the *globuli cells*, which form the second optic neuropil (or *glomerulus*). Bundles of globuli cell processes cross over to the other side of the brain, forming the *bridge*. The complex of bridge, glomerulus, and globuli cells is referred to as the *corpora pedunculata*. The posterior association center, the central body, is not only the connection site for the visual pathway but also a motor and association center.

The visual centers of web spiders are not as well developed; globuli cells and glomeruli are completely lacking, and instead of the bridge there is only a small anterior visual commissure (Fig. 78b). It is believed that the well-developed central body of the orb-web spiders is related to their ability to construct elaborate webs.

Neurosecretion (Stomatogastric System)

As their names implies, neurosecretory cells exhibit characteristics of both nerve cells and gland cells, for they have axons and produce secretions. Functionally, these cells are a link between the nervous system and the hormonal system. The activity of neurosecretory cells in spiders is probably correlated within certain events in their life cycle, such as molting or sexual maturation. (That hormones control development in insects has long been established; the respective endocrine organs are the corpora cardiaca and the corpora allata.)

The neuroendocrine system of spiders consists of several groups of neurosecretory cells in the CNS and several "retrocerebral" organs that act as reservoirs or even as production sites of neurosecretions (Gabe, 1955). Clusters of neurosecretory cells are present in the supra- as well as in the subesophageal ganglion (Fig. 79). In the subesophageal ganglion a serial (metameric) distribution of these cells is evident. Neurosecretory cells can be identified histologically by specific stains, such as paraldehyde-fuchsine or chrome-hematoxylin-phloxine. Behind the brain ("retrocerebral") lie several neuroendocrine organs: *Schneider's organs* (also known as stomatogastric ganglia or sympathetic ganglia), the *Tropfenkomplex*, the *stomadeal bridge*, and the *esophageal ganglion* with the nervus recurrens. The arrangement of this complex is shown in Fig. 79a.

Schneider's organs 1 lie directly behind the supraesophageal ganglion and are continuous with the Tropfenkomplex, where the neurosecretions are released into the hemolymph. Schneider's organs 2 are situated along the lateral walls of the sucking stomach, close to the aorta (Fig. 74). The "stomatogastric system" consists of the stomadeal bridge, the anterior rostral nerve, and the posterior nervus recurrens. The nervus recurrens terminates in the small esophageal ganglion, which has not yet been shown to be a source of neurosecretion (Kühne, 1959). The specific functions of the neuroendocrine organs are largely unknown. Definite neurosecretory cells appear only shortly before the spider reaches matu-

Fig. 79.   Neuroendocrine and stomatogastric systems. (*a*) Dorsal view of the supraesophageal ganglion (SEG). Stbr = stomadeal bridge, nsc = neurosecretory cells, Schn. 1, 2 = Schneider's organs 1 and 2, TrK = Tropfenkomplex, SeG = esophageal ganglion with nervus recurrens, St = sucking stomach. (After various authors.) (*b*) Detail from Schneider's organ 1 of *Tegenaria.* Many nerve fibers possess dark neurosecretory granules and also make synaptic contacts (S). 3,900×. *Inset:* 15,000×.

rity, and it is believed that maturation of the reproductive cells is closely related to neurosecretion (Babu, 1973). Whether or not the molting process is controlled by neurosecretions is still very uncertain (Kühne, 1959; Streble, 1966; Eckert, 1967).

The CNS and Behavior

We want to examine here a few examples of the ways that a spider's CNS works to integrate a variety of sensory information, enabling the spider to respond "appropriately" to environmental stimuli, and, especially, to orient itself. External sensory input, as well as proprioceptive input, can be stored in the memory and be recalled later. Actually, the process of learning may occur within

seconds: a single run out of the retreat is often sufficient for the
sheet-web spider *Agelena* to return to it in a direct course (Bartels,
1929; Görner, 1958). Such "engrams" can be formed either
through visual or kinesthetic input. Usually the behavior of a spider is the result of the integration of several kinds of sensory input.

When *Agelena* catches prey on its sheet web and then carries it
back to its retreat, it uses visual and kinesthetic cues to make the
return run. Additionally, the inclination of the web (gravity) and
the pattern of elasticity of the web may play a role in the spider's
navigation (Bartels, 1929; Bartels and Baltzer, 1928; Holzapfel,
1933; Görner, 1958, 1966). Even when all external cues are eliminated, *Agelena* can still return to its retreat in a straight line; in
this case the spider's orientation has to be purely kinesthetic
(idiothetic). If one designs an experiment in which visual and kinesthetic cues contradict each other, the spider reacts with a compromise. For instance, if the position of a light source is shifted immediately after prey is captured, *Agelena* initially turns in the
correct direction, toward the retreat. While running back, however, the spider gradually drifts off to one side in an attempt to correct its course according to the new position of the light (Fig. 80a).
This deviation from the correct course shows that a comparison

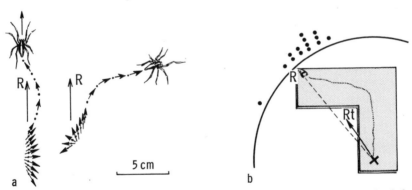

Fig. 80.   Direction of return runs to the retreat by *Agelena*. (a) On the left,
a control run; on the right, a run after the light source had been displaced
clockwise by 110°. The spider is influenced by the visual cue; shifting the
light causes it to deviate markedly from the straight course of return (R).
(After Görner, 1972.) (b) Choice of starting direction on return runs of *Agelena* in a right-angle frame under polarized light. The spider was lured to
prey (X) via a detour (stippled line). The black dots give the initial direction of each individual return run. Note that the average starting direction
of all the returns (Rt) is very close to the ideal return route XR (dashed
line). (After Görner, 1958.)

must take place in the CNS between the course as judged visually and that based on kinesthetic cues. Indeed, recent investigations show that visual and kinesthetic information seem to enter a common storage site, where they are integrated to give a compromise solution to the problem of direction (Görner, 1966; Dornfeldt, 1972). Apparently one of the two means of orientation can also be "switched off": some spiders orient themselves purely kinesthetically despite existing visual cues (Moller, 1970).

The ability of spiders to evaluate sensory information to alter their behavior has been seen in many experiments. For instance, *Agelena* returns straight back to its retreat even if it had been forced to make a detour on the way out (Fig. 80b). This means that during the run out onto the web the spider processes visual and kinesthetic information in the CNS and then "calculates" the shortest return. Besides the ability to orient themselves, *Agelena* and *Cupiennius* can also estimate distance (Dornfeldt, 1975; Seyfarth and Barth, 1972). This is evident when the spider searches for lost prey: at first the spider returns in a straight line to the capture site; when it nears the site it changes its course into irregular "searching" loops (Fig. 62b).

Integration of information by the CNS also occurs in the visual system of salticids (Land, 1971). A jumping spider adjusts the long axis of its body to be perpendicular to the path of a moving object so that the object can be fixed with the main eyes. The turn is triggered by input from the secondary eyes and is executed without any visual feedback. Thus when an object appears 80° to the left, the information coming from the retinas is sent to the legs as the command "turn 80° to the left, then stop." Each retinal area receives a slightly different image and therefore conveys slightly different information to the leg muscles. The CNS has to transform the information about the position of an object provided by the secondary eyes into a complex motor pattern that results in a precise and "precalculated" turn. When a moving object enters the visual field of the *secondary* eyes, a jumping spider will not always react by turning towards it. Sometimes the spider simply sits there and shows no apparent reaction at all. However, a closer examination reveals that the muscles of the main eyes are active, although the legs do not move. Apparently the CNS receives the stimulus from the secondary eyes but transmits the information only to the main eyes and not to the leg muscles (Land, 1971).

To attribute specific functions to specific areas of the brain is not yet possible. Short exposures of the supraesophageal ganglion to a laser beam have produced several irreversible changes in the web pattern of *Araneus*, but such experiments have not led to a mapping of the centers responsible for web building (Witt, 1969).

We can speak of *learning* as the alteration of behavior by experience. Although spiders are better known for their stereotypical behavior, many experiments have demonstrated their capacity to learn and their behavioral plasticity. In one such experiment, dead flies that had been soaked in either a 6% glucose solution (sweet) or a 0.5% quinine solution (bitter) were thrown into the orb webs of *Araneus diadematus*. The spiders were then lured to the quinine flies with a tuning fork of the frequency of middle C and to the glucose flies with a fork of the frequency C_1 (one octave above C). Glucose flies were always bitten and eaten, but the quinine flies were rejected. If the flies were replaced by glass beads and touched with a C_1-tuning fork, the spiders still tried to bite into them. In contrast, glass beads vibrating at the frequency C were rejected, indicating that the spider associated the frequency C with the bitter taste of the quinine flies (Bays, 1962).

Another experiment showing a spider's ability to learn from experience involved the araneid *Zygiella*. When prey hits the web (Fig. 98a), the spider will rush down along the signal thread; at the hub it chooses the radial thread that leads to the prey. When returning to its retreat it uses exactly the same path, in reverse. If the entire web is turned upside down, and the spider is then lured onto the web by a fly or tuning fork, the spider can still quickly reach the source of vibration. However, it has great difficulties on its way back. At first the spider runs in the original direction, which leads it to the periphery of the web. Only after some searching and several periods of rest does the spider find its way back to the retreat. If this experiment is repeated many times, the spider returns much faster (Le Guelte, 1969). Such improvement depends on the number of trials and also on the amount of time that elapses between trials. Definite improvement occurs only if trials are separated by less than four hours, suggesting that spiders have something akin to a "short-term memory." Long-term effects can also be demonstrated. Spiders tested after 24 hours do not return to the retreat quickly on their first attempt, yet in subsequent trials they learn the way faster than inexperienced control spiders do.

A clear example of memory in spiders is provided by web spiders, which can relocate prey previously captured. If a spider is busy feeding on a fly when a second fly gets stuck in the web, she leaves the first prey at the hub and rushes to the new one. After wrapping it up, she will leave it at the capture site and return to the first fly. If that fly has been removed in the meantime, the spider makes typical searching movements. The same is true if the "storage prey" is taken out of the web (Grünbaum, 1927; H. Peters, 1951). In both cases the spider seems to remember the existence and location of a previously captured fly. Jumping spiders can even remember uncaptured prey. They will often make detours while pursuing prey they have spotted at a site (for example, on a leaf) that is not directly accessible, but they retain a memory of the relative position of the prey at all times. This is expressed in the form of quick turns that reorient the spider to face the expected position of the prey (Hill, 1979).

From these descriptions it is clear that spiders are not simply reflex machines; they can react quite differently to the same stimulus. Their behavioral plasticity was highlighted when two *Araneus diadematus* built their orb webs under condition of weightlessness in the space capsule Skylab (Witt et al., 1977). This is particularly remarkable because gravity is normally an essential factor in the orientation of *Araneus* (H. Peters, 1932).

5

Spider Webs

The evolution of spider silk has been an event comparable in importance to the evolution of flight in the insects, or warmbloodedness in the vertebrates.

M. R. Gray, 1978

THE most characteristic feature of spiders is their ability to produce silken threads. Although certain insects (for example, some lepidoptera, hymenoptera, and neuroptera) are also capable of silk production, this ability is usually restricted to a single stage in their life span, such as building a cocoon prior to pupation. In contrast, *all* spiders possess spinning glands, which they use not only for making egg sacs (cocoons) and draglines but also for building snares.

Spider Silk

Silk is the secretory product of the spinning glands. Although different spinning glands produce different kinds of silk, all silks are proteinaceous and belong to the fibroins. The molecular weight of the fibroin from the orb weaver *Nephila* has been determined to be 30,000 (Braunitzer and Wolff, 1955). This value refers to liquid silk inside the spinning gland; the molecular weight of a solidified silk thread is 200,000–300,000, or about ten times higher. The transition from the water-soluble liquid form into the insoluble, solid silk thread is not yet fully understood, but apparently the molecules of the polypeptide chain change their orientation from an α-configuration that is soluble (with predominantly intramolecular hydrogen bonds) to the insoluble β-configuration (a pleated sheet form with intermolecular bonds). From the silk moth it is known that the liquid α-fibroin can be transformed into the β-configuration simply by pulling it.

The tenacity of spider silk can be compared to that of nylon. The dragline thread of the garden spider (*Araneus*) has a tenacity of 7.8 g/denier (denier = weight in grams of 9,000 meters of a fiber); the corresponding value for nylon is 8.7 (Lucas, 1964). The tenacity value of 7.8 g/denier becomes more significant if one calculates the corresponding "breaking length": the dragline would have to be 80 km long before it would snap under its own weight. With respect to elasticity, the dragline is even superior to a nylon thread, for it can be stretched by 31%, compared with only 16% for nylon.

Spider silk is a highly unusual protein in its amino acid composition (Table 2). Amino acids with short side-chains (alanine, glycine, serine) constitute 50–60% of the total fibroin (Peakall, 1969). It is quite remarkable that the silk proteins of the spider's web are largely conserved during successive web building (Peakall, 1971). Before building a new web, the spider (*Araneus*) eats its old web. When the old web is labeled radioactively with alanine-H^3, 80–90% of the initial radioactivity appears in the new web. Since this occurs after only 30 minutes, either the silk of the old web has been incompletely broken down by digestive enzymes, or the amino acids are so rapidly absorbed by the glandular epithelium that little is diverted into making body proteins. In any case, the old

Table 2. Amino acid composition (%) of the silk of *Araneus diadematus*. (After Witt, Reed, and Peakall, 1968.) The amino acids arginine, aspartic, isoleucine, lysine, phenylalanine, threonine, tyrosine, and valine make up 1–6% of the total fibroins.

Amino acid	Total web	Frame (*ampullate gl.*)	Cocoon (*tubular gl.*)	Attachment disc (*piriform gl.*)
Alanine	27	33	25	29
Glycine	20	24	12	25
Serine	5	6	19	5
Glutamic	9	18	14	15
Proline	13	2	4	5

silk is apparently quickly recycled, and hardly any body proteins are needed for its synthesis.

Silk Glands

All silk glands are located inside the abdomen. Each gland leads to a specific spinneret, which opens to the outside in the form of a tiny spigot. As one might expect, the largest variety of spinning glands is found in the orb-weaver family Araneidae, yet ground-dwelling spiders also have at least four different types of silk glands (Mullen, 1969; H. Peters, 1955; Richter, 1970). Morphologically and histologically, one distinguishes ampullate glands, aciniform glands, tubuliform glands, aggregate glands, piriform glands, and flagelliform (or coronate) glands. Each type of gland secretes a different kind of silk with its own specific characteristics. Fig. 81 surveys the location as well as the function of the various silk glands. The tubuliform glands provide the silk thread for the egg sac and are thus found only in female spiders. The aggregate glands are typical of the araneids; they produce the glue substance for the web's catching spiral. The entire set of spinning glands of a tropical orb weaver is depicted in Fig. 82.

Structure

Each spinning gland comprises the gland proper and a thin duct. Most glands are pear-shaped and always consist of a single layer of epithelial cells (Fig. 83). Silk is secreted into the glandular lumen in the form of tiny protein droplets and can be stored in the sack-

Fig. 81.   Location and function of the various silk glands.

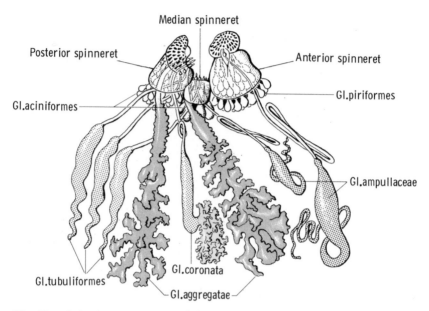

Fig. 82.   Spinning apparatus of the golden silk spider *Nephila*. Only one half of the paired set of silk glands is depicted. (After H. Peters, 1955.)

like middle part of the gland. The extrusion via the glandular duct is most likely caused by an increase of the spider's abdominal hemolymph pressure and sometimes also by the active extraction of silk from the spigots with the hind legs. The transition from liquid silk into a solid thread has nothing to do with exposure to air but is simply brought about by tension that orients molecules of the fibroin so that they are parallel to each other.

Unlike poison glands, spinning glands do not possess any musculature for expelling their secretions. In orb-web spiders, though, the amount of silk leaving the gland can be controlled by valves situated just in front of the spigots (Fig. 84). The diameter of the valves can be regulated by muscular action, thereby varying the thickness of the thread (R. S. Wilson, 1962a, b). Most silk threads have a diameter of only a few micrometers (Fig. 85), and many are even thinner than 1 μm. A well-known example of extremely fine silk threads is found in the catching silk ("hackle band") of cribellate spiders, where the individual fibers measure only 0.01–0.02 μm (Fig. 92c).

Fig. 83.   Ampullate gland of the garden spider *Nuctenea cornuta. (a) Inset:* the gland consists of a coiled tail (T), a sacklike midpiece (S), and a looped duct (D). 75×. The glandular epithelium of the "sac" exhibits basally located nuclei (N) and apically concentrated secretory droplets (S). 1,400×. (*b*) Secretory droplets (S) just prior to discharge into the glandular lumen. 8,200×.

Fig. 84.   Diagrammatic representation of dragline formation in *Araneus*. If the valve is almost closed, as shown here, the transition of liquid to solidified silk takes place directly behind the valve. When the valve is in the "open" position, the lumen of the spigot is filled with liquid silk and a solid thread is first formed at the tip of the spigot. (After R. S. Wilson, 1962b.)

Physiology

The most thoroughly investigated silk glands are the ampullate glands (*gl. ampullaceae*); they will therefore serve as a representative example for the other types of glands. The ampullate gland consists of a tubular tail portion, a sacklike midpiece, and a thin,

Fig. 85.   Silk threads from the cocoon wall of the pirate spider *Ero furcata*. The thick sinuous threads, which rise above the surface of the egg sac, apparently consist of several fused single threads. 83×.

looped duct (Figs. 82, 83). Experiments using radioactive marker substances have shown that the synthesis of silk is restricted mostly to the tail portion, while the "sac" functions mainly as a reservoir (Peakall, 1969). The secretory cells are typical columnar epithelial cells with basally located nuclei and apically concentrated secretory granules (Fig. 83a). The granules consist of protein and are a product of the endoplasmatic reticulum; Golgi bodies are lacking in these gland cells (Bell and Peakall, 1969). The secretory granules move toward the apical cell membrane and empty into the glandular lumen (Fig. 83b). Resorption of water presumably takes place within the lumen of the long duct.

The silk thread that exits from the ampullate gland serves as a dragline. In many spiders such a dragline is continually left behind as the spider walks around. It is anchored at intervals to the substrate by the action of the piriform glands. This results in distinct "attachment discs" (Fig. 86), which are barely perceptible as tiny white dots. Aside from draglines the ampullate glands also provide the material for the frame threads of orb webs and for the gossamer threads of young spiderlings.

When the reservoir of a silk gland becomes depleted, new syn-

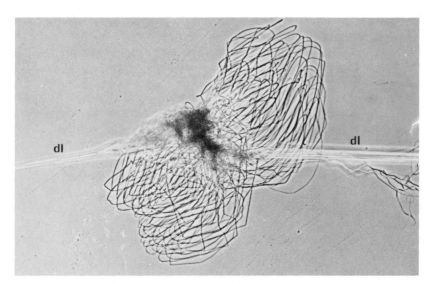

Fig. 86. Attachment disc of the crab spider *Xysticus* on a glass slide. The horizontal dragline (dl) can be clearly distinguished from the many delicate threads of the attachment disc itself. The symmetrical arrangement of these threads is due to their origin from the *paired* anterior spinnerets. 175×.

thesis of fibroin starts within a few minutes in the tail portion of the gland. Many spinning glands seem to have two different cell types that contribute chemically different secretory products (Kovoor, 1972; Kovoor and Zylberberg, 1980). While one type secretes only fibroin, the other apparently synthesizes mucopolysaccharides, which are perhaps responsible for the hygroscopic properties of the sticky spiral of orb webs.

It is interesting to note that even old, abandoned spider webs are not attacked by fungi or bacteria. It has been shown that the sticky substance of the orb web is acidic (pH 4) and hence resistant to decomposition by bacteria. A chemical analysis of the sticky substance revealed the presence of nitrate (KNO_3), phosphate (KH_2PO_4), and pyrrolidone (C_4H_7NO) (Schildknecht et al., 1972). The pyrrolidone, a hygroscopic substance, probably prevents the desiccation of the sticky catching thread. The axial threads of the web are apparently protected from bacteria by the hydrogen ions that arise from the dissociation of the phosphate. On the other hand, the acidity due to the hydrogen ions would denature the proteins and the stickiness would be lost. Since this is not the case, the presence of nitrate ions probably prevents denaturation of the proteins.

Spinnerets

A spider has three pairs of spinnerets on its abdomen; phylogenetically they represent modified extremities. The spinning glands terminate in little "spigots" on the surface of each spinneret (Fig. 87). All three pairs of spinnerets, anterior, median, and posterior (Fig. 88), are extremely mobile because they are equipped with a well-developed musculature (Fig. 89). In some "tarantulas" the spinnerets can be seen moving in step with the legs, alternating as the spiders walk (Seyfarth, personal communication). Like the other extremities, the spinnerets have more flexors than extensors. If the muscles are attached at the joint membrane between two segments of a spinneret, then both segments are moved with respect to each other. Some muscles traverse the spinneret and can shift the entire spigot-studded terminal area (R. Peters, 1967). During the construction of a web or cocoon the spinnerets must move independently, yet must also be able to work together in a highly coordinated manner. The spinnerets can move in several ways; lifting, lowering, twisting, and also a synchronous spreading of all spinnerets can be observed. The effective working range of the

Fig. 87. (*a*) Median spinneret of the cribellate orbweaver *Uloborus* show-ing three different types of spigots. 570×. (*b*) Spigots of the piriform glands on the anterior spinneret of *Zygiella*. The emitted silk threads (arrows) are the basic elements of the attachment discs (see Fig. 86). 850×. (*c*) Spigots from the cribellum of *Hypochilus*. 2,400×. *Inset:* Cross section of a spigot from the cribellum of *Amaurobius*. The silk thread lies within the circular lumen and measures only 0.08 μm in diameter. 52,000×.

spinnerets is enhanced to a great extent by the movements of the abdomen itself.

Phylogenetically, spiders originally had four pairs of spinnerets (Fig. 90), but among extant spiders this ancient trait is retained only in some Mesothelae, that is, those spiders which also have

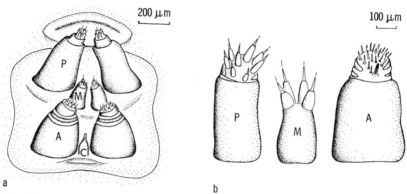

Fig. 88. Spinning apparatus of *Segestria senoculata. (a)* Arrangement of the three pairs of spinnerets and the colulus (C). (*b*) The anterior spinnerets (A) consist of three segments, the posterior (P) of two, and the median (M) of only a single segment. The different spigots belong to four different kinds of silk glands. (*a, b* after Glatz, 1972.)

other "primitive" characteristics. In the less "primitive" Orthognatha we find two to three pairs of spinnerets, and sometimes even a reduction to one pair (Glatz, 1972, 1973). For instance, in *Nemesia* the anterior spinnerets are lacking, the median pair is rudimentary, and only the posterior spinnerets carry functional spigots. Most extant spiders possess three pairs of functional spinnerets. They develop embryologically from the *anlagen*, or primordia, of the extremities of body segments 10 and 11. Each anlage splits in half so that two further pairs of spinnerets originate medially, re-

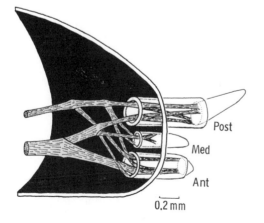

Fig. 89. Musculature of the spinnerets in *Tegenaria*. Lateral view of one abdominal half. (After R. Peters, 1967.)

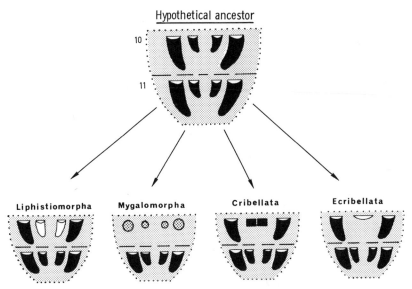

Hypothetical ancestor

10

11

Liphistiomorpha   Mygalomorpha   Cribellata   Ecribellata

Fig. 90. Diagram of the arrangement of spinnerets in different spiders and their possible origin from an ancestral form. The numbers 10 and 11 indicate body segments 10 and 11. Functional spinnerets are drawn in black, residual ones in white, and those lacking are stippled. The cribellum is represented as two black rectangles, the colulus as a white crescent. (After Marples, 1967.)

sulting in eight spinnerets altogether. However, the anterior median pair (on body segment 10) is often extremely reduced, and many ecribellate spiders (such as Araneidae, Linyphiidae, Theridiidae, and Thomisidae) have only a vestigial bump, which is referred to as the *colulus*. This rudimentary structure is probably now without any function (Marples, 1967). In many spiders the colulus is absent altogether.

Cribellate spiders possess an additional spinning organ, the *cribellum*, a small plate located in front of the three pairs of spinnerets (Fig. 91a). It is assumed that the cribellum and the colulus are homologous organs, since both develop from the primordia of the anterior median spinnerets. The cribellum can take the form of a single small plate (as it does in *Hypochilus*), or it may be divided into two (as it is in *Amaurobius*), or, rarely, even into four parts (as in *Dresserus*). The cribellar area is densely covered with many tiny spigots (cf. Fig. 87c). In an adult *Stegodyphus pacificus* (Eresidae)

Fig. 91.   Cribellum and calamistrum of *Amaurobius*. (*a*) The cribellum (cr) consists of a divided platelet, which is normally hidden in front of the spinnerets. 380×. (*b*) The calamistrum is formed by a row of strong bristles on the metatarsus of leg 4. Each bristle is equipped with fine cuticular teeth (see Fig. 57b), which comb out the cribellate silk from the cribellum. 600×.

the cribellum contains over 40,000 spigots (Kullmann, 1969); young spiders have fewer spigots, but the number increases with each molt. These delicate spigots produce the extremely thin silk threads (0.01 μm) of the "hackle band" (Lehmensick and Kullmann, 1957; Friedrich and Langer, 1969); they are combed out of the cribellum by rhythmic movements of the *calamistrum,* a row of comb-shaped hairs situated on the metatarsi of the fourth legs (Fig. 91b).

Webs

Ecologically one can divide spiders into two groups: the wandering spiders and the more sedentary web spiders. Only web spiders use their ability to produce silk for the construction of snares. The various web spiders have developed quite different webs and prey-catching strategies. The well-known orb-shaped web is one of the many kinds of webs built by different spider families. The funnel weavers (Agelenidae) and the sheet-web weavers (Linyphiidae) construct horizontal sheets, whereas the cobweb spiders (Theridiidae) and the daddy longleg spiders (Pholcidae) build somewhat irregular meshes. "Primitive" web builders, such as the cribellate *Amaurobius* or the ecribellate *Segestria,* weave only a tubular retreat with simple signal or catching threads radiating from its entrance. The greenish cribellate spider *Dictyna* usually lives on leaves on which it lays down its catching threads in a zigzag fashion on top of underlying radial supporting threads (Fig. 108).

   The catching threads ("hackle bands") of cribellate spiders are especially interesting because they function without any gluey substance—unlike the sticky threads of ecribellate spiders. Cribellate catching threads work mainly because of their structure: one or two straight axial threads are surrounded by sinuous support threads and a dense network of cribellate silk (Fig. 92). Prey is easily entangled in this "wool." Additionally, the cribellate silk has some adhesive properties, although these properties are not well understood. Because these threads do not contain any glue (which deteriorates quickly), they are effective much longer than are the sticky threads of ecribellate spiders. However, within a few weeks they also age, gradually losing their adhesiveness (Foelix and Jung, 1978). Cribellate silk, incidentally, is found not only in the rather simple snares of *Amaurobius* and *Filistata* but also in the orb webs of *Uloborus* and in the reduced orb of *Hyptiotes.*

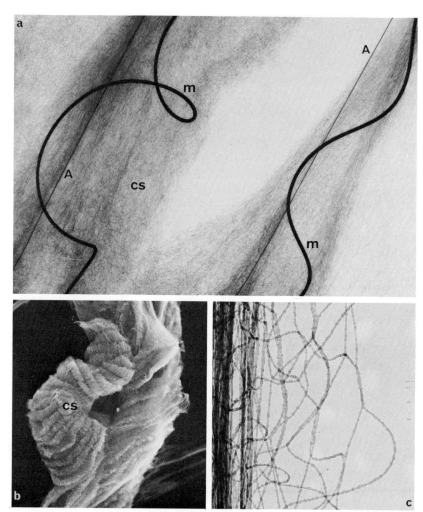

Fig. 92.   Details of cribellate catching threads. (*a*) Two thin, straight axial threads (A) support two coiled threads (m) and the surrounding "catching wool" of cribellate silk (cs) (*Amaurobius*). 1,200×. (*b*) The cribellate silk (cs) is brushed in regular bundles onto the axial threads by means of the calamistrum (*Mallos*). 140×. (*c*) The extremely fine threads of cribellate silk measure only 0.015 μm in diameter and often appear beaded (*Amaurobius*). 38,000×.

Sheet Webs and Frame Webs

Sheet webs are built by Agelenidae and by Linyphiidae, yet those sheets differ as much in their structural details as does the behavior of their respective inhabitants. The Agelenidae weave a flat, slightly concave silk mat with a funnel-shaped retreat at one end. There the spider hides and rushes out only when prey has blundered into the web. The webs of *Tegenaria* commonly bridge the corners of rooms in European houses; the corresponding agelenid in North America belongs to the genus *Agelenopsis*. The much smaller *Agelena* prefers the outdoors and is abundant in grass and low bushes. Its web consists of a sheet measuring, at most, 40–60 cm, suspended by oblique and vertical threads. Flying insects hit these vertical threads and drop onto the sheet (Fig. 3b).

The very delicate webs of the linyphiids are also horizontal, but convex, sheets with similar vertical threads that serve as tripping lines for insects (Fig. 93). Some silk threads of the linyphiid web contain sticky droplets, but these play an insignificant role in catching prey. In most cases an insect simply gets trapped between the vertical suspension threads. In contrast to agelenid spiders, linyphiids always hang beneath their dome. When prey is trapped

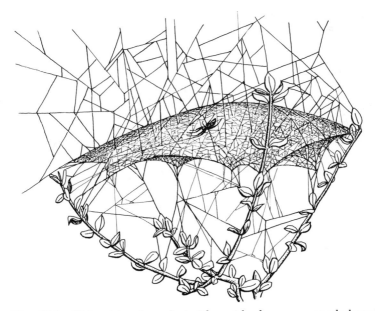

Fig. 93.   Web of *Linyphia triangularis.* The spider hangs suspended upside down under the dome of the horizontal sheet web. (After Bristowe, 1958).

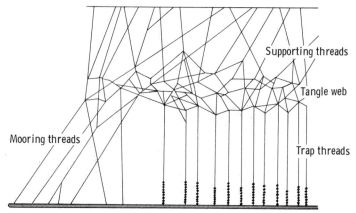

Fig. 94. Diagram of the web of *Steatoda castanea* (Theridiidae). The vertical trapping threads are studded with glue droplets. (After Wiehle, 1949.)

by the threads, the spider shakes the web until the victim falls onto the sheet, then bites through the web and pulls the victim down. The damage done to the web is mended after feeding.

To a certain extent the frame webs of the theridiids resemble those of linyphiids. The structure of the sheet, though, is very loose and irregular, and the trapping threads are studded with glue droplets (Fig. 94; Wiehle, 1949). These threads are attached tightly to the substrate and break easily when an insect (often an ant) touches them. The insect is then glued to the broken thread and suspended helplessly in the air. While trying to free itself, the animal contacts neighboring catching threads and becomes progressively more entangled. Meanwhile the alerted spider quickly climbs down and throws further sticky threads over the victim before biting it. Some theridiids build special retreats inside or outside the frame web. A well-known example is *Achaearanea saxatile,* which constructs an open silk tube that hangs vertically in the middle of the web. The spider camouflages the tube by adding plant and soil material to its surface.

The more primitive webs, which consist only of a tubular retreat with radial catching threads, have already been mentioned, but one of the most extraordinary variations on such a "retreat" is the silken tube of the purse-web spider *Atypus*. This catching device is about 15–30 cm long and 1 cm in diameter; most of it is buried vertically in the soil, and only a short, fingerlike end extends horizontally on the ground. The spider lives inside the silken

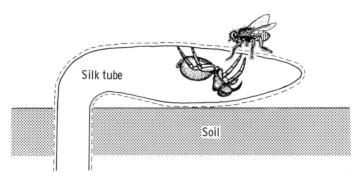

Fig. 95. The silken tube of the purse-web spider *Atypus*. The spider bites the prey through the wall of the silk tube and then pulls it inside. (After Bristowe, 1958.)

tube and attacks insects that happen to crawl over the tube (Fig. 95). The long chelicerae pierce through the walls of the tube into the victim, which is then dragged inside. The two slits cut into the wall of the tube by the action of the cheliceral teeth are quickly repaired before feeding.

Orb Webs

The orb web is certainly the best known of all webs. Essentially it is made up of three elements (Fig. 96): (1) *radial threads*, which converge in a central spot, the *hub;* (2) *frame threads*, which delineate the web and serve as insertion sites for the radial threads; and (3) the *catching spiral* (Wiehle, 1927, 1928, 1929, 1931). The scaffolding of the orb web is provided by the radial and frame threads; neither type is sticky. The catching spiral, in contrast, consists of a thread studded with glue droplets (Fig. 97). The microscope reveals that there are in fact two axial threads (1–2 μm in thickness), which are embedded in a gluey substance.

The hub usually consists of irregularly interconnected threads. In some orb weavers (such as *Tetragnatha*) the hub is removed after its construction and the web then appears with a large hole in the center (an "open hub"); in other genera (such as *Argiope*) the hub may be covered with a fine sheet of silk. Immediately surrounding the hub is the so-called strengthening zone, but this part of the web cannot always be determined as separate from the hub itself. More important is the next part, the "free zone," which is crossed only by the radial threads. Here the spider can easily change from one

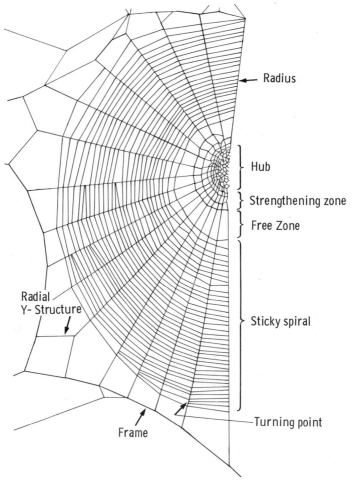

Fig. 96. Structure of an orb web. Drawing was traced from a photograph of a web of *Araneus diadematus.*

face of the web to the other. The actual catching area is that part of the web covered by the sticky spiral.

Wherever two threads cross in the web, they form a solid connection. It is still a matter of debate, however, whether these connections represent a genuine fusion of two threads or whether another substance cements them together. Several studies have demonstrated that spiders do use a cement that can form either stiff or flexible connections (Eberhard, 1976; Kavanagh and Til-

Fig. 97. Microscopic views of threads from an orb web. (*a*) Sticky spiral of *Araneus diadematus* regularly covered with glue droplets. 150×. (*b*) The same thread after contact with a glass slide; two axial threads can be recognized inside the homogeneous glue substance. 380×. (*c*) Union of a radial and a sticky thread from the web of a *Zygiella x-notata*. Note the collar at the connecting site. 360×.

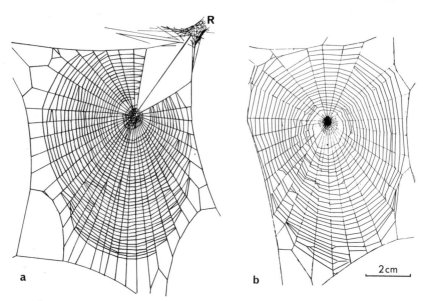

Fig. 98. (a) Typical web of the sector spider *Zygiella*. During daytime the spider hides in the retreat (R), but keeps contact with the hub by means of a signal thread (tracing of a photograph by Witt). (b) First web built by a cross spider (*Araneus diadematus*). (Photo: Witt.)

linghast, 1979). Altogether, an orb web contains 1,000–1,500 connection points, most of which occur between the radii and the spiral thread (Jackson, 1971).

The number of radii varies little within a particular species of orb weaver, and is often characteristic of that species. The web of the garden spider *Araneus diadematus*, for instance, usually has 25 – 30 radial threads forming fairly regular angles of 12–15°. Webs of very young *A. diadematus* often have many more radii than those of adults (Witt, Rawlings, and Reed, 1972). In the horizontally inclined orbs of *Tetragnatha* one finds fewer radii (about 18), whereas 50–60 are present in the webs of the small araneid *Mangora*. These numbers of radii imply that many orb weavers show a species-specific geometry in their webs. It is thus often possible to identify a certain spider solely by its characteristic web structure.

Zygiella, for instance, typically builds a web with a "free sector" that is crossed only by a sturdy signal thread (Fig. 98a); this thread connects the hub with a silken retreat outside the web. To observe how this free sector comes about is quite interesting. While laying down the sticky spiral, the spider always stops before reaching the signal thread and reverses its course from a clockwise to a counter-clockwise direction, and vice versa. Thus the sticky spiral actually results from the spider's moving like a pendulum. During the day *Zygiella* hides in a retreat, keeping one leg touching the signal thread to detect any vibrations occurring in the web. Although *Zygiella* typically builds free-sector webs, closed orb webs are often built by the juveniles. Even adults occasionally produce orbs without the free sector; this happens if the signal thread deviates from the plane of the web by more than 40°. Signal threads leading to a safe retreat, a curled leaf, for instance, occur in many other araneid spider webs. Having such a signal thread means that the spider is less exposed to predators (such as birds or wasps), for it needs to be present on the web only when actually catching prey.

Another common structural variation in the orb web are the so-called *stabilimenta* (Figs. 99, 126). These silken bands leading to the hub are added to neighboring radii in a zigzag manner. Whether these structures have any stabilizing effect, as their name

Fig. 99. Stabilimenta. (*a*) *Argiope aurantia* weaves a vertical zigzag line through the center of its orb web. (*b*) Close-up view of the hub threads (H) and of the draping with stabilimental threads (St) from the orb web of *Uloborus*.

would suggest, is dubious. More likely the stabilimenta serve as some kind of camouflage, because they are built only by those spiders that always sit in the hubs of their webs. *Cyclosa* is one of the best examples of such a spider. In its web the stabilimenta extend vertically from the hub to the catching area; additionally, they are adorned with remnants of prey and old shed skins (Rovner, 1976). The spider itself, sitting in the hub with its legs pressed tightly to its body, blends perfectly with the brownish stabilimentum. But the stabilimenta in the webs of the brightly colored *Argiope* species hardly render the species less conspicuous. Quite probably, different functions must be attributed to the stabilimenta of different types of orb webs (Robinson and Robinson, 1973). Aside from camouflaging the spider (such as *Cyclosa* or *Uloborus*), stabilimenta may also serve as a molting platform (as for *Nephila*) or as a protective shield against heat radiation from the sun.

Most orb webs are built vertically, but *Uloborus* builds an orb web that is usually oriented in a horizontal plane. With the exception of cribellate catching silk it closely resembles the araneid orb web, even in details. This remarkable example of convergence is interesting from a phylogenetic viewpoint and will be discussed later.

All orb webs presented so far have been basically two-dimensional. Several orb weavers, however, add further silk lines to the orb and thus make it three-dimensional. A good example is *Theridiosoma*, which builds a complete orb web but attaches a thread laterally to the hub. When this thread is tightened, the web bulges, resembling an inside-out umbrella. The spider itself sits as a living bridge: its hind legs grasp the radii near the hub while its front legs pull on the tension thread. When an insect flies into the web, *Theridiosoma* at once releases its front legs so that the web jerks back into the two-dimensional plane and entangles the hapless victim.

A similar spring trap is built by the cribellate spider *Hyptiotes* (Uloboridae). Its triangular web is most likely a reduction from an orb (Fig. 100). Four radial threads, which enclose three sectors, converge into one mooring thread. Again, the spider forms a living link by holding the mooring thread tightly with its front legs. When prey is encountered, the tension is released and the web collapses. Obviously, the web becomes so damaged during the capture that a new one has to be constructed after each catch.

Since there are more than 2,000 orb-weaver species, I cannot touch upon all the structural variations that orb webs may exhibit, but in many cases the differences are relatively minor and concern

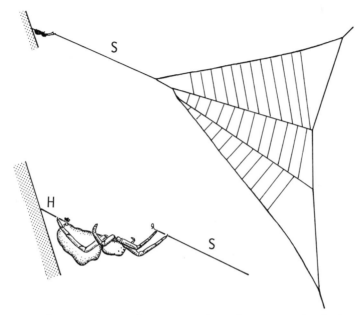

Fig. 100.   The spring trap of *Hyptiotes*. The web consists of only three sectors of an orb. The spider itself forms a living bridge between a tension thread (S) and an attachment thread (H). (After Wiehle, 1927.)

only the symmetry of the web. *Nephila*, for instance, builds a broad orb web in which the lower half is much larger than the upper. Consequently, the sticky spiral does not really spiral around the center but only crosses the lower half of the web in a "pendulum" fashion. A further characteristic of the Nephila web is that an auxiliary spiral persists in the finished web. *Nephila* also constructs a three-dimensional mesh above the hub, called a barrier web.

The rather different web of the "orb weaver" *Cyrtophora* also consists of a three-dimensional network but has a central tentlike construction (Fig. 101). This "canopy" resembles an orb web inasmuch as it also contains radial threads and a spiral thread. However, the number of radii is much higher (around 200 split radii), and the spiral is not sticky. Perhaps the *Cyrtophora* web represents an intermediate step between the sheet web of the linyphiids and the orb web of the araneids: the transition to the orb could have evolved by a reduction of the irregular network and a tilting of the central sheet (Kullmann, 1972a). However, the opposite opinion has also been expressed, namely, that the *Cyrtophora* web is derived from an orb web (Lubin, 1973). Indeed, this is more likely,

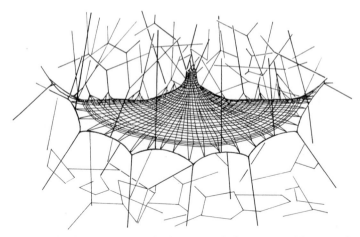

Fig. 101.   Web of *Cyrtophora*. The horizontal sheet resembles an orb web; it is surrounded by an irregular mesh of threads above and below the sheet. The spider sits underneath the tentlike center of the sheet web. (After Wiehle, 1927.)

since *Cyrtophora* is morphologically (as determined by its genital structures) a specialized araneid.

Finally, an extreme variation of orb-web symmetry occurs in the ladder-web spider *Tylorida* from New Guinea (Robinson and Robinson, 1972). These webs are about 1 m high but only 15 cm in width. The hub is situated close to the top so that the spiral threads run almost horizontally—hence the name *ladder web*. A very similar web, yet turned 180°, has been discovered in South America for *Scoloderus* (Eberhard, 1975). Such elongated webs are most likely an adaptation for catching moths. Whereas moths can rather quickly escape from regular orb webs (see chapter 6), they slide down a ladder web; not only are they exposed longer to the attacking spider, but they also lose scales and thus get stuck more easily on the sticky threads.

Construction of an Orb Web

The building of an orb web follows three distinct phases: (1) the construction of the frame and radii, (2) the laying down of the auxiliary spiral, and (3) the establishment of the sticky (or catching) spiral. The following description of orb-web construction is based on the behavior of *Araneus* (H. Peters, 1939a, b):

Frame and radial threads. The spider starts with a horizontal

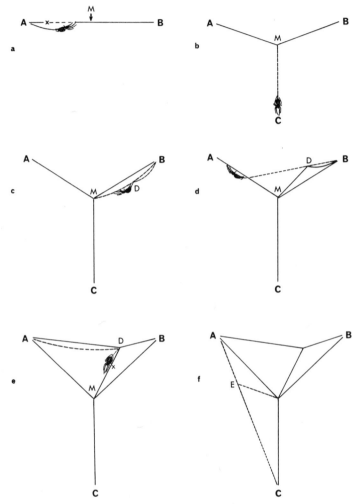

Fig. 102.   Construction of an orb web. (After H. Peters, 1939a.)

thread by simply exuding a silk thread into the air while sitting on
an elevated point. This thread is carried away by wind or even the
slightest draft until it gets caught on some object, a twig, perhaps.
Actually, this horizontal thread is only a provisional structure; the
spider bites through it (Fig. 102a, at X), grasps the cut thread with
its front legs and moves from point A toward point B. At the same
time a new thread is reeled off behind the spider while the original
thread AB is curled up by the front legs. About halfway (at M), the

old and the new thread are connected. Since more silk is used for the new thread AM, the entire thread AMB sags a bit. At M the spider descends vertically until it reaches the surface to which it fastens the thread (Fig. 102b, at C). The resulting Y-structure is essentially the basic framework of the future orb, with M being the center.

The next step establishes additional radial threads. This is a rather complicated procedure, especially because the spider is constantly producing a new thread wherever it goes. The first radial threads are always made together with a frame thread, that is, in one move. The spider walks on the existing radius from M to B and fastens the new thread at B (Fig. 102c). There it turns around and uses the new thread MB as a guide line. Obviously, while walking back on MB, it is spinning a new thread again. After a short distance the spider attaches this thread to the new MB at the point D. The spider now keeps running via M toward the starting point A, where it attaches the thread (Fig. 102d). From A the spider returns to D, again doubling the thread AD (Fig. 102e). This produces the final frame thread AB and, at the same time, the radius DM, which is, however, replaced immediately, because the spider bites through at X (as it did with the first horizontal thread) while running back to the hub (M). The new thread XM becomes transformed into the final radius DM. The rather sharp buckle at D is somewhat compensated for by letting out more thread so that the new radius DM is longer than the previous one.

Following the same pattern, the next frame-thread-plus-radial-thread is executed (Fig. 102f). The basic scaffold of radial threads is then "filled up" with further radii. Again, these are produced twice; that is, an existing radius serves as a guide line while a new (temporary) radius is pulled behind as the spider walks from the center to the periphery. This radius is fastened only briefly to the frame, then bitten through at the periphery and subsequently replaced while the spider returns on it to the hub.

The sequence of the placement of radial threads is by no means haphazard but follows two basic rules: (1) the direction of placement of a new radius alternates, and (2) the first radial threads, which fill the gaps between the original radii, are always constructed directly below an already existing (original) radius. This procedure of consecutive placement of radii becomes clearer in Fig. 103.

The spider always decides at the hub in which sector the next radius is to be placed. As soon as it has completed a radial thread and has arrived back at the hub, it briefly tugs on all the finished

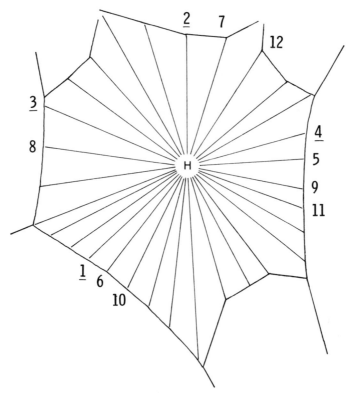

Fig. 103. Partially completed orb web. The numbers give the sequence of placement of the first radial threads; the earliest radii (1–4) are underlined. H = hub. (After H. Peters, 1939a.)

radii with its front legs. The observer gets the impression that the spider "measures" the angle between two neighboring radii. That an oversized angle would determine the placement of the next radial thread seems plausible, and various experiments, such as burning out radii while they were being laid down (Hingston, 1920), provided support for this hypothesis. But other factors, like web tension, also seem to be involved.

Although the precise mechanism triggering the placement of radial threads is not yet known, it is clear that the front legs do have a measuring function (Reed, Witt, and Jones, 1965). If the front legs are removed, the regularity of the angles between adjacent radial threads is impaired. Normally, the angles between the 20–30 radii of an orb web (for *Araneus diadematus*) are astonishingly constant, about 15°. It is true, though, that the upper half of the orb

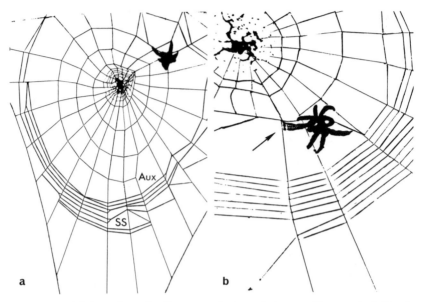

Fig. 104. (*a*) An orb web after completion of the auxiliary spiral (Aux). The first turns of the sticky spiral (SS) can be seen in the lower part of the web. (*b*) *Araneus diadematus* in the process of laying down the sticky spiral. Note that one front leg quivers briefly while touching the next radius (arrow). (Single frame from a movie by Witt.)

web contains fewer radii (and thus larger angles between neighboring threads) than the lower half.

Auxiliary spiral. While the spider is still busy building the radii, it is also interconnecting these threads by a few narrow circles in the center of the web. This hub region is then extended into the so-called strengthening zone by further peripheral turns. After construction of the radial threads has been completed, the strengthening zone is continued into a wide spiral toward the periphery, forming the auxiliary spiral (Fig. 104a). Although the auxiliary spiral has only a few turns, it ties the radii together and helps stabilize the half-finished orb web. The auxiliary spiral thread also serves as a handy guide for the spider when it comes to laying down the catching spiral. Without an auxiliary spiral the spider can cross the radii only awkwardly, since each radial thread would sag greatly under the spider's weight. After the auxiliary spiral is finished, the spider pauses for a moment before it tackles the last step of orb-web construction.

Catching spiral. The auxiliary spiral begins at the hub and ends well before reaching the peripheral framework (Fig. 104a). When laying down the sticky spiral, the spider starts at the periphery and uses the auxiliary spiral as a guide line. While crossing the radial threads in a spiral fashion, it constantly fastens the sticky thread to each radius. In this process both the front legs and the hind legs play an important role. One front leg reaches for the next radius and touches it with a quick, brushing movement, apparently to ascertain its position. At the same time one of the fourth legs pulls the thread out of the spinnerets and dabs it against the radius (Fig. 104b).

As the construction of the sticky spiral proceeds, the auxiliary spiral is simultaneously taken down. In the finished web only the remnants of the crossing points can be recognized. The catching spiral is not continued into the center of the web but terminates shortly before it. This results in a rather open space between the catching area and the hub, termed the *free zone*. The sticky spiral is by no means a continuous spiral. It often reverses its course from clockwise to counterclockwise, and vice versa. Such turning points can easily be seen at many points in the web (Fig. 105). Since the position of the hub is slightly off center, (that is, shifted toward the upper part of the web), most of the sticky spiral is confined to the lower half of the web.

The laying down of the sticky spiral is the most time-consuming stage of the orb web's construction. Whereas building the framework and the radii takes only about 5 minutes, the sticky spiral requires at least 20 minutes. That the entire orb web in all its complexity is created in less than half an hour is astounding. The total

Fig. 105. Placing of the sticky spiral. Spiral construction begins at the periphery (0′); the numbers indicate the time elapsed in minutes. (After Wiehle, 1927.)

length of the threads is about 20 meters. Since most threads are only 1–2 μm thick, the weight of an orb web is extremely low, between 0.1 and 0.5 mg. These values become even more impressive if one considers that a female *Araneus diadematus* easily weighs 500 mg.

It is also remarkable that the construction of the orb web is controlled only by the sense of touch, without any visual feedback. Even when all eight eyes are covered with opaque paint, the spider still builds a perfectly normal web. This achievement is quite routine for the spider, for it usually builds its web at night anyway. More surprisingly, perhaps, is the fact that gravity is also dispensable for the orb web's construction. This was most convincingly demonstrated by the two garden spiders that were sent into orbit with the space capsule Skylab in 1973. Despite complete weightlessness they still built regular orbs (Witt et al., 1977).

Relation of Structure and Function in the Orb Web

The ultimate purpose of any spider web is to capture prey—and the orb web is certainly no exception. Its highly geometrical construction suggests its special effectiveness and economy as a trap. As we have just seen, the orb web is built with a minimum of material (0.1–0.5 mg of silk) and time (20–30 minutes). The tightly strung radial threads converging in the web's center give the spider two advantages: (1) they transmit vibration signals from the periphery to the center, where the spider usually sits, and (2) they provide direct and quick access routes (Witt, 1975; Barth, 1982). The web can thus be regarded as an extension of the spider's sensorium. The spider's first reaction to a fly that has hit the web is to jerk the radial threads several times with its front legs. Only when the prey has been located in relation to the center does the spider rush out on a directed course—in most cases exactly on that radial thread leading straight to the prey.

The radii serve as communication channels not only during prey capture but also during courtship, when the male approaches the female's web. Usually the small male sits at the edge of the web and rhythmically plucks the threads, apparently in order not to be mistaken for prey. The mechanical properties of the sticky spiral, especially its great elasticity, are also very important: it can be stretched several times its original length without breaking. This is of course advantageous when a vigorously struggling insect is trapped in the web. Aside from these mechanical stimuli, the web can also carry chemical signals, which stem from the spider's secretion of pheromones. It is known that a female's empty web may elicit courtship behavior of the male (Blanke, 1973). The carrying of chemical stimuli is not restricted to orb webs alone but applies also to the draglines of wandering spiders (Tietjen and Rovner, 1980).

Most orb webs have a vertical orientation in space, or, to be more precise, they are slightly tilted. The spider sits almost invariably on the "underside" of the hub, with its head facing down (two exceptions are *Verrucosa* and *Cyclosa*). In case of a disturbance or danger, the spider can simply drop to the ground on a safety thread—a response that is typical of many orb weavers.

Although orb webs have a species-specific structure, many Araneid spiders can move with ease in a foreign web. The pioneer French entomologist J. H. Fabre has already successfully transferred an *Argiope bruennichi* to a web of *Argiope lobata* (cited by Wiehle, 1928). Similarly, *Araneus diadematus* has no difficulties catching prey in the foreign web of *Argiope aurantia* (Richardson, 1973). On the other hand, *Zygiella* does not feel at home in a web of *Araneus*, since it keeps climbing to the web's periphery and then dropping from the frame (Wiehle, 1927). Incidentally, it seems that some spiders can and do take over foreign webs under natural conditions (Enders, 1974; Eberhard, Barreto, and Pfizenmaier, 1978).

In nature orb webs must be replaced often, because they quickly become damaged or destroyed by wind, rain, or early morning dew. As a rule, a garden spider (*Araneus diadematus*) builds a new web every day (Wiehle, 1927). Only the previous framework may be used again for the new construction. If the web is only slightly damaged, as, for instance, after catching small prey, the spider may or may not mend the hole. In general, repair does not consist of reconstructing the original design but of patching the holes to make the web stable again. The cribellate orb weaver *Uloborus*, however, often performs elaborate repairs, sometimes replacing the entire half of a web in an orderly fashion (Fig. 106; Eberhard, 1972).

"Drug Webs"

In 1948 the German zoologist H. M. Peters, who had always been bothered by the fact that his garden spiders built their webs at an ungodly hour (between 2 A.M. and 5 A.M.), asked his colleague from pharmacology, P. N. Witt, for a stimulant that might shift the spider's web building to an earlier hour. Unfortunately, the drug (amphetamine) did not yield the desired effect. The spiders built at their usual hours, yet, surprisingly, the web structure was definitely altered: the radial threads as well as the catching spiral were placed irregularly. In the following years Witt tested a great variety of drugs (for instance, caffeine, mescaline, and strychnine) on orb-web spiders and investigated how these substances affected web construction (Witt, 1956). It was soon clear that certain drugs produced specific effects. For instance, a certain dosage of caffeine results in a typical "caffeine web" (Fig. 107) that is distinctly different from a mescaline web or an amphetamine web.

The drugs can affect the size and shape of the web, the number of radii and spiral turns, the regularity of placement of the radial and spiral threads, the mesh width, and so forth. Relatively small doses of caffeine (10 μg/animal) result in smaller but wider webs than normal; the radii often form oversized angles, yet the regu-

Fig. 106.   Web repair. After destruction of the left half of the web, the spider (*Uloborus diversus*) first gathered all broken threads into a seam (S) and then started to rebuild the missing sector. Note the turning points of the spiral thread. The right half of the web was left unchanged, but the hub was built anew. (Photo: Eberhard, 1972.)

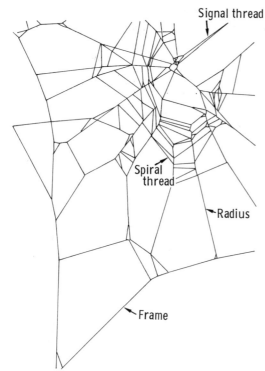

Signal thread

Spiral thread

Radius

Frame

Fig. 107. Drug web of a *Zygiella x-notata* constructed after the administration of a relatively high dose of caffeine. Compare with the normal web in Fig. 98a. (Tracing of a photograph by Witt.)

larity of the catching spiral is not affected. At higher doses (100 μg/animal) the alterations in the webs become much more noticeable and their regular design disappears. Most drugs tend to have a negative influence on web regularity. Only with very low doses of the hallucinogen LSD-25 could an increase in web regularity be observed. If the drug concentration was raised by one order (to 0.1 – 0.3 μg/animal) the regularity of the angles between radial threads decreased slightly.

Testing a drug on a spider is actually a rather simple procedure. The substances do not have to be injected but are simply dissolved in sugar water. A drop of such a solution is then touched to the mouth of the spider, and it is imbibed quickly. For quantitative studies, small drops of the drug of known concentration and exactly determined volumes are delivered from a microsyringe to the spider's mouth. To study the effects of the drug, photographs of the spider's web are taken before and after the drug is administered. Structural alterations of the web can then be measured directly on the photographs. The use of statistical methods allows one to detect even very subtle changes that would not be apparent from a purely visual comparison of the control and "drug" webs.

Is Web Building Genetically Determined or Learned?

The elaborate and highly regular structure of the orb web provokes the question as to whether the first webs of a spider exhibit the same complexity of those built by adults or whether some learning process leads by degrees to the "complete" orb web. The question is answered if we inspect the very first web built by a young garden spider: it is already a perfect, miniature orb (Fig. 104b). Detailed measurements have even shown that the early webs are often more regular than the webs of adults (Witt, Rawlings, and Reed, 1972). Learning from previous experience does not seem to play a role in web building. This finding was further demonstrated in experiments in which young spiderlings were confined to narrow glass tubes so that they could not build any webs. When they were released after several months, they could weave orbs as regular as those of their normally reared siblings, which served as a control.

However, one cannot conclude that web building is an entirely stereotyped process. A certain plasticity of this behavior has been shown in many experiments. For instance, if one burns out a radial thread with a hot wire just after it has been constructed, the spider will replace it immediately. One may repeat this game more than twenty times before the spider gives up replacing the radial thread and proceeds to build the auxiliary spiral (Hingston, 1920). This shows clearly that already existing structures influence the further construction of the web. Apparently the spider can integrate the feedback from its sensory input and adapt its behavior to a given situation. On the other hand, the spider does not replace the burnt out radii indefinitely, but at some point simply proceeds to the next phase of web construction, even though the previous phase has not been completed.

Similar conclusions can be reached if one transfers a spider engaged in building a web to another web that is at an earlier stage of construction (P. J. Peters, 1970). The spider then usually repeats phases (for example, laying down the auxiliary spiral) that it had already completed in its own web. In some cases, however, it was observed that necessary steps in web construction were *not* repeated, resulting in a rather irregular web. In the first instance the spider apparently reacted to its sensory feedback in completing the web; in the latter case the spider seems to have followed the original "program" coded in its CNS. This explanation is certainly an oversimplification, since other factors, like sensory feedback from the silk glands, may also determine the extent to which stages of web building are repeated.

The statement that even very young spiderlings can already build perfect orb webs needs to be scrutinized. When spiderlings leave their cocoon, they do not build an orb web right away, although they are capable of silk production. Rather, they live communally in a mesh of irregular threads, and only after two weeks do they separate and start building their first orb webs (Burch, 1979). If the young spiderlings are taken out of the cocoon prematurely and kept isolated from one another, they can trail draglines and sometimes build a small retreat (H. M. Peters, 1969). Some days later irregular orb webs appear. Successive webs are improved to perfection within a few days. Most likely, however, this improvement is not owing to a learning process but is rather a reflection of the fact that the central nervous system is still developing. At the time the spiderling hatches from the egg, its CNS contains only neuroblasts. The precise correlation between differentiation of the CNS and the type of web built at specific times in early development still needs to be established.

The juvenile webs of the cribellate orb weaver *Uloborus* are especially interesting (Szelp, 1961; Eberhard, 1977a). The spiderlings build an orb web immediately after leaving the cocoon, but this first web differs from the adult web in three major respects: (1) the catching threads are lacking, (2) the auxiliary spiral is not removed, and (3) instead of a catching spiral many "extra" radial threads are filled in between the original 15–20 radii. The main reason for this deviation from the normal orb web is that before the second molt *Uloborus* does not have a cribellum or a calamistrum; thus it cannot produce cribellate silk for the catching thread. After the second molt a cribellum and a calamistrum are present and the spider weaves a regular orb web for the first time. Again it seems likely that the stage of maturation of the CNS plays a role in determining which kind of web will be built during the ontogeny of *Uloborus*.

In conclusion, then, juvenile spiders often build different webs than adults do. However, these early webs cannot be regarded as merely incomplete versions of the adult's web. Learning does not seem to be involved in the "adult" orb web.

Orb Webs and Evolution

The orb web is often considered the evolutionary summit of web-building spiders. It is rather hard to imagine how such a complex structure could have come about at all, yet it is even more difficult to explain how an orb web could develop in two different groups of spiders, the cribellate Uloboridae and the ecribellate Araneoidea (Araneidae, Tetragnathidae). Was the orb web "invented" in both groups independently or in only one group, which gave rise to the other (Kullmann, 1972)? There are in fact good reasons to assume convergence in the evolution of the orb web. The two groups use quite different catching threads (cribellate silk versus ecribellate glue-coated threads), and it is hardly plausible that this difference developed only after the structure of the orb had been achieved. One hypothesis then is that the orb web developed independently twice, starting from simpler precursors in both groups (Fig. 108).

According to this hypothesis the ancestral forms of web were merely a retreat with threads radiating from its opening. Cribellate spiders (like *Filistata* and *Amaurobius*) have a "hackle band" along the radial threads, whereas the corresponding plain tripping threads of ecribellate spiders (like those of *Segestria* or *Ariadna*) have only a signaling function (stage I). At the next level of evolution (stage II), the area of the catching plane is enlarged and extends somewhat into open space. In ecribellate spiders this led to the formation of three-dimensional webs (like those of linyphiids and theridiids). The next step postulates the omission of the primary retreat (stage III); secondary retreats may develop at the web's periphery or in its immediate surroundings. In the sheet webs of linyphiids and the cobwebs of theridiids we begin to find glue droplets on some threads to facilitate the ensnarement of flying insects. Still later (stage IV) the web becomes centric and the spider now sits in the hub. The last step would then lead to the typical orb web (stage V), which has a catching spiral with cribellate silk in cribellate spiders, while it is equipped with glue droplets in ecribellate orb weavers. A recent consideration of orb-web phylogeny suggests that the orb was already present in webs of common ancestors of uloborids and araneids but subsequently evolved in different directions, one with cribellate silk, the other with sticky silk (Levi, 1980). This interpretation, unfortunately, does not really shed light on the evolution of the orb web itself.

The orb web in fact is probably *not* the terminal point of the evolution of spider webs. Many orb webs of both cribellate and ecribellate spiders show various degrees of reduction and modifica-

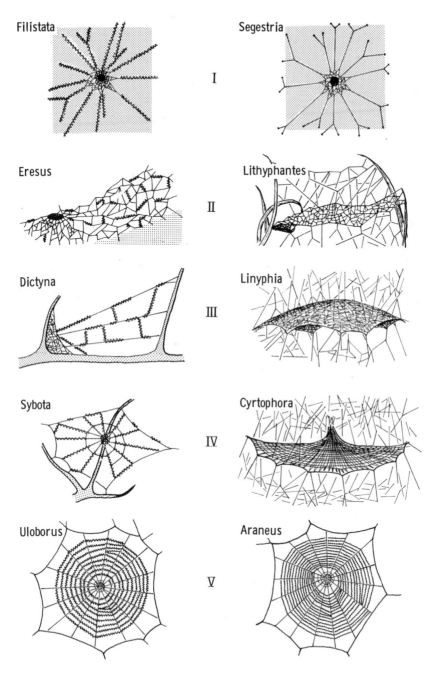

Fig. 108. Evolution of the orb web in cribellate (left) and ecribellate (right) spiders. (After Kullmann, 1972, and Wiehle, 1931.)

tion. The araneid *Zygiella* leaves the center of the web and uses one isolated radius as a signal thread leading to its retreat (Fig. 98a). Since this signal thread is not crossed by the sticky spiral, two sectors of the web remain open. The uloborid spider *Hyptiotes* goes much further in reducing the original orb: only three sectors remain (Fig. 100). *Miagrammopes*, likewise a cribellate spider, spins only a single horizontal thread, which is dressed with catching silk in its middle (Lubin, Eberhard, and Montgomery, 1978).

Corresponding reductions are also found on the ecribellate side, that is, among the Araneidae. The bolas spider (*Mastophora* in America, *Dicrostichus* in Australia) uses only a short thread with a big drop of glue on its end (Fig. 123). This bolas is thrown after insects which fly close by. In *Archemorus* the orb web is also abandoned entirely. The spider sits patiently on the upper surface of a leaf, mimicking detritus or bird droppings. When an insect passes nearby, it is detected visually. *Archemorus* suddenly leaps at the victim and seizes it with its well-armored front legs (Robinson, 1980). Another curious "bird dropping" spider is *Celaenia* from Australia and New Zealand. While simply dangling on a short thread, it grabs moths that fly by (Forster and Forster, 1973). Since the moths caught are invariably males, it is believed that *Celaenia* exudes an attractive scent that mimics the sex pheromone of the female moth.

Other quite fantastic modifications of the orb web are known from the tropical *Poecilopachys* and *Pasilobus* (Robinson and Robinson, 1975). *Pasilobus*, for example, builds a triangular horizontal web consisting of three radii and 4–11 drooping, sticky threads. When a moth brushes against such a strand, the sticky thread ruptures at a predetermined point near one of the marginal radial threads. The insect becomes stuck to the broken sticky thread and finds itself suspended and tethered in flight (Fig. 109). The alerted spider rushes out along the middle radial thread and hauls in its line with the attached prey.

These examples show that evolution has not stopped at but has gone beyond the orb web. In some instances the modifications and reductions have been so radical that there is no hint at all of the original structure—as in the case of the bolas spiders. In another case (*Pachygnatha*) it has been claimed that juvenile spiders build orb webs but that the adults forsake web building altogether and return to a free, hunting way of life (Balogh, 1934). These claims have been confirmed only recently after a long period of uncertainty (Martin, 1978).

A very basic issue not yet dealt with is how spider webs *per se*

Fig. 109. Pasilobus from New Guinea constructs an extremely modified "orb" web. The sagging threads of the sticky "spiral" rupture when an insect brushes against them. (After Robinson and Robinson, 1975.)

could have evolved. It is speculated that the spinning threads were originally used only for wrapping the eggs in an egg sac (Kaston, 1964). Perhaps a retreat was also present at an early stage, and tripping threads emanating from it could alert the spider to insects passing by. At this stage, however, the silk threads were only a means to detect and not to trap prey. A definite improvement was achieved when special catching threads could hamper or even detain prey, making it much easier for the spider to overpower its victim. In conclusion, we can safely assume that snares developed from enlarged living quarters or retreats. The "modern" hunting spiders, such as lycosids, salticids, and pisaurids, have probably secondarily reverted from snare building to a nomadic way of life.

6

Locomotion and
Prey Capture

IN keeping with their varied life styles and different habitats, spiders have developed diverse modes of moving about and capturing prey. Both are complicated by the fact that they can move in all three dimensions. Vertical locomotion is accomplished sometimes by jumping, but mostly, however, by climbing on vegetation or on their own silk thread. Many spiders are able to "fly," that is, they emit a line of silk that is caught by the wind, which, in turn, carries the spider aloft. Almost everyone has witnessed this phenomenon in autumn when watching gossamer strands drifting through the air. Usually, however, only the shiny silk threads are noticed, the tiny passengers are easily overlooked.

Walking

Any regular kind of walking is characterized by a specific *rhythm* or *stepping pattern*. If we look at all eight legs of a spider at the same time, it becomes obvious that two sets of legs always move alternately. For instance, legs 1 and 3 on the left side (L_1, L_3) are active together with legs 2 and 4 on the right side (R_2, R_4). In other

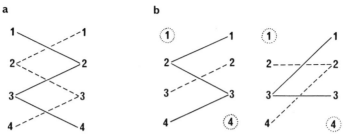

Fig. 110. (*a*) Regular walking pattern: diagonal rhythm. Synchronously moving legs are connected by solid or dashed lines. (*b*) Two possible walking patterns for a spider lacking the first left leg and the fourth right leg. The spider uses the stepping pattern on the right. (After D. M. Wilson, 1967).

words, while legs $L_1-R_2-L_3-R_4$ are moving, legs $R_1-L_2-R_3-L_4$ are at rest (Fig. 110a). Such a *diagonal rhythm* is quite commonly observed among arthropods, regardless of the number of legs they use. In insects, for example, the typical walking pattern is $L_1-R_2-L_3$ and $R_1-L_2-R_3$.

The movements of the different legs are not absolutely synchronized but show slight temporal delays. The onset of activation is quite obviously metachronous in slowly moving spiders, when a wavelike motion passes over the legs on each side of the body. As a consequence, we can also define the walking pattern by watching the stepping sequence on the right or left side. The most common stepping sequence in spiders is described by the formula 4– 2– 3– 1 —or 2– 3– 1– 4, 3– 1– 4– 2, or 1– 4– 2– 3—since any leg can take the first step (D. M. Wilson, 1967). If a spider is moving extremely slowly, the sequence 4– 3– 2– 1 occurs, and the wavelike motion of the legs becomes especially apparent. In contrast, during running one set of legs moves practically synchronously and alternates more strictly with the other set of legs. This gives the impression of a very precise and "mechanical" run.

If a spider loses a leg, it quickly adjusts its gait to the new condition. First of all, the position of the remaining legs is corrected in such a way that the "gap" is more or less compensated for. The spider also modifies its walking pattern, and the length of the steps may increase. This behavioral plasticity is probably caused by an altered proprioceptive feedback: certain sensory inputs are now lacking altogether, and because of the new positions of the legs, the remaining joint receptors provide the spider with slightly different information than before.

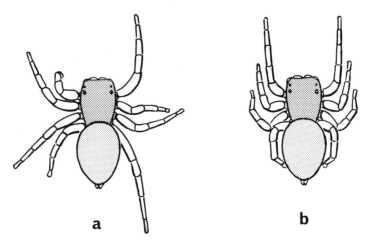

Fig. 111. (*a*) Walking and (*b*) jumping positions of the salticid *Philaeus*. (After Ehlers, 1939.)

Even if several legs are missing, a spider can still change its walking pattern to achieve smooth locomotion. An interesting experiment with a large "tarantula," from which two legs from opposite sides (L_1 and R_4) were amputated, should be mentioned here (D. M. Wilson, 1967). Theoretically two possibilities to compensate for the loss of these two legs exist (Fig. 110b). The spider could either retain a diagonal rhythm and move four legs (R_1–L_2–R_3–L_4) synchronously while balancing its body on the two legs R_2 and L_3, or it could move three legs at a time (R_1–L_3–R_3 or L_2–R_2–L_4), although this would completely offset the diagonal rhythm. The experiment showed that the spider adopts the second alternative, which is indeed the mechanically more stable. The fact that certain pairs of legs (R_2–L_2 and R_3–L_3) now move together proves that the diagonal rhythm is not rigidly "programmed."

Most spiders run in a jerky fashion. At intervals of several centimeters the animal halts abruptly, and after a brief pause it starts again, often changing its direction slightly. When a wolf spider stops, it often freezes the position of its legs momentarily, making the diagonal walking pattern particularly noticeable. In contrast, when a jumping spider stops, it typically arranges its legs symmetrically around its body (Fig. 111); this stance allows for a sudden leap. When web spiders stop moving, many of them also draw their legs close to the body in a kind of resting or protective stance (Ehlers, 1939).

Mechanics of Walking

Since all the legs of a spider are anatomically equal (except in length), they also move basically in the same manner. Yet quantitative differences may play a role, especially with respect to torsion of the leg axis. As a rule, legs 1 and 2 are directed forward and pull, whereas legs 3 and 4 point backward and push (Fig. 112).

During the motion of a single leg, one can differentiate a pulling or pushing phase (*remotion*) and a lifting phase (*promotion*, a forward motion made without contacting the ground). To move the animal ahead, the joints of the first two pairs of legs must bend, while the joints of the hind legs (legs 4) must stretch. The third legs are laterally directed, so bending or stretching of their joints hardly contributes to forward movement; however, a *torsion* of their coxal joints does (Figs. 112, 113).

The legs must move in a coordinated fashion not only in time but also in space. For instance, if the spider makes a left turn, the legs on the right side must increase their stride (Ehlers, 1939). Walking is not necessarily limited to a forward direction. Many spiders—especially crab spiders and jumping spiders—can run adroitly sideways, or even backwards. In the latter case the walk-

a

1   2   4

Fig. 112. (*a*) Contribution of the different legs to the propulsion of the spider. The initial leg position is shown with dotted lines. The first and fourth legs operate mainly by bending and stretching; legs 2 and 3 show torsion. Here only the torsion of the patellar joint is shown for leg 2. (*b*) Working range of the legs of a wolf spider during slow walking (5 cm/sec). Dotted line = propulsion by torsion; vectors = relative contributions to propulsion by bending and stretching. (*a, b* after Ehlers, 1939.)

b

Fig. 113. Sequence of leg movements of a slowly walking wolf spider (*Alopecosa*). Only the left legs are pictured. Note the simultaneous movements of the first and third legs, and of the second and fourth legs, respectively. Bottom: Footprints as recorded on smoke paper. Whereas legs 1 and 2 touch the substrate only with their claws (dots), legs 3 and 4 leave long scratch marks. (After Ehlers, 1939.)

ing pattern still follows the diagonal rhythm, but in reverse. This explains why jumping spiders can walk backwards just as fast as forwards. If the spider turns on the spot, all the legs on one side of the body move forward as usual while the legs on the other side move in the opposite direction (Land, 1972).

   The walking speed of a spider is typically only a few centimeters per second, but large spiders such as *Lycosa* or *Tegenaria* can easily reach a speed of 40–50 cm/sec. The length of the steps increases with the spider's speed: at 6–7 cm/sec a *Tegenaria* takes steps of only 1 cm, but doubles that at 30 cm/sec. As mentioned earlier, spiders can perform impressive sprints, although they become exhausted after a few seconds.

In general, spiders with legs that are equal in length are better runners than those with legs that vary in size. This can be easily confirmed if one compares the running of wolf and garden spiders. Garden spiders have a short third pair of legs and cannot run as quickly on the ground as wolf spiders can. However, while running on a thread the web spider can use its short third legs quite efficiently (Ehlers, 1939; Jacobi-Kleemann, 1953). Apparently the araneid's legs are well adapted for hanging from threads and less well for supporting the weight of the body above the legs. They also lack the traction that adhesive hairs (scopulae; see chapter 2) provide for efficient locomotion in wandering spiders.

Locomotion on a Thread

For a spider the simplest form of locomotion is to let itself drop by its own silk thread. This can be done without any help from the legs, but usually one of the fourth legs pulls the thread sideways when the spider wants to stop (Fig. 114a). Orb web spiders often use their fourth legs to reel out the thread from the spinnerets, thus regulating the speed of the downward motion (Ehlers, 1939). While descending by a thread, the garden spider stretches out its first pair of legs in anticipation of contact with the ground; the second

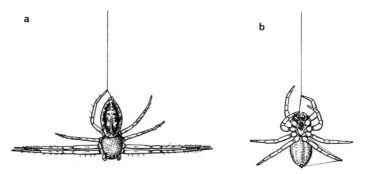

Fig. 114. (*a*) Crab spider *Diaea* dropping on its own thread. (After Bristowe, 1958). (*b*) Jumping spider *Philaeus* climbing back on its own thread. Only the two pairs of front legs grasp the thread, while the palps reel it in. (After Ehlers, 1939.)

pair of legs is spread horizontally to keep the spider from spinning around (Jacobi-Kleemann, 1953).

Climbing back up a vertical thread is accomplished mostly with the aid of the two pairs of front legs (Fig. 114b), while the third pair of legs or the palps gather up the loose thread. During this process the connection with the spinnerets is always maintained so that the spider can quickly drop down again. When moving upside down on a horizontal thread the garden spider uses all of its legs. In this case, the hind legs are moved more rapidly than the front legs, and the third legs often move twice as fast as the others (Jacobi-Kleemann, 1953).

The mode of locomotion during web building does not differ in principle from the spider's normal walking in the completed web. It simply appears more complex because, aside from a merely locomotor purpose, some leg movements also function in placing the threads. For instance, a third and a fourth leg together always pull a radial thread close to the spinnerets so that the spiral thread can be fastened to the radius (Jacobi-Kleemann, 1953).

Jumping

Jumping is most obvious in the salticids, although many other hunting spiders (lycosids, clubionids, and oxyopids) are also capable of at least short leaps. We shall take a closer look at the mechanism of a salticid's jump.

It was believed formerly that the strong front legs are responsible for propelling the spider in a leap. Actually, however, the front legs are often lifted above the ground just before the spider takes off (Figs. 115, 7). The front legs play a role only in landing and, of course, in seizing prey. The thrust for the takeoff comes from the hind legs, either from the fourth or third pair, and sometimes from both. Which technique is used depends on the species. *Evarcha* jumps off with the third pair of legs, *Salticus* with the third and fourth, and *Sitticus* with only the fourth. Just before taking off, the spider fastens a safety thread to the ground. Then the legs are pulled close to and symmetrically around the body. A very quick extension of the fourth pair of legs, a torsion and extension of the third pair of legs (or both), initiates the leap. The stretching of the legs is largely caused by an increase in hemolymph pressure and probably by a concomitant sudden relaxation of the flexor muscles.

Besides capturing prey, salticids utilize their jumping ability for escape. Normally they will jump only a few centimeters, but in

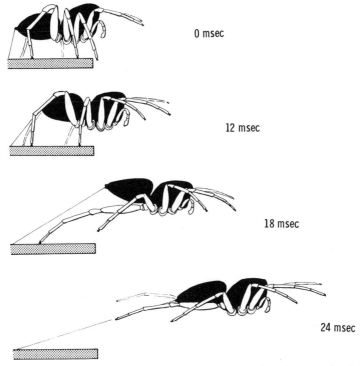

0 msec

12 msec

18 msec

24 msec

Fig. 115.   Takeoff of the jumping spider *Sitticus*. The jump results from a rapid stretching of the fourth pair of legs. (Tracings of slow-motion pictures by Parry and Brown, 1959b.)

some cases they cover up to 25 times their own body length (Ehlers, 1939). Compared with the jumps of some insects (grasshoppers or fleas, for instance) this may seem like a modest performance, yet after all, salticids do not have any oversized jumping legs. Short leaps are often interspersed in the normal walking pattern whenever the spider has to bridge a small gap. This leaping is also seen in other wandering spiders which live predominantly on vegetation. Again, the takeoff is caused by the action of the third and fourth pairs of legs (Ehlers, 1939).

Locomotion on and under Water

Some spiders are not capable of walking on water; among them are the salticids, thomisids, linyphiids, and theridiids. Many pisaurids and lycosids (such as *Dolomedes*, *Pardosa*, and *Pirata*), how-

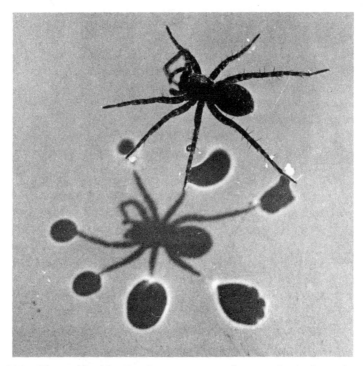

Fig. 116.   The wolf spider *Pardosa amentata* afloat on the surface of water, cleaning its first right leg with its mouth parts. The tips of the other legs indent the water surface slightly. The sun rays project these indentations as large shadowy patches onto the bottom of the shallow pond.

ever, can walk on water as well as they do on land. Propulsion is mainly by means of the second and third pairs of legs. The first legs are used as feelers and are stretched forward, while the fourth pair of legs is dragged behind. The smaller, light weight species can raise their bodies high above the water (Fig. 116). The larger and heavier species walk rather flatfootedly on the water's surface so that the entire tarsus (and sometimes the metatarsus) is in contact with the water. In the large "raft spider" *Dolomedes*, the body rests on the surface of the water as well. Incidentally, *Dolomedes* does not make use of the diagonal walking pattern when running on water. Instead, the third pair of legs and, after a short delay, the second pair of legs are pulled back in synchrony. *Dolomedes* thus moves in a manner similar to that of the water striders (Gerridae) among the insects. The legs are moved only at their insertion sites in the cephalothorax or at the coxal joints, the other leg segments

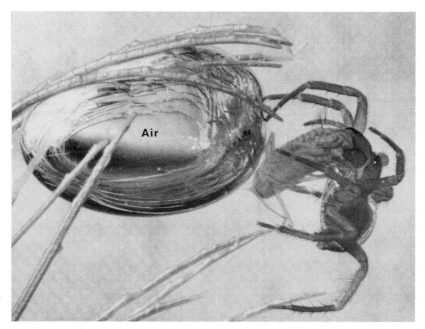

Fig. 117.   The water spider *Argyroneta aquatica* carrying an ephemerid larva to its diving bell (Air). (Photo: Vollrath.)

being neither bent nor stretched (Ehlers, 1939). Thus the spider rows across the water.

The orb web spider *Tetragnatha*, which is usually found near lakes or ponds, can also walk nimbly on the water's surface. Here only the first and second pair of legs move in the diagonal rhythm, whereas legs 3 and 4 are pulled behind passively. Despite this unusual technique *Tetragnatha* can attain the remarkable speed of 15–20 cm/sec. This is faster than this spider walks on land (Ehlers, 1939).

The only spider that can walk and swim under water is the water spider *Argyroneta aquatica* (Fig. 117). Because of the airbubble which surrounds its abdomen, this spider is always in a labile, ventral-side-up position. The legs are in direct contact with the water and are not covered by air; this would increase buoyancy to such an extent that the spider could no longer dive. The legs are used not only for walking under water (along plants or silk threads), but also for free *swimming*. Although they move according to the diagonal rhythm, they also beat up and down, that is, the joints are bent and stretched, yet none of the customary lateral torsion of the coxal or body joints occurs (Ehlers, 1939).

Locomotory Activity

Most spiders are active at night. Notable exceptions are the jumping spiders, which move about during daytime but withdraw into their silken nests at dusk (Jackson, 1979). They are diurnal, of course, because of their dependence on vision. Similarly, lynx spiders (Oxyopidae), crab spiders (Thomisidae), and many wolf spiders (Lycosidae) are also active mostly during the day.

In contrast, many wandering spiders are hardly ever seen in the daytime; they venture from their retreats only at dusk. Before *Cupiennius* leaves its hideout, it goes through a fixed sequence of preparatory steps, each of which is correlated with a particular light level (Seyfarth, 1980). When the light intensity drops to about 15 lux, the animal turns around and stands above its retreat; there it waits until the illumination has decreased to 0.1 lux. Only then does the spider start to wander around. Maximum activity is reached within two or three hours after dark. The duration of both the activity and the resting times is controlled endogenously. This can be concluded from the observation that *Cupiennius* shows almost the same activity rhythm, namely, of 24.9 hours, when kept continuously in the dark that it does under natural conditions. Such a circadian rhythm of locomotory activity is probably present in many other spiders (Cloudsley-Thompson, 1978).

The large "tarantulas" have also been known as strictly nocturnal animals (Cloudsley-Thompson, 1968). Although this is true as far as their hunting and free-wandering activity is concerned, it does not mean that they are completely inactive during day. Weaving activities, such as silking over the openings of their burrows, take place during daylight (Minch, 1978).

The activity rhythm of web-building spiders has been studied mainly among the araneids (Ramousse and Davis, 1976; Ramousse and LeGuelte, 1979; Ramousse, 1980). Most species of *Araneus* build their webs preferentially at the beginning or at the end of the nocturnal period. Surprisingly, the first nymphs of *Araneus* are active mostly during light phases, but this behavior reverses itself after the spiderlings molt (Le Berre, 1979).

Many araneids are strictly nocturnal and may even destroy their web before daybreak (Eberhard, 1976; Stowe, 1978). Quite a few species have therefore been overlooked previously, since most spider watchers tend to be diurnal.

Prey Capture

The many ways in which prey is captured in a web have already been dealt with in chapter 5. The wandering spiders, however, do not rely on a snare, but must locate and overpower their prey directly. First we will take a close look at the predation strategy of wandering spiders and then compare the effectiveness of different methods of prey catching in some web spiders.

Wandering Spiders

The ctenid spider *Cupiennius* shall serve as a typical example for the events that take place during prey capture (Melchers, 1967). *Cupiennius* usually lies in ambush rather than hunts its prey actively. An attack is launched only when a prey animal comes very close. Most impressive is the speed of capture: the entire sequence, from attacking to subduing of the prey, can occur in less than 0.2 seconds (Fig. 118). One would expect that the spider's extremely fast grasping movements would follow a rigid motor pattern. However, high-speed cinematography (at 1,000 frames/sec) has shown that these movements are by no means stereotyped but are well adapted to each specific situation.

First of all, the prey must be noticed and located. Visual cues

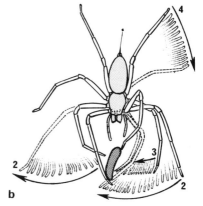

Fig. 118. Prey capture in *Cupiennius.* (a) The spider in its attentive posture hanging upside down on a wall. (b) Only the tarsi of the front legs handle the prey. The rapid change in the position of the legs (in the time of 25 msec!) is indicated by the dashed lines and the arrows. (After Melchers, 1967.)

Fig. 119.   Prey capture in a wolf spider (*a, b, Lycosa*) and a nursery-web spider (*c, Dolomedes*). (*a*) The wolf spider has seized a cricket and is catapulted through the air. (*b*) Often the spider lands on its back, clamping the prey tightly above with all its legs (Photos *a, b:* Rovner.) (*c*) After the bite prey is held only with the chelicerae.

play hardly any role for *Cupiennius*, for an experimentally blinded animal can catch its prey just as efficiently as an unblinded one. Instead, vibrations of the substrate or of the air (by wing beats) or the immediate contact with a victim elicit directed catching movements: the spider turns very rapidly toward the prey and grasps it with the front legs. The first gentle touch with the forelegs is quickly changed into a power grip. The legs are able to improve their secure hold by means of the adhesive hairs (scopulae) on the tarsi. The prey is quickly pulled toward the spider's body and the chelicerae and their fangs move apart. Then follows the bite into the nearest part of the victim's body. Immediately after the bite the tips of the legs release their grip so that the prey is held in the air only with the chelicerae, thereby minimizing danger to the spider from the prey's weapons. This too is advantageous because the victim has no contact with the substrate and therefore cannot apply any directed force to free itself. (Fig. 119). Only after the prey has become immobilized by the poison does actual feeding (the chewing and the exuding of digestive juice) begin. For extra measure, large prey items are fastened to the ground by some silk threads before the spider feeds.

In summary, the entire prey capture passes through the following stages:

1. Locating the prey
2. Turning toward the victim and grasping it with the tips of the front legs
3. Pulling the prey to the chelicerae and biting it (venom injection)
4. Releasing the grasp with the legs and holding the prey only with the chelicerae
5. Fastening of some silk threads over the immobilized prey
6. Feeding

Some wolf spiders (for instance, some species of *Pirata*) use visual clues to orient themselves toward prey (Gettmann, 1976); most likely such spiders react to the prey's movements (Homann, 1931). Classic examples for that type of prey capture are the jumping spiders (Fig. 120; for details see chapter 4).

As noted for *Cupiennius*, some hunting spiders place silken threads over the paralyzed victim and attach it to the substrate. The advantage of this behavior is that spiders which roam in the higher foliage strata can secure their prey near the catching site. If the spider is disturbed, the prey can then be left and still be relocated quickly (Rovner and Knost, 1974; Greenquist and Rovner, 1976).

The method of prey capture described for *Cupiennius* gives a general idea of how spiders hunt and capture their prey but does not apply equally to all wandering spiders. Even among the "ancient" Orthognatha we find many different levels of complexity with respect to predation (Buchli, 1969). On a rather simple level are some "tarantulas" (Theraphosidae) which merely move about until they come across potential prey. Other "tarantulas" (Aviculariidae) climb in trees and jump at passing prey animals. The sedentary trap-door spiders show a somewhat more complex behav-

Fig. 120.   Prey capture in the jumping spider *Salticus scenicus.* (*a*) The spider sits vertically on a glass wall and fixates its victim, a young wolf spider. (*b*) *Salticus* stalks the prey and is now within jumping distance. (*c*) The victim is seized with the front legs and the bite is applied.

ior: they hide in a silk-lined, earthen tube, which is covered by a hinged lid, the "trap door". At night the spider lifts the trap door slightly and stretches out its front legs. The more "primitive" representatives of trap-door spiders jump out and chase passing prey, whereas the more advanced species leave the tube only if prey is within easy reach. A further improvement was achieved when radial threads (signal or tripping threads) were added to the entrance of the burrow. This method is also used by the "ancient" Mesothelae (Bristowe, 1975; Klingel, 1966). Finally, in the orthognath Dipluridae we find sheet webs similar to those of the Agelenidae. As soon as a prey item falls on the web and sets up vibrations, the spider rushes out of its hiding place to attack it.

Web Spiders

Prey capture by web spiders does not differ in principle from that seen in wandering spiders. But there are many variations in the specifics of predation among the web spiders. For example, web spiders do not usually feed at the capture site but carry their prey to a safer place (into a retreat or to the hub of an orb web). The orb weavers (Araneidae) and the comb-footed spiders (Theridiidae) show another pecularity: they often subdue their prey by first wrapping it with silk before biting it.

The funnel-web spider *Coelotes* (Agelenidae) provides a good example of how sheet-web spiders capture their prey. *Coelotes* preys mainly on beetles, which blunder onto its sheet web (Tretzel, 1961a). The slightest vibrations in the web cause the spider to dart out from its subterranean retreat. In several quick sprints it takes a straight course toward the victim. When the spider has reached the beetle, it turns the insect on its back and tries immediately to puncture the segmental membranes of the abdomen with its chelicerae. The poison takes 8–10 minutes to produce any paralysis, and during this time the spider holds on firmly with its chelicerae. Only after the movements of the victim begin to weaken is the grasp somewhat loosened and digestive juice poured over the wound. When the beetle is severely paralyzed, its wings often open up, and the spider now has easy access to the softer parts of the body. The actual feeding begins only after the prey has been carried into the spider's retreat. There the immobilized prey may still be fastened to the ground with a few silken threads (Tretzel, 1961b), as was described above for some wandering spiders.

Prey capture has been most thoroughly studied in the orb weavers. Their methods of catching prey are even more variable than in other kinds of spiders. The common garden spider *Araneus diadematus*, for example, often follows this sequence: (1) locating the prey in the web; (2) rapidly moving toward the prey; (3) immobilizing the prey; (4) transporting the prey to the hub.

Quite different strategies may be utilized, however, for the last two steps (H. Peters, 1931, 1933). When a fly becomes entangled in the sticky spiral thread of the orb web, it produces specific vibrations which immediately excite the spider. Even if the fly then remains quiet, the spider will pluck several radial threads, apparently to probe the load on each radius. In other words, it tries to find the exact position of the prey. Especially if the fly moves its wings again, the spider will rush out of the hub using exactly that radial thread which leads to the prey. The victim is briefly touched with the front legs and palps; then the hind legs wrap silk around it. Only thereafter follows a *brief* bite. Using its legs and chelicerae, the spider then cuts the neatly wrapped "package" from the web and carries it to the hub. There it is attached by a short thread be-

Fig. 121. The tropical orb weaver *Argiope argentata* during "offensive wrapping" of a cricket. (Photo: Robinson.)

fore it is eaten. The feeding process always takes place in the hub, never at the actual capture site.

This rather general description must be made more specific. The main point is that the garden spider usually wraps its victim *before* biting it. This is in contrast to most wandering spiders. However, if the prey is very small (such as a fruit fly), it is simply grasped with the chelicerae and carried to the hub. Large insects, which set up strong vibrations in the web, are also bitten immediately, but then the bite lasts many seconds or even minutes. Such a *long* bite probably prevents a possible escape of strong prey animals. On the other hand, aggressive prey, such as wasps, are always wrapped first, and then bitten. Apparently in this situation it is safer for the spider to keep the dangerous prey at a distance. These few examples demonstrate that the biting behavior is not rigid but depends on the type of prey.

The same can be said for the spider's methods for transporting the subdued prey: if the victim is relatively light (about 10 mg), it is always carried with the chelicerae; heavier prey (about 80 mg) is

Table 3. Strategy of attack of *Argiope argentata* toward different prey. (After Robinson and Robinson, 1974.)

	Strategy		
Prey	Wrap → Bite	Bite → Wrap	Bite → Pull out
Grasshoppers	100%	–	–
Flies	74%	2%	24%
Moths	17%	75%	8%

always attached to a short thread and hauled behind with the fourth leg (H. Peters, 1933).

Other orb weavers (for example, *Argiope* species) behave like *Araneus;* that is, the prey is first wrapped and then bitten (Fig. 121). As a regular exception *Argiope* uses the bite first when dealing with moths (Table 3; Robinson and Robinson, 1974).

Many moths get stuck in the web only very briefly. They merely lose some wing scales on the sticky threads but afterwards escape quickly (Eisner, Alsop, and Ettershank, 1964). To capture a moth, then, the spider must be at the point of impact immediately. Even flies remain in an orb web for an average of only five seconds before they can free themselves (Barrows, 1915). Usually, however, this is plenty of time for an alert orb-web spider to rush out for the capture. Once the spider has left the hub, most prey animals have hardly any chance for escape.

Unlike *Argiope,* the tropical orb weaver *Nephila* attacks *all* of its prey with a bite first and then performs the wrapping while sitting in the hub (Robinson and Mirick, 1971). This strategy can be inefficient and even risky if the "wrong" prey animals are encountered. This was shown in experiments with bombardier beetles (*Brachynus,* Carabidae) which were released into the webs of *Nephila* and *Argiope* (Eisner and Dean, 1976). Bombardier beetles possess a fantastic defensive weapon: they can aim explosive secretions toward an aggressor. When ejected from the beetle's abdomen, these secretions have a temperature of 100°C! Whereas a *Nephila* will be completely repelled by this weapon as it tries to bite the insect, an *Argiope* has already tightly wrapped the beetle, before the explosion can be triggered. Only when *Argiope* tries to bite through the swathing silk does the beetle try to defend itself. This has, however, little effect and leads only to further wrapping. Whereas *Argiope* can always overpower the bombardier beetle with the wrapping method, *Nephila* never succeeds with the biting strategy. Of course, it is true that bombardier beetles are not an essential item in the large prey spectrum of araneids. On the other hand, there are a number of insects which do use defensive chemical secretions. For instance, some stinkbugs (Pentatomidae) can defend themselves against a *Nephila* but not against an *Argiope* (Robinson, 1975).

In general, the offensive wrapping of prey yields two advantages for the spider: (1) there is less danger of being harmed by strong prey (a biting grasshopper or stinging wasp); (2) it takes less time than applying the *long* bite. This second point becomes even more important when several prey items get caught in the web within a short period of time. The spider can fasten the first victim securely at the hub and can then rush toward the second. Such additional prey is also wrapped and bitten but is left at the capture site as a "reserve."

Within the araneid family we find at least three related strategies of prey capture, which suggest successive steps in the evolution of their predatory behavior (Robinson, 1975; Fig. 122). *Strategy 1* is sometimes encountered in all araneids, especially if the prey is small. *Strategy 2* is typical of *Nephila*. Wrapping at the capture site makes it much easier to handle and carry bulky prey like butterflies or dragonflies. *Strategy 3* is preferred by *Araneus* and *Argiope;* the advantages have already been mentioned. In the cribellate orb weavers (Uloboridae) one can find a fourth strategy: the

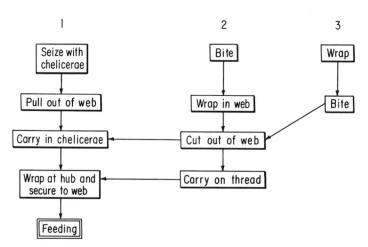

Fig. 122. Different strategies of predation in orb weavers (Araneidae). (After Robinson, 1975.)

prey is wrapped but not bitten at all. A bite would not be of much use anyway, as uloborids do not have poison glands. The offensive wrapping of prey is probably a more recent step in evolution, which might have derived from the defensive wrapping that takes place at the hub. In summary, about four different levels in the predation strategies of spiders can be distinguished (Eberhard, 1967):

1. Grasping and biting	no web	theraphosids, clubionids, and salticids
2. Grasping and biting	web on the ground	agelenids
3. Grasping, biting, and occasional wrapping	aerial web	linyphiids
4. Grasping, biting, wrapping; or wrapping and biting; or wrapping only	aerial web	theridiids, araneids, and uloborids

Predation Specialists

So far I have tried to establish some general principles underlying the many different approaches spiders use to capture their prey. Some spiders, however, have developed highly specialized methods of predation which do not fit any general scheme. A few representatives of such spiders were mentioned earlier, for instance, the spitting spider *Scytodes* and the triangle spider *Hyptiotes*. The bolas spider *Mastophora* was briefly touched upon in chapter 5 but deserves a more detailed discussion here. One would think that the method of a bolas spider—to throw a sticky droplet after a flying insect (Fig. 123)—could hardly be successful. Such a strategy seems even more absurd if we consider that these spiders hunt at night. However, bolas spiders are quite adept at capturing certain moths (*Spodoptera*), or, to be more precise, only the male *Spodoptera*. The explanation of this baffling phenomenon is that bolas spiders apparently secrete a volatile substance which imitates the sex pheromone of the female *Spodoptera*. The male moths are attracted by this scent and fly in circles around the spider. Thus the spider has a much better target at which to throw its bolas. On the average, a bolas spider catches two or three moths a night. This is comparable indeed to the number of prey a regular orb weaver catches with its web (Eberhard, 1977b).

Some spiders have specialized for a certain prey type and have developed appropriate capture methods. Well-known examples are the pirate spiders (Mimetidae), which prey exclusively on other spiders, and the Zodariidae, which hunt only ants. The pirate spider *Ero* attacks other spiders by very briefly biting into one of their extremities. The injected poison acts very quickly—the victim is paralyzed within a few seconds. *Ero* then approaches again and starts sucking the prey from the bite hole. An even more specialized method is used by *Ero* when it is after the orb weaver *Meta segmentata*: *Ero* uses the courtship thread of the male and plucks it, supposedly imitating the courtship signals. The female *Meta* is apparently tricked, since she comes out of the hub—only to fall victim to *Ero* (Czajka, 1963). In a similar manner *Zodarium* (Zodariidae) will bite an ant in a leg joint and then wait for the prey to become paralyzed (Harkness and Wehner, 1977). Exclusive ant hunters are sometimes also found in other spider families, such as the Salticidae (*Stoidis aurata;* Edwards, Carroll, and Whitcomb, 1974) and Drassodidae (synonym: Gnaphosidae).

One member of the gnaphosid family, *Callilepis nocturna*, has a highly specialized method of hunting ants (Heller, 1974, 1976). *Callilepis* runs in short bursts; the motion resembles that of certain ants (for example, *Formica*), but the body does not have an antlike appearance at all. Thus *Callilepis* cannot be considered as an ant mimic. The ant is always attacked head-on (Fig. 124a). The tarsi of the spider's front legs contact the ant's head and probe for the base

Fig. 123.   Hunting method of the bolas-spider *Mastophora.* (*a*) A front leg holds a short thread with a glue droplet (arrow) at its end. (*b*) When a moth passes close by, the bolas is hurled at it. (*a, b* from Eberhard, 1977; Copyright © 1977 by the American Association for the Advancement of Science.)

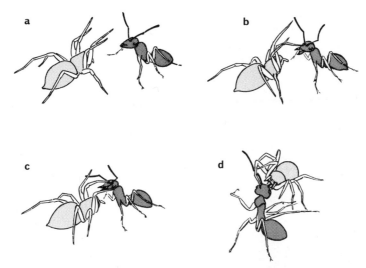

Fig. 124. Prey capture technique of the ant spider *Callilepis.* (*a*) The spider assumes a jumping position and raises its front legs. (*b*) One tarsus contacts the base of an antenna. (*c*) Both tarsi of the front legs locates the bases of the antennae. (*d*) Bite at the base of one antenna. (After Heller, 1974.)

of the antennae (Fig. 124b, c). Then follows a quick bite (0.2 sec) at the base of one antenna, and the spider withdraws completely. A minute later *Callilepis* searches for the victim again and applies a longer bite. Initially the bitten ant is quite aggressive, but within a few seconds its injured antenna becomes limp and the ant starts walking in small circles (right-hand circles if the left antenna was bitten and vice versa). Thus the ant hardly moves away from the spot where it was first attacked, and therefore it can easily be relocated afterwards. *Callilepis* tucks the paralyzed ant underneath herself and runs quickly for a hiding place. During this maneuver she is often attacked by other ants, but somehow she manages to dodge them. Once she has reached a safer place, she closes it off with a silken cover and starts feeding. The prey is never chewed but is sucked from the neck and abdomen. After one or two hours the undamaged cuticular shell is all that remains of the ant.

The very rapid and precise capture method of *Callilepis* represents an adaptation to cope with strong and potentially dangerous prey. The bite is placed only at the vulnerable base of an antenna, and the legs are immediately removed from the reach of the ant's formidable mandibles. The predation strategy of *Callilepis* is

Fig. 125.   Prey catching in the Australian ogre-faced spider *Dinopis*. The spider extends a rectangular web with cribellate catching threads between its front legs (*a*, *c*). (*b*) When an insect comes within reach, the web is swept over the prey. (From Kullmann and Stern, 1975). (Inset: Land.)

rather rigidly "programmed": if both antennae of the ant are cut off, the spider still attacks but never bites it. Apparently the bite is "blocked" when *Callilepis* cannot locate the antennal bases. On the other hand, if one glues two antennae on the ant's abdomen, the spider will bite there. The antennae must therefore be considered the key stimulus for the spider's bite (Heller, 1976).

We want to conclude this chapter with a description of the unique prey capture of the ogre-faced spider *Dinopis*. This tropical spider hangs upside down in a vertical frame of threads, somewhat similar to an orb weaver (Robinson and Robinson, 1971). The actual catching web, however, is held between the front legs (Fig. 125). Although the spider hunts mostly at night, it locates its prey visually. This is made possible by two huge posterior median eyes (1.4 mm in diameter), which are similar to the main eyes of jumping spiders (anterior median eyes; 0.4 mm diameter). Unlike the main eyes of jumping spiders, the enormous eyes of *Dinopis* do not have better resolution but are 2,000 times more sensitive to light (Blest and Land, 1977). For a nocturnal hunter this is, of course, a definite advantage.

When an insect comes within reach of *Dinopis*, its front legs spread the rectangular catching web and throw it like a sweep-net over the prey. The elastic web is jerked several times so that the victim becomes completely entangled in the hackle threads. Additionally *Dinopis* uses its hind legs to pull out silk threads from the spinnerets to wrap the prey. During this process the prey is bitten once, or several times, and thereafter actual feeding begins. It is curious that the spider often starts constructing a new catching web while it is still busy feeding. This is possible because the wrapped prey is handled only with the palps, and the legs are thus free for building a new capture web.

Although spiders always catch live prey, this does not mean that they do not also feed on dead animals. In the laboratory they accept crushed insects and even animals that have been dead for several days (Knost and Rovner, 1975). Whether scavenging is common in nature has not been thoroughly investigated; yet there are some indications that it occurs regularly in some wandering spiders (Gettmann, 1978). Given the variety of techniques that spiders have mastered to capture their prey, and the diversity of their habitats and diets, such a finding would not be surprising.

7

Reproduction

SPIDERS are always dioecious; that is, they invariably have separate sexes. Aside from a few exceptions (for example, *Argyroneta*), the females are larger than the males. This sexual dimorphism is especially obvious in many tropical orb weavers (such as *Nephila*, *Gasteracantha*, and *Micrathena*), where the males appear to be dwarfs (Fig. 126). There has been a lot of speculation about the biological meaning of the small body size of male spiders, but so far no consensus has been reached (Vollrath, 1980). In any case, the small spider males are very agile, and some can even "fly" on their own thread, just as young spiders do.

Because of their small body size, males need fewer molts to reach maturity than do females; consequently, males mature earlier. After their last molt the males have conspicuously thickened palpal tarsi and can thereby be distinguished easily from the females. The female palps represent simply a kind of shortened leg (without a metatarsus), but the male palps have tarsi that are specialized for the storage and transfer of sperm. This function of the male palps as copulatory organs is highly unusual, and nothing comparable exists in other arthropods.

In contrast to females, most male spiders change their habits

Fig. 126. Size dimorphism of the orb weaver *Argiope aemula* from New Guinea. The dwarfed male approaches the female sitting in the hub. (Photo: Robinson.)

after their last molt. They leave their retreats or webs and become vagabonds; often they do not even catch prey anymore. As soon as they have charged their palps with sperm, they start wandering around, searching for a female. Usually they are rather cautious

Fig. 127. Position of the external sexual organs of *Araneus diadematus;* ventral view. The genital opening lies inside the epigastric furrow (arrow). The epigynum (E) is situated in front of this furrow. Book lungs are outlined with dots. B = bulb of palp. (After Grasshoff, 1973.)

when approaching a female, because they always risk being dealt with as prey. Spiders have therefore developed a special courtship behavior that generally precedes mating. The common belief that spider males are eaten by the females during or after copulation is true only for a very few species. In most cases a male either walks away or beats a hasty retreat right after copulation. His palps are then refilled with sperm. This procedure, however, can be repeated only a few times, since most male spiders have rather short lives; many die soon after copulation. Females usually live much longer, since they must still lay eggs and build cocoons. In some species the females also exhibit brood care for the developing young.

Internal Sexual Organs

The internal sexual organs, the testes and ovaries, lie as paired structures inside the abdomen. The reproductive cells, the sperm and the eggs, are released to the outside in both sexes through a ventral opening (the epigastric furrow) that is situated between and slightly behind the book lungs (Fig. 127). The males exude their sperm through this opening onto a special sperm web and then transfer it to their palps. The internal sexual organs are more complex in females, which also have a special storage site for sperm, the seminal receptacles.

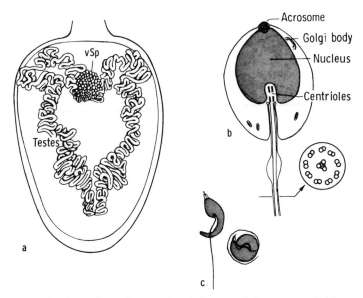

Fig. 128.   (*a*) Testicular tubes in the abdomen of the tarantula *Grammostola.* The genital pore is covered by a ventral spinning field (vSp); these "epiandrous glands" contribute to the male's sperm web. (After Melchers, 1964.) (*b*) Spermatid of the lynx spider *Oxyopes.* The cross-section of the flagellum shows the unusual 9 + 3 arrangement of microtubules 3,800 ×. (Drawn from electron micrographs by Osaki, 1972.) (*c*) Differentiation of the mature sperm cell by rolling the flagellum around the nucleus. (After Bösenberg, 1905.)

Testes and Sperm Cells

The two testes are highly convoluted tubes (Fig. 128) that merge into a common duct that leads medially into the epigastric furrow. The differentiation of sperm cells (spermiogenesis) takes place in the epithelium of the testicular tubes. Only a little is known about the structure and physiology of spider sperm. The early stages of sperm cells (spermatids) are flagellated, although the flagella have a rather unusual arrangement of their axial tubules; spider sperm axonemes are assembled according to a 9 +3 rather than the common 9 + 2 pattern (Fig. 128b; Osaki, 1969; Bacetti, Dallai, and Rosati, 1970). During spermiogenesis this flagellum is apparently resorbed (Reger, 1970), so that one would expect the sperm to be nonmotile. However, examinations of freshly deposited sperm droplets have shown that the sperm move vigorously after water is added to them (Bösenberg, 1905; Gerhardt and Kaestner, 1938). It has been known for a long time that the differentiating sperm cell

Fig. 129. (*a*) Cross-section of a testis of *Zygiella*. The lumen of the testicular tube is filled with ring-shaped sperm cells. 540×. Inset: 1,500×. (*b*) Differentiated sperm cell as seen in the electron microscope. The flagellum (arrows) has been incorporated into the cytoplasm. A = acrosome, N = sections through the nucleus. 24,000×. (Photo *b*: Reger.)

forms a ringlike structure by rolling the flagellum tightly around the head (containing the nucleus) of the sperm cell (Fig. 129). In the lumen of the testicular tube, these disk-shaped sperm are then surrounded by protein capsules and therefore become nonmotile (Boissin, 1973). It is at this stage that the sperm cells are transferred into the palps (and later into the seminal receptacles). At egg-laying time the protein layer probably dissolves inside the female's seminal receptacles, and the sperm cells again become motile.

In the course of spermatogenesis, cell divisions (mitosis and meiosis) can be studied particularly well. In those cells that are just in the process of dividing, the chromosomes can be made visible by special staining techniques. Under favorable conditions the entire set of chromosomes can be counted under the microscope. The spider species investigated to date exhibit 20–30 chromosomes in the diploid stage. Crab spiders have about 22 chromosomes, wolf spiders 22–28, and jumping spiders 28–30 (Hackmann, 1948; Mittal, 1964; Painter, 1914).

Aside from the "regular" chromosomes (the *autosomes*, A), two special chromosomes represent the *sex chromosomes* (X-chromosomes). Whereas female spiders possess a dual set of these X-chromosomes ($2A + X_1X_1X_2X_2$), male spiders have but a single set

(2A + X_1X_2). Consequently, after meiosis the haploid egg cells have A + X_1X_2 chromosomes, but the sperm cells are of two types: either they likewise possess A + X_1X_2 or they lack sex chromosomes altogether (A + O). Sex determination is thus dependent on the type of sperm cell that fertilizes the egg. Some species of spiders have only one X-chromosome in the male, others may have males with three X-chromosomes. A Y-chromosome, typical of some insects and mammals, is lacking in spiders.

Ovaries and Egg Cells

The ovaries are paired, elongated structures situated in the ventral part of the abdomen (see Fig. 30). They are reminiscent of the ovaries of birds, because the egg cells (*oocytes*) bulge into the body cavity (Fig. 130a) and are connected to the ovarian epithelium by a short stalk (the *funiculus*). How the egg cells are released is still a matter of conjecture. The so-called oviducts represent the inside of the ovarian epithelium and are therefore not in an adequate position to take up the maturing egg cells to enter the lumen of the "oviduct" (Sadana, 1970).

In many spider families the egg cells contain a typical structure that has been called the *vitelline body*, or *Dotterkern* (von Wittich, 1845). It consists of several concentric lamellae (Fig. 130b), which have been identified as endoplasmic reticulum (Sotelo and Cenóz, 1957; André and Rouiller, 1957). Nothing definite is known about the function of the vitelline body, but ostensibly it represents an organizing center for yolk formation (Osaki, 1972). Yolk accumulation occurs in two steps (Seitz, 1971). At first, very fine grained yolk particles aggregate in the young egg cell until the cell reaches a diameter of approximately 100 μm. Only after copulation does a second accumulation of yolk begin, this time in the form of much larger granules. The second phase of yolk accumulation can take place only if enough food is available. After copulation female *Cupiennius*, for example, voraciously attack their prey. Within two weeks the volume of an egg cell increases ten- to twelvefold. Accordingly, the female's abdomen swells visibly, and just prior to egg deposition four-fifths of her opisthosoma is taken up by the ovaries.

The total mass of the eggs that a female spider produces is impressive. *Cupiennius*, for instance, produces 1,500–2,000 eggs for her first cocoon, equivalent to a weight of 1.5–2.5 grams (Melchers, 1963). The subsequent four or five cocoons are each made at intervals of 45 days; they contain successively fewer eggs.

Fig. 130.   Egg cells. (*a*) Dissected ovary of a *Zygiella.* The egg cells (EC) sit on the outside of the ovary (Ov). 65×. (*b*) Histological section of two young egg cells. A large pale nucleus (N) with a distinct nucleolus (Nc) is seen in the cell on the right; in the cell on the left a conspicuous vitelline body (VB) is surrounded by fine granular yolk. 370×. (*c*) The yolk granules are much larger in mature egg cells. 270×. (*d*) The periphery of a mature egg cell contains various yolk droplets and microvilli projecting into the chorion layer (Ch). 5,200×.

External Sexual Organs

Male spiders lack primary copulatory organs. Instead, their pedipalps have been modified to transfer sperm. In many "primitive" spiders (Orthognatha, Haplogynae—but not Mesothelae) the males have only slightly modified pedipalps and the females correspondingly rather simple copulatory organs. On the other hand, in entelegyne spiders a good correlation between the highly differentiated palp of the male and a complex epigynum of the female is evident. The external sexual organs are often so species-specific that systematicists use them as decisive characters for species identification. It is tempting to postulate that the highly specialized "lock-and-key" mechanism of male and female copulatory organs serves to prevent cross-breeding between different species. However, we have no experimental proof for this assumption. More likely, hybridization is already inhibited at the behaviour level: courtship is discontinued if one of the spiders does not react in a species-specific way. In fact, many male spiders do try to court females of the "wrong" species (Fig. 131); they are, however, always unsuccessful, because the females are responsive only to males of their own species (Crane, 1949; Grasshoff, 1973).

Fig. 131.   A female garden spider (*Araneus pallidus*) immediately after her final molt. Note the two males waiting: on the left an *A. pallidus*, on the right an *A. diadematus*. (Photo: Grasshoff.)

Fig. 132. (*a*) Simple type of a male palp in *Segestria florentina*. The spiraled spermophor can be seen through the bulb (B). Ta = tarsus, Ti = tibia. 120×. (After Harm, 1931.) (*b*) Complex type of a male palp in *Araneus diadematus*. The diagram shows the expanded state. Cy = cymbium. Sclerites: C = conductor, E = embolus, mA = median apophysis, R = radix, St = stipes, ST = subtegulum, T = tegulum, tA = terminal apophysis. The extensible hematodochal areas are lightly stippled. (After Grasshoff, 1968.) (*c*) Scanning electron micrograph of the left palp of a male *Meta menardi*. 35×. (Photo: Opell.)

Male Copulatory Organs

The simplest form of a male palp is seen in the haplogyne and orthognath spiders. The tarsus of the palp (the *cymbium*) carries an extension in the form of a pear-shaped *bulb*, or palpal organ, which acts as a reservoir for the sperm (Fig. 132a). A blind duct spirals through the bulb and opens at its very tip; the narrow portion of the tip is called the *embolus*. The bulb functions like a pipette and can take up a droplet of sperm. The sperm cells are then stored inside the duct (*spermophor*) until mating. It is not quite clear how the sperm are expelled, since an elevated hemolymph pressure does not seem to be involved. Presumably the mass of sperm becomes displaced by a glandular secretion which is discharged into the spermophor (Harm, 1931).

The male palps are much more complex in entelegyne spiders (Fig. 132b), because the wall of the palpal organ consists of hard, sclerotized parts (the *sclerites*) and soft areas (the *hematodochae*); both can bear special protrusions (*apophyses*) that play an essential role during copulation. The soft hematodochae are inflatable and allow the palpal organ to expand hydraulically (Homann, 1935). Normally the entire bulb is collapsed so that the fragile embolus is protected from mechanical damage. When the hemolymph pressure is increased, the hematodocha expands and the sclerites become erect and project from the rest of the palp (Fig. 133). Theses sclerites assume defined spatial positions, and this is a precondition for a secure coupling with the female's epigynum.

The various sclerotized parts of the palpal organ have their own names. The spoon-shaped base of the tarsus is referred to as the *cymbium*, the basal appendage of the tarsus as the *paracymbium*. The arrangement of the different sclerites (*tegulum, subtegulum, median apophysis, conductor, embolus*) is shown in Fig. 132b. In some entelegyne species the embolus can be drawn out into a long, spiraled thread, sometimes several times the length of the male's body. These lengthy emboli often break off during copulation and

Fig. 133. A mechanical diagram depicting the coupling of the bulb and the epigynum in *Araneus*. (*a*) The spine of the median apophysis (M) hooks onto a process (Sc, the *scapus*) of the epigynum (Ep). (*b*) The median apophysis twists and becomes enveloped by the scapus. The sclerites R, St, and E shift their position so that E (the embolus) becomes situated in front of the epignal opening. The inflation of the hematotocha (H) causes a rotation of the tegulum (T), which in turn presses the conductor (C) to one side of the scapus and the embolus into the epigynum. (After Grasshoff, 1973.)

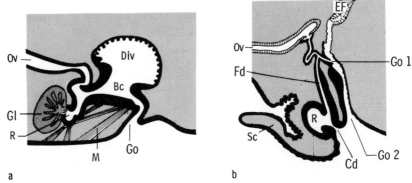

Fig. 134.   (a) Simple copulatory apparatus in a female *Dysdera crocata;* longitudinal section. Bc = bursa copulatrix with a dorsal evagination (Div); Gl = gland attached to the seminal receptacle (R); Go = genital opening; M = muscles; Ov = oviduct. (After Cooke, 1966.) (b) Complex copulatory apparatus in a female *Araneus diadematus.* Cd = copulatory duct; EF = epigastric furrow, Fd = fertilization duct; Go1 = internal genital opening; Go2 = external genital opening; Sc = scapus. (After Gerhardt and Kaestner, 1938.)

remain stuck in the epigynum of the female. This happens regularly in the golden silk spider *Nephila clavipes* and in the black widow *Latrodectus* (Wiehle, 1961) and, of course, prevents either sex from mating again.

Female Copulatory Organs

The terminal part of the oviduct is referred to as the *uterus externus*. In the Orthognatha and the Haplogynae it ends in the primary genital opening (*gonopore*) and is situated between the anterior book lungs. The spermathecae, or seminal receptacles, connect directly with the uterus externus, which is also the site of fertilization. Thus, in the Haplogynae the copulatory duct is at the same time a fertilization duct (Fig. 134). In the Entelegynae the females possess a special copulatory organ located in front of the genital opening, the *epigynum*. This is a slightly raised sclerotized plate with several cuticular infoldings which constitute the connecting ducts (sperm ducts) and the seminal receptacles (Fig. 135).

A closer look at the epigynum shows that it is quite complex. Aside from the primary genital opening (gonopore)—which lies hidden in the epigastric furrow—we find other orifices that play a

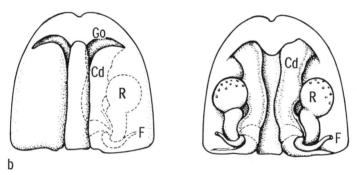

Fig. 135. (a) Diagram of an epigynum, ventral view. Cd = coiled ducts; EF = epigastric furrow; F = fertilization duct; Go = genital opening, R = seminal receptacle; Ut. int., Ut. ext. = uterus internus and externus. (After Wiehle, 1967.) (b) Epigynum of *Cupiennius salei*. External view of the sclerotized parts on the left, internal view on the right. Abbreviations as in (a). (After Melchers, 1963.)

role in reproduction. Those of the coiled connecting ducts (or sperm ducts) lead to the seminal receptacles (Fig. 136), and from there, special fertilization ducts connect with the uterus externus. During mating the male's embolus is inserted through the external genital opening into the sperm duct. Both structures must match;

Fig. 136. Epigynum of the black widow (*Latrodectus mactans*); internal view of sclerotized parts after dissolution of soft tissue with KOH. Cd = coiled ducts; EF = epigastric furrow; R = seminal receptacles. 200×.

that is, a long, convoluted sperm duct usually requires a lengthy, coiled embolus. The embolus may penetrate right up to the seminal receptacles, where the sperm cells are deposited. Only when the female starts laying her eggs do the sperm in the receptacles become active and migrate through the fertilization ducts to the egg cells. The expulsion of the sperm cells is most likely caused by special glands whose secretions displace the sperm mass (Cooke, 1966). Fertilization occurs in the uterus externus.

The sperm ducts and seminal receptacles are lined with cuticle. In some spiders which continue to molt even in their adult stage (Mesothelae and Orthognatha), the lining of the seminal receptacles is also shed. This means that female "tarantulas," for example, which have mated previously, become "virginal" again after each molt; they need to mate again in order to produce fertile eggs. Male tarantulas do not molt anymore once they have reached sexual maturity. Usually they die within a few years after their last molt.

Filling the Palps ("Sperm Induction")

Before a male spider goes in search of a female, he charges his palpal organs with sperm. First he spins a sperm web which is usually
a small triangular structure (2–4 mm²) that is suspended horizontally. The male presses his abdomen against the rim of the triangular web and moves his abdomen up and down until a drop of
sperm emerges from his genital opening. Thereafter the male (of
many species) moves to the underside of the sperm web and
reaches with his palps around the margin of the web. The palps are
dipped alternately into the sperm drop (Fig. 137). Most likely capillary forces play a role in the uptake of sperm, since the tips of the
palps are often "soaked" between the mouth parts before the bulbs
are filled. This process is sometimes called "palpal lubrication."
    Sperm can be taken up either directly—as just described—or
indirectly, in which case the sperm cells must be sucked through
the mesh of the sperm web (Gerhardt, 1929). Different spider families use different methods of transferring the sperm to the palps. In
some species (*Scytodes*, for example) the sperm web is reduced to a
single thread, which is held by the third pair of legs and drawn
across the genital opening. The exuded sperm droplet adheres to
this thread and is then drawn into the bulb (Gerhardt, 1930).
    For a long time arachnologists thought that "sperm induction"
was a precondition for the courting behavior of the male. In a series of elegant experiments this idea has now been refuted. Male
spiders with their palps removed or with a covered genital opening
display themselves quite normally toward a female (Rovner, 1966,

Fig. 137.   A male *Tetragnatha* hanging suspended beneath his sperm web,
charging the palps with a droplet of sperm. (After Gerhardt, 1928.)

1967). It is likely that the initiation of courtship is triggered by the central nervous system, probably via hormones, some days after the spider's last molt. Perhaps this explains why newly molted males, which have not yet filled their palps with sperm, do not court in the first days following molting.

Courtship

Courtship can be defined as those ritualized behavioral patterns which are preparatory to mating. Paramount for male spiders is to avoid being mistaken for prey. Furthermore, females, which appear rather passive at first glance, need to be sufficiently stimulated before copulation can take place. Of course, female spiders are not completely passive during courtship. Female wolf spiders, for instance, indicate their willingness to mate by vigorously waving their legs (Rovner, 1968a). The fact that the females seem passive can also be interpreted as a lack of the aggression that they normally exhibit. In other words, seemingly passive behavior may nevertheless be an active element of courtship.

Since almost every spider species has developed its own courtship, it is hardly possible to make generally valid statements about this behavior, but to give at least an outline, we shall group the courtship behaviors into three categories or levels. Each level is defined by the mechanism that triggers the male's courting (Platnick, 1971): level 1 requires direct contact between male and female; level 2 needs female pheromones to stimulate the male's courtship behavior, and level 3 postulates a visual recognition of the female by the male.

Level 1. Crab spiders (Thomisidae) and sack spiders (Clubionidae) have only a very modest courtship. Typically, the male simply crawls over the female, pulls the female's abdomen close, and inserts one palpal organ into the female's genital opening. Many Haplogynae and "tarantulas" also show little in the way of preliminaries (Baerg, 1928; Gerhardt, 1929). After direct body contact, the male and female exchange a brief interplay with their front legs and palps before they copulate. Some crab spiders (*Xysticus*, *Tibellus*), however, have developed a rather interesting courtship: the male "ties" the female with some strands of silk before mating (Fig. 138). These threads do not hold the female captive, though, for she has no trouble freeing herself after copulation. Similar "ties" are also used by *Nephila* (Araneidae) when the minute male

Fig. 138. Copulation of the crab spider *Xysticus.* The male "ties" the female to the ground and then crawls under her abdomen to start mating. (After Bristowe, 1958.)

places a few threads over the legs of the large female (Robinson and Robinson, 1973); again, these ties can have only a "symbolic" significance.

Level 2. Courtship at this level is somewhat more complex. Often male spiders (for example, *Filistata, Segestria,* and *Amaurobius*) will lure females by pulling or drumming on their webs. Female pheromones are usually involved as well. The males use their contact chemoreceptors, and perhaps also olfaction, to recognize the silk of the females. Draglines of female wolf spiders are known to induce "following behavior" and courtship in the male (Tietjen, 1977, 1979a, b; Tietjen and Rovner, 1980). In *Amaurobius ferox* direct body contact is necessary to elicit courtship behavior, whereas in *A. similis* and *A. fenestralis* the presence of pheromones alone suffices to stimulate the male. The males of the different *Amaurobius* species use various vibratory signals, which they generate with their legs, palps, and abdomens. Each species has its own code (Fig. 139; Krafft, 1978), and a male of *A. similis,* for example, will court only at a web of its own species.

In some clubionids and gnaphosids the males apparently recognize the nests of the immature females and spin their own nests right next to them (Bristowe, 1941). Immediately after the final molt of the female—that is, during a period of time when the female is essentially defenseless—copulation takes place. To refer to such behavior as "rape" may just reflect our anthropomorphic point of view. It may well be that copulation is possible only during that time, when the cuticle of the female is not yet fully sclerotized. Mating right after the female's final molt is also common among many orb weavers, such as *Argiope.*

Palps   Abdomen   Palp

Fig. 139.   Recording of male vibratory signals from two different *Amauro-bius* species courting at the webs of the respective females. *A. similis* drums only with his palps, whereas *A. ferox* strums with one or two palps and additionally vibrates his abdomen. (After Krafft, 1978.)

When a male web spider (for instance of Araneidae, Agelenidae, and Linyphiidae) approaches a female in her web, he is particularly prone to being dealt with as prey. Another risk is that the female might disrupt the courtship because prey has entered the web or because another male has appeared on the scene. The male tackles these problems in different ways, mostly, however, by somewhat restraining the mobility of the female.

Araneid males initially remain at the periphery of the web and make their presence known by plucking the threads with their front legs. Their actual approach of the female can be a tedious and lengthy procedure. Usually the male attaches a special thread, the *mating thread*, to the female's web. By plucking and beating this thread rhythmically with his front legs, and especially with his third pair of legs, the male entices the female to move from her web onto the mating thread (Fig. 140a). If she is receptive she will advance toward the male. After a short exchange of foreleg dabbing, the female assumes a typical copulatory posture (Fig. 144).

Pheromones, which are emitted a few days after the last molt (Blanke, 1972), often play a role in helping the male find the opposite sex. Male araneids apparently can recognize the female pheromone chemotactually on the web and also seem to be guided by olfaction, at least for short distances of about 60–80 cm (Blanke, 1975b).

Although the courtship behavior of araneids may appear rather uniform at first glance, we find some remarkable variations from the usual pattern. The males of *Nephila* and of some *Argiope* species do not use any mating threads but climb directly into the hub of

Fig. 140. (*a*) Courtship of *Araneus pallidus*. The male keeps plucking the mating thread while approaching the female, which has already assumed the mating position. (Photo: Grasshoff.) (*b*) Courtship of the European house spider *Tegenaria atrica*. The female falls into a passive stance and is then dragged onto the sheet web by the male. One palp (P) is in the process of being inserted.

the female's web, where they start a tactile courtship. In other *Argiope* species the male also crosses the female's web but then cuts a hole near the hub, attaches a short mating thread, and commences a vibratory courtship. From an evolutionary point of view a tactile courtship at the web's hub may represent the original type of courtship in araneids (Robinson and Robinson, 1978, 1980).

Normally a rather lengthy courtship is necessary before the female spider allows the male free access to her web. In the case of *Linyphia triangularis*, however, the male is always dominant and conquers the female's web without encountering any resistance (Rovner, 1968b). The female never attacks him; on the contrary, if prey happens to fall on the dome of her web (Fig. 93), the male will chase the female away and feed alone. During courtship the male destroys most of the female's web; within a few minutes the dome may be reduced to a small silken band. The female remains entirely passive during this action and her passivity probably signals to the male that she is willing to accept him. At any rate, copulation occurs immediately after her web has been destroyed. The reduced web provides the male with the advantage of eliminating other male competitors. Furthermore, the female cannot interrupt courtship or copulation because of prey entering the web—as she would normally do if the web were intact.

Courtship is somewhat more complex for many wolf spiders (Lycosidae) and nursery-web spiders (Pisauridae). The behavior of the male is influenced not only by tactile and chemotactile stimuli but also by vibratory and visual signals.

When a male *Lycosa rabida* notices a female passing by, he assumes a typical courtship posture (Fig. 141a): the front legs are raised, the palps touch the substrate, the body is lowered (Rovner, 1968a). The subsequent behavior of the male consists of characteristic courtship movements and intermittent periods of resting. First the palps are waved alternately in a circular fashion, called *palpal rotation* (Fig. 141b); then they contact the substrate again. One front leg is stretched forward and is raised and lowered several times. At the same time the abdomen vibrates up and down. The palpal rotation is soon changed into palpal "drumming," which is audible to the human ear. Recently it has been shown that the palpal drumming includes a stridulation that is produced in the tibio-tarsal joint of the palp (Rovner, 1975): a cuticular spur scratches over parallel ridges (the "file") of the tibia, thus producing sounds. After the stretched front leg is snapped back into a flexed position, the male remains inactive for about 15 seconds, or he may approach the female slightly.

Fig. 141. (*a*) Courting attitudes of the male wolf spider *Lycosa rabida*. In the initial phase (1) the first pair of legs is raised and flexed; the tibiae are extended horizontally; the abdomen vibrates vertically. (2) Stretching of leg 1. (3) Fully extended leg 1. (After Rovner, 1968a.) (*b*) Palp rotation as an element in courting by male wolf spiders. (After Bristowe and Locket, 1926.)

It is during those pauses that the female becomes active. About five seconds after the male's palpal drumming, the female responds by briefly waving her front legs. Usually she also takes a few steps toward the male. The male now repeats and intensifies his courtship movements—leg stretching, palpal rotation, abdominal quivering. When he is within reach of the female, he cautiously extends one front leg, but he does not actually touch the female. The first contact is always initiated by the female and apparently signals her readiness for copulation.

From this description it is evident that *Lycosa rabida* exhibits a reciprocal courtship; that is, both partners take turns exchanging signals. The visual signals are largely confined to perception of motion. This can be concluded from the observation that a male often initially directs his courtship toward other males (although he receives only a threat in response). Males without their palps or front legs can still court successfully and be accepted by the female. This means that the acoustical and vibratory signals are not necessary components of courtship. On the other hand, leg waving by the females has been elicited by playing back the acoustical signals of the male over a tiny loud-speaker (Rovner, 1967). It is plausible that acoustical and vibratory signals play a major role in courtship only in the dark. In fact, *Lycosa rabida* is active at night as well as during the day.

Chemotactile signals seem to be the most important factors in the male wolf spider's courtship behavior. When male spiders are put into empty boxes that have previously housed conspecific females, they start exhibiting their typical courtship behavior (Bristowe and Locket, 1926; Kaston, 1936; Rovner, 1968a; Dijkstra, 1976). They show no reactions, however, if males or immature females have been kept in these boxes. If a male wolf spider comes across the dragline of a mature female, he will stop immediately and will commence probing the substrate with the tips of his legs and palps. His front legs start quivering and the entire courtship sequence may follow, just as if the female were present.

Other species of wolf spiders show courtship movements that are similar to yet distinctly different from those of *Lycosa rabida*. Legs and palps can be waved together or alternately; the palps may be held in a certain position, or vibrate excitedly, or describe aerial loops. Each species has its own, typical repertoire.

The nursery-web spider *Pisaura* is famous for its extraordinary courtship. The male first catches a fly, wraps it in silk, and carries it in his chelicerae to the female. If the female is receptive, she seizes the "bridal gift" and starts feeding on it. At the same time the male begins copulating with her. Despite such tricks males are not always safe from female attacks; *Dolomedes* (Pisauridae) males are often eaten, probably because they approach the female from the front and without the necessary caution (Gerhardt, 1926). Incidentally, a synchronization of the male's courtship with feeding in the female is known to occur in several other spider families, for example in the araneid *Meta segmentata* (now *Metellina segmentata*) (Blanke, 1974) and the uloborid *Uloborus geniculatus* (now *Zosis geniculatus*) (Gerhardt, 1927).

Level 3. In salticids and oxyopids visual signals are the primary releaser for courtship, although tactile and chemical stimuli are also involved (Jackson, 1977, 1978). It is presumed that courtship of these spiders has developed from courtship levels 1 and 2.

All male jumping spiders display their specific courtship movements in front of the females. These movements range from the simple lifting of a leg to the complex, sequential movements of several extremities. Usually, those extremities which are mostly used in the courtship display are also conspicuously colored (Bristowe, 1929; Crane, 1949; Kaston, 1936). When a male notices a female, he approaches her in a zigzagging dance. At the same time, he displays species-specific courtship movements such as raising his front legs, vibrating his palps, and twitching his abdomen (Fig. 142). The female remains rather passive, yet she watches the male. In some species the female responds by vibrating her palps, and sometimes she may even weakly imitate the male's courtship routine. During this initial phase of courtship the primary objective of the male is to identify himself as a mate of the "right" species. If the female is receptive toward the performing male, she assumes a quiet, crouching position. The next phase, which leads directly to copulation, is very similar for all jumping spiders. The male extends his forelegs so that they are parallel and touches the female. After further fondling he simply climbs on the female's back and begins copulation.

The strong dependence of jumping spiders' courtship on visual clues becomes evident when one covers a male's main eyes with black paint. He still shows signs of excitement if a female is present, but he no longer performs the typical courtship dances (Homann, 1928; Crane, 1949). Conversely, when the main eyes of the female are painted black, she will not accept a courting male. This demonstrates that the courtship in salticids is indeed a reciprocal visual affair. If a male addresses the female of another species—and this occasionally happens in nature—the female withdraws at some point in the first phase of courtship. Apparently, without the species-specific movements of the male, there will not even be a chance for him to copulate.

Aside from the important visual signals (movement, and size and shape of the mate), chemical stimuli also play a role in salticid courtship. Chemical cues alone do not suffice to trigger the courtship dances—as they do in lycosids—yet contact with the female's silk still seems to have a stimulating effect on the male. Furthermore, it seems that very young females (1–2 weeks after their final

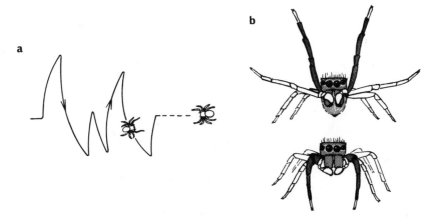

Fig. 142. (*a*) Zigzagging dance of a male jumping spider in front of the female. (After Homann, 1928.) (*b*) Two courting stances taken by the male jumping spider *Euophrys frontalis* (After Bristowe, 1958.)

molt) are preferred by the courting males. Older females (6 weeks postmolt) are less attractive to the males, probably because their pheromone production has already decreased.

Within the large family of jumping spiders we can find species with a rather "primitive" courtship, which relies on the spider's chemotactile or olfactory sensitivity, as well as gradually more "advanced" species that use almost exclusively visual cues when they court (Crane, 1949). Recent investigations have shown that even within the same species different courting strategies are employed (Jackson, 1977a). For instance, if a male *Phidippus johnsoni* encounters a female outside the nest, he will perform the usual visual type of courtship. If the same male comes across a nest in which a female is hidden, however, he shows a completely different courting behavior: the tarsi of his front legs are rubbed over the surface of the female's nest, and his whole body oscillates up and down. After a while, the male enters the nest and mating ensues. It seems interesting that only the first type of courtship is light-dependent, but not the second. When both sexes are put together under dark red light, no courtship behavior is elicited from either spider, even if they bump into each other. As soon as a white light is turned on, though, the male begins the visual type of courtship within a few minutes.

Lynx spiders (Oxyopidae) also can recognize each other from a distance of several centimeters. The males often possess darkly colored palps which they wave in front of the females (Gerhardt, 1933; Bristowe, 1962). Each species has its own sequence of palp, leg, and abdominal movements; they also show an exchange of leg stroking before mating.

Copulation

The mechanics of the copulatory organs were already briefly explained earlier. During copulation, the palpal organ of the male is inserted into the female's genital opening, and the sperm is deposited in her seminal receptacles. Haplogyne spiders insert the entire bulb of the palp into the female's genital opening; in entelegyne spiders only the bulb's tip, the embolus, enters the copulatory duct. Characteristic of the Entelegynae are their extensible hematodochae; such spiders can inflate the normally collapsed palpal organ and thereby push the embolus into the sperm duct of the female's epigynum. Only after the palpal organ has been coupled with the epigynum do the hematodochae swell to their maximum

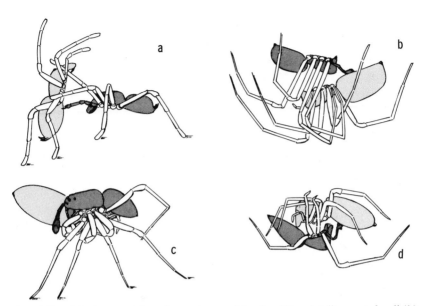

Fig. 143. Mating positions in various spider families: (*a*) "tarantulas," (*b*) linyphiids, (*c*) lycosids, (*d*) clubionid *Cheiracanthium*. (After von Helversen, 1976.)

size. This hydraulic action also leads to the erection of the leg spines. In some species the hematodochae swell only once and very briefly before the palps are withdrawn from the epigynum. This is the case in most species of araneids. In other species (as in most linyphiids) the hematodochae pulsate rhythmically for several hours. There are also differences as to whether the palps are inserted simultaneously or consecutively: most Haplogynae employ both palps at the same time, whereas the Entelegynae insert first one and then the other palp.

The mating behavior of spiders and its impressive diversity have been studied extensively from a comparative point of view (Bristowe, 1941; Gerhardt, 1911–1933). The many variations of the mating positions of spiders can be reduced to three or four basic types (Fig. 143).

Type 1 is characteristic of the "primitive" wandering spiders (Mesothelae, Orthognatha, and Haplogynae). The male approaches the female from the front (Fig. 143a), the female raises her prosoma, and the male inserts one or both palps into the female's genital opening. Afterwards both spiders separate cautiously. *Type 2* is widespread among web spiders. The spiders mate in essentially the same position as in type 1, but with both partners hanging upside down from the web (Fig. 143b). The male's palps are inserted into the female consecutively. *Type 3* is found among the "modern" wandering spiders (the Clubionidae, Lycosidae, Salticidae, and Thomisidae, for example). The male climbs over the prosoma of the female and then turns toward either the left or right side of her opisthosoma. The female twists her abdomen in such a way that one of the male's palps can be inserted (Fig. 143c). Each time the other palp is used, the male changes to the other side of the female's abdomen.

Most likely type 1 is the original mating position for spiders, and types 2 and 3 are derived from it (von Helversen, 1976). *Cheiracanthium* (Clubionidae) uses a modified, fourth kind of position: the spiders face each other with their ventral sides in contact (Fig. 143d). It should also be mentioned that a certain kind of mating position is not necessarily stereotyped within one family. Most agelenids, for instance, copulate according to type 3, yet some *Tegenaria* species follow type 1.

Fig. 144.   Copulation in two *Araneus* species. (*a*) *A. diadematus:* the male embraces the female's abdomen and inserts one bulb. (After Gerhardt, 1911.) (*b*) *A. pallidus:* the small male turns a somersault of 180° and falls directly in front of the female's chelicerae. He is bitten immediately and thus fixed in the mating position. (After Grasshoff, 1964.)

The supposed aggressiveness of the female spider toward the male is largely a myth. When a female is ready for mating, there is little danger for the male. If a male courts at the wrong time, however, he may well be attacked and eaten by the female. In general, most species separate quite peacefully after copulation. Only in some exceptional cases does the male fall victim to the female, for example in certain *Argiope* and *Cyrtophora* species. The infamous black widow (*Latrodectus mactans*) does have a bad reputation, but—quite contrary to popular belief—the male usually withdraws unharmed.

The small male of *Araneus pallidus* is not so lucky, however. He initiates copulation by jumping toward the ventral side of the female's abdomen and fixing one palp to the epigynum. During this process he tumbles backward so that his abdomen rests right underneath the female's prosoma. The female immediately seizes his abdomen with her chelicerae and within a few minutes starts feeding on him (Fig. 144). Apparently, this is more of a technical necessity than pure cannibalism. If the female is prevented from biting the male, he constantly slips off her abdomen and is unable to insert his palp (Grasshoff, 1964). A very similar mating behavior has also been observed in *Cyrtophora cicatrosa* (Blanke, 1975).

Agonistic Behavior

So far we have dealt only with those reproductive behaviors that take place between sexes. Of course different types of behavior are elicited when two males of the same species meet during courtship. All those activities which are related to a competitor (for example, threatening, fighting, or fleeing) are referred to as *agonistic behavior,* and among spiders such behavior occurs in both sexes but is more elaborate in males.

When two male wolf spiders (*Pardosa*) encounter each other in the presence of a female, they assume specific threat postures and sometimes start to fight (Fig. 145). Usually the attacking male will be the winner. Once he has established his dominance, he is likely to maintain it during further bouts (Dijkstra, 1970). The loser tends to slink away, while the winner flaunts about jerkily. He will then soon encounter the female and circle her, walking sideways. Rising as if on tiptoe, he waves one or both palps in the air and then starts his usual courtship. The agonistic behavior has a selective advantage for the species: the winner has a better

Fig. 145.   Agonistic behavior of male wolf spiders (*Schizocosa crassipes*). (*a*) The primary reaction to another male is the cautious extension of one front leg. (*b*) The dominant male (left) threatens the submissive male which remains in a resting position. (*a, b* After Aspey, 1975.)

chance of mating with the female (Aspey, 1975) and thus of passing on his genome.

When two male linyphiids (*Linyphia triangularis*) meet, they also exhibit specific threat and fighting behaviors, which they never show toward females (Rovner, 1968b). Both males spread their large chelicerae, extend their front legs perpendicularly from their bodies, and vibrate their abdomens rapidly. If neither of the two opponents is impressed, they will move closer and finally begin to fight. First they push each other with the tips of their legs, and later they interlock their chelicerae. The loser drops quickly from the sheet web on which they had been vying for the female; usually the larger male turns out to be the winner. The males may also start to fight without a female present. It seems that the first male to reach the female's web will defend "his" territory, the dome of her web. Females will defend their web only against other females, but not against courting males.

In most jumping spiders, threatening behavior between males is strongly ritualized (Fig. 146b); actual fights are rare (Crane, 1949). By no means does the bigger male always win the ritualized contest, but simply the more aggressive male. The threat signals are visual, as are normal courtship signals, and they consist mainly of raising and lowering the legs. In the more "primitive" jumping spiders the threat movements are identical with regular courtship movements, probably because the male cannot distinguish between a female and a male spider at greater distances (Bristowe, 1929). In the most "advanced" jumping spiders, in contrast, the threat movements clearly differ from the courtship movements (for instance, different legs are used). A key stimulus for a male's threatening behavior lies in certain contrasting patterns on the palps or on the carapace of a potential competitor. Such markings occur only in the males (Crane, 1949). When a female is not ready

Fig. 146. Agonistic behavior. (*a*) Two male *Linyphia triangularis* threaten each other with wide open chelicerae. (Photo: Rovner.) (*b*) Two male jumping spiders (*Euophrys parvula*) face each other with their third legs raised and their abdomens swiveling sideways. (Photo: Forster.)

for mating, she may also threaten a male: she moves her legs up and down as she walks sideways in a zigzagging fashion (Forster and Forster, 1973).

Brood Care

Within a few weeks after copulation the female is ready to begin laying her eggs and produce an egg case (or cocoon). Fertilization takes place just before the eggs are deposited; the sperm cells that had been stored in the seminal receptacles are released as the eggs pass through the uterus externus. The fertilized eggs are then squeezed one by one through the genital opening. Generally, they are surrounded by a clear, viscous liquid, and after a short time this fluid dries up, cementing the eggs together. Normally egg laying takes only a few minutes, even when there are very many eggs. *Araneus* lays almost 1,000 eggs within ten minutes (Pötzsch, 1963), *Cupiennius* as many as 1,500–2,500 in about eight minutes (Melchers, 1963)—quite an impressive performance, especially if one considers that each egg measures at least 1 mm in diameter (Fig. 147a, b). Evidently, egg laying is a rather energy-consuming process. This is reflected in the increase of the heart rate, which in *Cupiennius* is elevated from a normal 60–70 beats/min to about 160 beats/min during egg laying. After all the eggs have been deposited into the egg sac, the female looks rather skinny because of her shriveled abdomen.

Egg-Case Construction

The eggs are never directly exposed to the environment but are always protected by silk. In the simplest case only a few silk threads are wrapped around the eggs (Fig. 147a). A typical cocoon, however, consists of a basal plate and a cover plate which enclose and protect the egg mass. One of the main advantages of an egg case is the favorable humidity level that is maintained inside; hence the eggs can develop without depending as much on climatic conditions. In order to understand the various types of cocoons, we shall take a close look at their construction; the cocoon of the orb weaver *Araneus quadratus* will serve as an example (Crome, 1956).

Before the spider starts making her egg sac, she withdraws for several days into her retreat. She then spins a thin layer of single, tightly woven threads. Using only abdominal movements she molds this first layer into a disk, the basal plate (Fig. 148a). This sheet is covered on both sides with flocculent, curly silk threads. The spider then crawls underneath the basal plate and keeps turning around in circles, spinning continuously. This motion leads to the construction of a cylindrical wall (Fig. 148b). The palps are constantly held in contact with one side of this wall while the side opposite is dabbed with the spinnerets (Fig. 150a). Thus the cylin-

Fig. 147. Egg sacs. (*a*) *Pholcus* wraps her batch of eggs with only a few strands of silk and carries it in her chelicerae. (*b*) An opened cocoon of *Araneus diadematus*. The basal plate is seen on the right; the tightly packed eggs rest on the cushion of downy silk threads. (*c*) The cocoon of the pirate spider *Ero furcata*. The closely woven cocoon wall is covered with stronger, sinuous silk threads (see Fig. 85). The young spiderlings have emerged through a hole at the top of the egg sac (arrow). 17×. (*d*) Opened cocoon of the theridiid *Argyrodes*, parasitized by wasps (W). 28×. (Photo *d*: Foelix and Vollrath.)

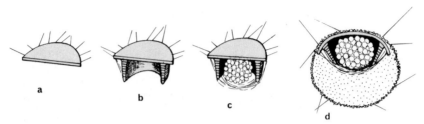

Fig. 148.   Stages in the construction of an egg sac in *Araneus quadratus*. (*a*) Basal plate with attachment threads. (*b*) Addition of the cylindrical wall. (*c*) Egg chamber with a cover plate below. (*d*) Section through the finished cocoon. The lower part is filled with a loose mesh of silk threads. Attachment threads suspend the cocoon. (After Crome, 1956a.)

drical wall gradually grows until it has reached a height of 5 mm after about two hours. The size of cocoon is directly correlated with the size of the spider but not necessarily with the number of eggs that will be deposited.

The spider pauses for a few minutes before she starts laying the eggs. When she has finished, she abruptly pulls away from the egg mass and begins to cover it with silk threads (Fig. 148c). This gradually becomes the cover plate, to which the spider keeps adding loops of thread. A loose mesh thus ultimately envelops the entire surface of the egg sac. Finally, the spider spins a few suspension threads to attach the egg sac to neighboring leaves or twigs (Fig. 148d). During the next days the spider will stay near the cocoon. If some suspension threads are severed, she will replace them and, if necessary, also tackle larger repairs. Most female orb weavers die only a few days after having built their egg sac. Outwardly the cocoon remains unchanged from October until spring, while inside the spiderlings develop. It is not until May that the offspring will emerge.

In summary then, the construction of an egg sac passes through the following stages:

1. Weaving a horizontal silk disk, the center of which is condensed into the basal plate.
2. Adding the cylindrical wall
3. Egg laying
4. Closing the egg chamber with a cover plate
5. Surrounding the egg case with a loose mesh of threads

6. In some species, spinning an additional tougher cocoon wall to which suspension threads are attached.

Wolf spiders follow basically the same sequence of steps as araneids in constructing their cocoons. However, instead of crawling beneath the basal plate the spider stays on top of it to form the cylindrical wall; and, she sits *above* the egg chamber when laying her eggs. Originally the egg case is white, but it is then tightly wrapped with bluish green threads rather than encased in a downy meshwork. The finished cocoon is lentil-shaped and has a tough, paperlike surface. It is attached to the spinnerets and carried around until the young hatch (Fig. 151a). If one tries to take the egg case away from the spider, she will vehemently defend it and will often even pierce her chelicerae into the cocoon wall in an effort to hold onto the cocoon. If one does remove the cocoon, the spider will search for it for hours. Often she will accept artificial substitutes like small paper balls or snail shells, which she then attaches to her spinnerets.

The construction of a spider's egg sac is often cited as an example of rigid or "programmed" behavior. For instance, if a *Cupiennius* is stopped while building her cocoon and placed on another cocoon that is in a more advanced stage of construction, the spider will resume her building at the point at which she was interrupted (Melchers, 1963). This may lead to the construction of another cylindrical wall, even though that structure was already present. On the other hand, one can also observe some degree of plasticity in this behavior. For instance, when *Cupiennius* is disturbed while building her own cocoon, she never returns to her half-finished product but starts making a new one. This means, however, that she has now to repeat the initial phases of egg-sac construction. Since this is done in a somewhat abbreviated manner, the result is a functional yet rather odd-looking egg sac. If that second cocoon turns out to be too tattered, the spider will simply eat it. From this behavior we can conclude that the spider is quite capable of perceiving the condition of the cocoon's surface.

Although egg-sac construction appears to be rather "programmed" in *Cupiennius*, this is by no means true for all spiders. If in *Cyrtophora*, for instance, the egg sac is tilted by 90° while it is under construction, the spider must deposit her eggs from the side rather than from below. *Cyrtophora* adapts easily to that condition and finishes a normal cocoon. Even if the cocoon is turned upside down, the spider tries to compensate for its new position; thus there is no question that her behavior can be flexible enough to meet new situations, (Kullmann, 1961).

Types of Cocoons

Many spiders lay their eggs inside their retreats, which can then be called egg nests. The jumping spider *Heliophanus* (Fig. 7b) spins only a few threads around her 20–40 eggs; she then guards them within her closed silken retreat (Fig. 149a). Another jumping spider, *Marpissa*, builds three to five flat cocoons which she stacks inside her nest (Fig. 149b). Each cocoon contains 20–40 eggs and is encased by a basal plate and a cover plate. Thus different types of cocoons may occur within the same family of spiders (here, in the Salticidae). The same is true of the Gnaphosidae, where some genera have only simple cocoons inside their nests, and others build more complicated egg sacs with impregnated and camouflaged cocoon walls. When the walls are camouflaged, the female's guarding of the eggs becomes superfluous (Holm, 1940).

One spider that makes a camouflaged cocoon is *Agroeca brunnea* (Clubionidae). Its egg sac is one of the most unusual types of cocoons and looks like a little Japanese lantern. The bell-shaped egg sac is attached by a short stalk to grass blades or to twigs. In its unmasked condition it is pure white, but usually the spider glues soil particles or plant material to the outside so that it blends well with its surroundings. The interior of the cocoon is divided by a horizontal "wall" (which is really the cover plate) into an egg chamber and a molting chamber (Fig. 150). About one week after hatching, the 40–60 young spiderlings crawl from the egg chamber into the molting chamber, where they stay for two or three weeks (Lüters, 1966). Some days after molting they cut a circular hole into the cocoon wall, and the spiderlings emerge one after the other.

a   **b**

Fig. 149. (*a*) Section through an egg nest of the jumping spider *Heliophanus cupreus*. The female guards the 20–30 eggs inside the closed silk nest. (*b*) Egg nest of the jumping spider *Marpissa rumpfi*. Cocoons are arranged in several layers and enclosed in an open silk chamber (n). (After Holm, 1940.)

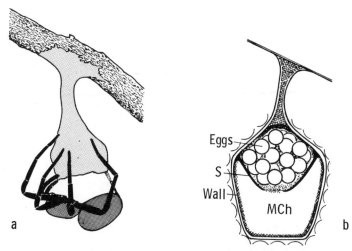

Eggs
S
Wall
MCh
a   b

Fig. 150.   Cocoon of the clubionid *Agroeca brunnea.* *(a)* Construction of the cylindrical wall. The diameter of the cocoon corresponds to the distance between palps and spinnerets. (Drawn from a photo by Lüters, 1966.) *(b)* Section through the finished cocoon. A septum (S) divides the cocoon into an egg chamber and a molting chamber (MCh). The cocoon wall is studded with camouflaging soil particles. (After Holm, 1940.)

It is true that the various spider families do not always have one type of cocoon, yet we can differentiate two basic types of cocoons among the entelegyne spiders. The Trionycha usually have an egg sac that is surrounded by a loose mesh of threads, whereas the Dionycha possess a tough, thin-walled egg sac (Holm, 1940). If the egg cases are rather simple, as in *Heliophanus* or in *Pholcus* (Fig. 147a), it must always be considered that this does not necessarily represent a primitive stage, but that it could as well be the result of a secondary reduction.

Brood Care

Many spiders do more for their offspring than just construct a cocoon. As we have seen, some species camouflage, guard, and defend their egg sac; others even care actively for the newly hatched spiderlings, either by protecting them in special ways or by directly feeding them.

A wolf spider mother will assist her offspring during "hatching" by opening the rim of the cocoon with her chelicerae (Fig. 151).

Fig. 151. Brood care in the wolf spider *Pardosa amentata*. (*a*) Carrying the cocoon (C) attached to the abdomen. (*b*) Opening the seam (S) of the cocoon wall with the chelicerae. (*c*) Spiderling, just hatched from the cocoon. (*d*) Two spiderlings climbing the legs of their mother. (*e*) About 80 young spiders sit closely packed on their mother's abdomen.

Without this help the young spiderlings are unable to leave the egg sac. Normally the newly emerged spiderlings climb immediately onto their mother's back, where they hold fast to her abdominal hairs (Rovner, Higashi, and Foelix, 1973). In all, there may be over 100 tiny spiderlings resting on top of each other in several layers (Higashi and Rovner, 1975). During the seven or eight days spent on the mother's back, the spiderlings live exclusively from their yolk supply. The mother likewise does not feed during the entire period of brood care. Whether the spiderlings gain any particular advantage by being carried around is still unclear. Certainly they enjoy some kind of protection from predators and to some extent from adverse microclimatic factors, yet experiments have shown that the young can survive easily when raised isolated from their mother and from each other (Engelhardt, 1964).

Several other experiments have demonstrated that young wolf spiders do not climb exclusively onto their own mother but will also try to climb onto male spiders—even those of a different species (Meyer, 1928; Engelhardt, 1964; Higashi and Rovner, 1975). In such experimental situations the males often simply eat the spiderlings. It is also possible to trick a female spider into accepting a foreign cocoon or young other than her own. Even spiderlings of another species are readily accepted, and they will soon settle down on the back of their "stepmother." From these experiments it is evident that a mutual recognition between the mother spider and her offspring does not exist (Engelhardt, 1964).

Nursery-web spiders (Pisauridae), which are related to wolf spiders, also care for their young. The female carries the globular cocoon in her chelicerae. Before the young hatch, the mother constructs a tentlike web and suspends the egg sac inside it. The emerging spiderlings stay for several days in this "nursery web." After molting they gradually disperse and start their regular free-hunting life.

In species where the mother spider provides food for the young spiderlings, one can differentiate between two levels of organization: (1) leaving caught prey passively at the disposal of the spiderlings, or (2) actively feeding them liquefied food from her midgut. Active brood care that involves feeding of the young is found in only a very few spider species (in about 20 of the 30,000 known species), namely, in certain theridiids, eresids, and in some agelenids, such as *Coelotes terrestris* (Tretzel, 1961b).

The young *Coelotes* remain for about one month in the funnel web of their mother. When the mother catches prey, the young "beg" for food by touching their mother's chelicerae with their palps or legs. Usually the mother simply drops the softened prey, and one of the young spiders quickly grabs it and carries it into a hideout to feed on it. As long as the prey is still struggling, the mother refuses to turn it over to a spiderling; her "message" comes across as she vigorously beats her hind legs against the sheet web. The mother can distinguish her young (and their vibrations) from prey or enemies quite well. Prey animals produce vibrations of higher amplitude and higher frequency than those of young spiders. Nevertheless, the mother often "checks" her young with one palp; only thereafter can they continue to run around in the web. It is clear that this discriminatory ability together with a tolerance toward the same species are necessary preconditions for any communal living (see chapter 9). The young spiderlings enjoy the advantage of being provided with much larger prey items than they could overpower themselves.

Among the cobweb spiders, *Theridion pictum* and *Achaearanea saxatile* also leave caught prey for their young (Hirschberg, 1969). When *Achaearanea* has caught prey, she performs stroking movements in the web to attract the young spiders. Conversely, plucking movements serve as warning signals that send the young ones scurrying to the retreat (Nørgaard, 1956). The cobweb serves here as a means of communication between mother and young spiders, just as does the sheet web in *Coelotes*.

The highest organization of brood care in spiders has evolved in a few species among the theridiids and the eresids. The mother feeds her young mouth-to-mouth with a special substance that she regurgitates. This kind of food transfer is well known from bees, ants, and termites but is extremely rare in spiders. *Theridion notatum, Theridion impressum*, and a few *Stegodyphus* species rank among these exceptions. The regurgitate consists of a mixture of predigested food and the mother's own intestinal cells, which are in a process of lysis (Nawabi, 1974). From time to time the mother exudes a drop of regurgitate at her mouth opening, and soon several spiderlings gather there to drink the liquid. Some spiderlings stroke their mother's legs, apparently to stimulate her to regurgitate. During the first days after hatching, the young are fed chiefly with regurgitate, and prey is offered only as an extra. In *Theridion impressum* the mother stops regurgitation feeding after the young have undergone their first molt. Prey animals, however, are still consumed communally (Kullmann, 1974). When the young spiders have grown further, they will be chased away by the mother (Hirschberg, 1969).

Regurgitation feeding has also been demonstrated by using radioactive markers such as labeled phosphorus (^{32}P). This method permits quantitative measurements of the regurgitated substances (Hirschberg, 1969; Kullmann and Kloft, 1969). In such studies the radioactive isotope (for example, $Na_2H^{32}PO_4$) is first fed to a fly. When the radioactively labeled fly is then given to the spider mother, she becomes radioactive herself (Fig. 152). After the young spiderlings have hatched from the cocoon, they are checked every day to see whether they have become radioactive or not. By measuring the amount of radioactivity in the spiderling one can also determine *how much* food it has received from the mother. It was

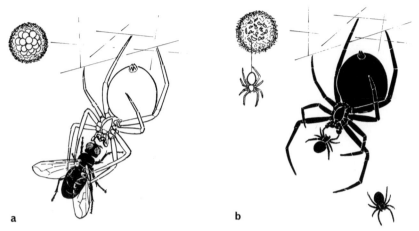

a   b

Fig. 152.   Use of radioactive isotopes to demonstrate regurgitative feeding. (*a*) After having built the cocoon, the spider is fed with a radioactively labeled fly and becomes radioactive herself. (*b*) The newly emerged spiderlings are fed mouth-to-mouth and in turn become radioactive. Radioactivity is represented in black. (After Kullmann and Kloft, 1969.)

surprising to learn that regurgitation feeding already becomes established on the first day after hatching. During the next days the young spiderlings feed additionally on prey animals. Thereby they quickly gain weight and are ready to molt after only one week.

The regurgitate is not absolutely necessary for the survival of the spiderlings. If they are kept in isolation and offered only the softened prey caught by their mother, they also grow up, although more slowly. Apparently the combination of regurgitate and the consumption of prey provides for the optimal development of the young spider (Hirschberg, 1969).

It is quite remarkable that regurgitation feeding is found in two completely unrelated families, namely, the ecribellate Theridiidae and the cribellate Eresidae. Probably, this highly developed brood care has evolved independently in both spider families (Kullmann, Sittertz, and Zimmermann, 1971; Kullmann, Nawabi, and Zimmermann, 1971/72). It also seems plausible that regurgitation feeding represents a first step in the development of communal (or social) life. This mode of feeding requires not only close contact but also tolerance and cooperation between conspecifics.

8

Development

THE ontogeny of a spider can be divided into three periods: an embryonic period, a larval period, and a nympho-imaginal period (Vachon, 1957). The embryonic period encompasses development from the time an egg is fertilized until the typical shape of the spider's body is established. During the subsequent larval period the prelarva and larva still lack certain morphological characteristics and hence are referred to as "incomplete stages" (Holm, 1940). The larval stages are unable to feed on their own and live solely on their yolk supply. Not until the nympho-imaginal period, when all the organ systems are finally present, do the young spiders become self-sufficient. The imago (adult) differs from the nymph (or juvenile) essentially by being sexually mature.

All stages from the prelarva to the adult are separated by a molting process. Growth occurs only *during* a molt, that is, between two consecutive stages, and thus takes place in graduated steps.

The Embryonic Period

Spider eggs are always enveloped by two layers, an inner *vitelline membrane* and an outer *chorion* (Fig. 130d). The chorion appears opaque and granular because the liquid that surrounded the egg during egg laying has dried onto it (Fig. 157a). Immersing an egg in paraffin oil renders the chorion transparent so that the internal egg structure and all developmental processes can be observed directly. Immediately beneath the vitelline membrane lies a thin plasmatic *cortical layer*. This peripheral zone gives off delicate extensions that radiate toward the center of the egg cell, where the nucleus is located. The main part of the egg, however, consists of yolk granules and "vitelline fluid." The yolk granules tend to be larger in the lower part of the egg; this does not reflect true polarity, though, because turning the egg upside down will reverse the yolk distribution (Holm, 1940).

Early Development

Actual fertilization, that is, the fusion of the egg and sperm nuclei to form a zygote, occurs about 3–4 hours after the eggs have been laid (Montgomery, 1908). The zygote begins a series of mitotic divisions called cleavage. A few hours after fertilization one can recognize two "cleavage nuclei" that shift their position from the center of the egg to the periphery; actual cell membranes have not yet formed. At the same time the cortical plasma divides into many polygonal patches (Fig. 153a–c). When the two cleavage nuclei have divided four more times (which for *Agelena* happens about 24 hours after the egg was laid) all 32 nuclei have moved to the periphery (Holm, 1952). Following three further nuclear divisions, each "cleavage cell" (nucleus) coalesces with from four to eight patches of the cortical cytoplasm, thereby establishing large, flattened cells. Thirty-five hours after egg laying, a thin *blastoderm* has formed by a process that can be called "superficial" cleavage, because the entire yolk mass, which does not divide, becomes concentrated in the center of the embryo. In this stage of development the embryo is called a *blastula*. The yolk granules now sink to the bottom part of the blastula, leaving behind a space, the blastocoel, that is filled with perivitelline fluid (Fig. 153d). The next stage is marked by the so-called contraction of the blastula (at 50–55 hours), which involves a transfer of the perivitelline fluid to the outside, so that the overlying blastoderm settles on top of the yolk mass.

The Metameric Phase

The polarity of the embryo first becomes apparent immediately after the contraction of the blastula, when one side of the flattened blastoderm is transformed into a columnar epithelium. Gradually

Fig. 153. Early embryonic stages of *Agelena labyrinthica.* (*a*) The cleavage cells spread within the cortical plasm (30 hours). (*b*) Blastula stage prior to contraction (48 hours). (*c*) Blastula stage after contraction. (*d*) Blastula of the tarantula *Ischnothele* in optical section. Pr = perivitelline space. (*e*) Formation of the primitive plate (pp) and of the cumulus (cp) (100 hours). (*f*) Beginning of segmentation of the prosoma (150 hours). (*g*) Primordia of the four pairs of legs (160 hours). (Photos: Holm.)

a diffuse germinal disk, which consists of rather small cells, develops (at about 75 hours after egg laying). Ten hours later a slight indentation called the *primitive groove*, or blastopore, appears in the center of the germinal disk. It is at this spot that the migration of the mesendoderm cells into the interior takes place (*gastrulation*). The area which is then underlaid by the mesendoderm cells is referred to as the *primitive plate* (Fig. 153e).

The primitive plate is initially flat, but soon one portion of it bulges outward to form the primitive knot, or *cumulus* (at about 100 hours). The cumulus gradually shifts toward the margin of the germinal disk. By this time the primitive plate is several cell layers thick, because most of the mesendoderm has already migrated into the interior. Between the cumulus and the primitive plate lies an area of flat cells called the *dorsal field*. This sector of the gastrula enlarges laterally while the cumulus becomes reduced in size and finally disappears completely (130 hours after fertilization).

When the sector of the dorsal field has spread half way around the developing embryo (180°), the first signs of segmentation appear in the form of two or three concentric furrows around the blastopore (Fig. 153f). At about 150 hours the germinal disk stretches into a broad *germinal band*, which consists of a cephalic lobe, a caudal lobe, and five intervening metameres (somites) that represent the respective segments of the pedipalps and the legs. The cephalic lobe soon gives off an additional segment, the cheliceral segment, while the caudal lobe splits to form the first abdominal segment. About the same time, the primordia of the extremities become visible as slight elevations on the prosomal segments; somewhat later (170–200 hours) similar budlike thickenings appear on the developing abdominal segments (Fig. 153g). Whereas the prosomal segments manifest themselves synchronously, the abdominal segments are added successively at the caudal end. In the interior of the body the coelomic cavities become established when the mesoderm separates (Fig. 154); the walls of these cavities later differentiate into muscle tissue.

Inversion of the Embryo

When the germinal band has reached its maximal length so that the cephalic and the caudal lobes almost touch each other (day 10), a longitudinal furrow appears in the midline of the germinal band (Fig. 155). This median furrow gradually widens, and the halves of the germinal band pull apart from each other laterally, again exposing the mass of yolk beneath the median furrow. The marginal

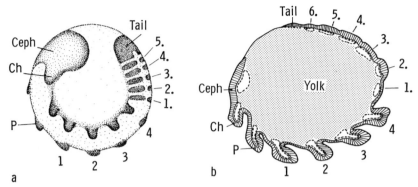

Fig. 154.   (*a*) Germinal band shortly before inversion (*Cupiennius salei*, 130 hours). The abdomen is clearly segmented (1.– 5.). On the prosoma the extremities differentiate. Ceph = frontal lobe, Ch = chelicerae, P = pedipalps, 1– 4 = legs. (After Seitz, 1966.) (*b*) Longitudinal section of an embryo shortly before inversion (*Agelena labyrinthica*). Note the metameric coelomic cavities (dashed lines). Abbreviations as in (*a*). (After Wallstabe, 1908.)

areas of the embryo extend laterally until they meet in the dorsal midline; thus the originally convex germinal band straightens and finally curls in the opposite direction (*inversion* or *reversion*).

In some "primitive" spiders (the Mesothelae and certain Orthognatha) the embryo develops *without* such an inversion process (Crome, 1963; Yoshikura, 1975). During the early developmental phases a *postabdomen* composed of nine segments appears. It is sharply flexed toward the ventral side, and at this stage of development the embryo very much resembles those of some "primitive" arachnids (scorpions, for instance). Inversion is typical of most labidognath embryos and, from an evolutionary point of view, is considered a more advanced form of development.

The anlagen of the pedipalps and legs initially have only two segments, but these soon divide into four and then into six or seven segments of equal length (Wallstabe, 1908). The anterior extremities of the abdomen gradually become smaller and move apart (Fig. 155d). Invaginations in the second and third abdominal segments represent the future book lungs and the tubular tracheae, respectively. The next abdominal extremities, on segments 4 and 5, shift toward the posterior end of the embryo and differentiate into spinnerets. A slight constriction of the first abdominal segment indicates the border between prosoma and opisthosoma. The initially distinct segmentation of the body becomes less apparent

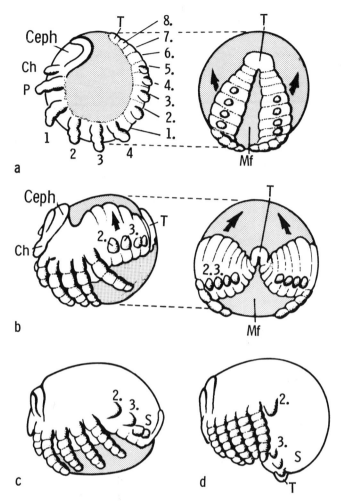

Fig. 155. Late embryonic development in *Agelena labyrinthica* (abbreviations as in Fig. 154). (*a*) Beginning of inversion, lateral view. Abdominal view of the same stage is seen on the right. The germinal band splits along the midline (Mf) and both parts expand laterally (arrows). The anlagen of the abdominal extremities appear on segments 2.– 5. (*b*) In the middle of the inversion process the extremities consist of 5 segments and rest on top of the ventral yolk mass. (*c*) The lateral body walls have merged along the dorsal midline, and to the legs has been added another segment. (*d*) Completed inversion. The yolk mass is completely grown over by the embryo; prosoma and opisthosoma are flexed toward each other. The abdominal appendages move apart and differentiate into respiratory organs (segments 2. and 3.) and spinnerets (S). The extremities have attained their final number of segments (15 days after the egg was laid). T = tail. (After Wallstabe, 1908.)

during later developmental stages. However, abdominal segmentation is often still noticeable in young spiders, either directly in the form of fine furrows or indirectly as a segmentally distributed pattern of abdominal hairs (Fig. 156). The typical shape of the spider's body emerges at the end of the inversion process. The embryo at this stage is then termed a *prelarva* by some authors (Vachon, 1957; Legendre, 1958).

The spider embryo has a marked capacity for regeneration, at least until segmentation begins. Even the loss of half of the embryo can be tolerated, and a normal embryo formed (Holm, 1952). The cumulus ostensibly acts as the organization center, for if it is extirpated, no dorsal field, and consequently no germinal band, develops. This observation has been challenged by experiments in which spider embryos whose cumuli had been destroyed by X-rays still developed normally (Seitz, 1970). However, it could be that some of the endodermal cumulus cells had survived the radiation and hence could still regulate the development of the embryo.

Organ Development

Most organ systems develop during the larval period from the cells of the three germinal layers. The nervous system, sensory organs, respiratory organs (book lungs and tracheae), poison glands, silk glands, foregut, and hindgut develop from the *ectoderm*. The *mesoderm* differentiates into the musculature, blood vessels, coxal glands, and reproductive organs. The *endoderm* provides the material for the midgut and the Malpighian tubules.

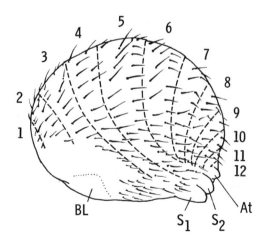

Fig. 156. Lateral view of the opisthosoma of a young spider (*Nuctenea umbratica*). The embryonic segmentation (dashed lines) is reflected in the serial distribution of hair sensilla. At = anal tubercle; BL = book lung; S_1, S_2 = spinnerets; 1–12 = abdominal segments. (Tracing of a photograph by Holm, 1940.)

Development of the nervous system. The primordia of the nervous system appear as medial, pillowlike thickenings of the ectoderm. Neuroblasts gather within each segment and form ganglia that sink into the interior of the embryo, where they aggregate to produce a coherent mass of nervous tissue. All abdominal ganglia migrate into the prosoma. There they combine with the ganglia of the extremities and form the large subesophageal ganglion. The cheliceral ganglion shifts anteriorly so that it comes to rest above the esophagus; topographically it is now a part (the tritocerebrum) of

Fig. 157. (*a*) Hatching spider larva. The granular egg shell is shed while the first molt takes place. 85×. (*b*) Larval leg of a black widow (exuvium). Note the few short hair sensilla (S) and the two little claws that are moved by long tendons (t). 240×. (*c*) First nymphal leg, still encased in the larval leg cast. Note the wrinkled surface of the new cuticle and the linear arrangement of hair sensilla. 270×.

the supraesophageal ganglion. The proto- and deuterocerebrum of the supraesophageal ganglion develop as invaginations of the cephalic lobe and become connected with the subesophageal ganglion only secondarily (Dawydoff, 1949). The outgrowth of nerve fibers gives rise to a neuropil (Fig. 75) and the peripheral nervous system.

Development of the gut. The abdominal yolk mass becomes cleaved by intersegmental membranes which later divide further to form the prospective midgut diverticula. The median axis of the embryo remains unsegmented, however, and will turn into the glandular part of the digestive canal. The foregut and hindgut are ectodermal invaginations and therefore possess a lining of cuticle. The union of the three independently formed parts of the intestinal tract does not take place until after hatching (Legendre, 1965).

In *Agelena* hatching occurs about two weeks after the egg was laid. Special cuticular denticles, or "egg teeth," which are situated at the base of the larval pedipalps, help to tear the chorion sheath of the egg. It is possible that transient hatching glands are also involved in perforating the egg membranes (Yoshikura, 1975). While these membranes are being shed, the spiderling molts for the first time (Fig. 157; Holm, 1940).

Classification of Developmental Stages

Normally it is the emergence from the egg which marks the transition from embryonic to postembryonic life. This can also be said of spiders (Holm, 1940); yet the stage at which they hatch may differ in different spiders. For instance, in most spiders it is the prelarva which sheds its egg membranes, but in some spiders this happens first at the larval stage. For this reason Vachon (1957) has classified the different developmental stages without regard to when the spider hatches; instead, he defined the completed inversion process as the end of the embryonic period. The subsequent larval period begins with a spiderlike *prelarva*, which after molting develops either into another prelarva or into a more advanced *larva* (see Table 4). After one or two additional molts, the first complete stage, *nymph* 1, appears (Fig. 158). The next 5–10 nymphal stages (juveniles) differ mainly by their increasing size. Only with the last molt do the spiders reach sexual maturity and begin adult life. The main criteria for determining the different developmental stages are summarized in Table 4.

Table 4. Developmental stages of spiders. (After Vachon, 1957.)

	Larval: not self-sufficient (yolk as food supply)		Nympho-Imaginal: self-sufficient (prey as food supply)	
Characteristic	Prelarva	Larva	Nymph	Adult
Mobility	none	very little	complete	complete
Leg segmentation	incomplete	complete	complete	complete
Hairs, spines	neither	both, but little differentiation	large variety of both	large variety of both
Claws	none	simple	differentiated	differentiated
Cheliceral claw	undifferentiated	differentiated, but no poison canal	differentiated with poison canal	differentiated with poison canal
Spinnerets	barely differentiated	differentiated, but without spigots	functional	functional
Reproductive organs	undeveloped	undeveloped	developed, but nonfunctional	functional

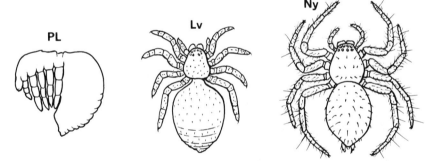

Fig. 158.   Prelarva (PL), larva (Lv), and nymphal stage (Ny). (After Vachon, 1957.)

Growth and Molting

The rigid exoskeleton of an arthropod rather limits the growth of the body. In spiders only the soft abdomen can expand—the prosoma and the extremities, which are encased in hard exocuticle,

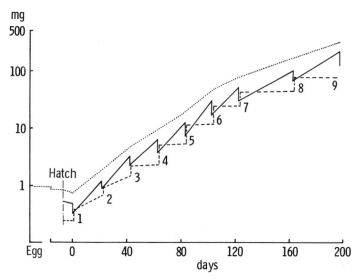

Fig. 159. Growth of a *Tegenaria agrestis* during nine molts (1–9). Dotted line = body growth, solid line = growth of opisthosoma, dashed line = growth of prosoma. Egg = time of egg laying (– 145 days). The ordinate is represented logarithmically. (After Homann, 1949.)

cannot. Actual growth can thus occur only during a molt. The new cuticle lies wrinkled beneath the old body shell (Figs. 157c, 162b) and can be stretched during and immediately after the molting process. It is this folding-extension mechanism that allows for a finite increase in size from one developmental stage to the next. In addition to an increase in size, some body proportions may also be changed, and certain sensory organs (such as hair sensilla) may increase in number or may appear for the first time.

Early nymphal stages may molt every few days, but later instars need several weeks to prepare for the next molt (Eckert, 1967). The intermolt intervals are, of course, dependent on nutritional conditions. If provided with an ample supply of food, young *Tegenaria* molt about the time at which their weight has doubled (Fig. 159; Homann, 1949). The number of molts undergone depends on the ultimate body size. Small spiders need only a few molts (about 5), whereas large spiders pass through about 10 molts to reach the adult stage (Bonnet, 1930). For most spiders the last molt marks the transition to sexual maturity; only in some exceptional cases do adult spiders still molt further (see below).

It has been claimed that the orb weaver *Argiope bruennichi* grows after the final molt (Crome and Crome, 1961). In one extreme case the prosoma stretched from 2.5 mm to 5.2 mm in length, the opisthosoma from 3.6 mm to 5.2 mm, and the first leg from 10.2 mm to 24.9 mm. Unfortunately, these results could not be duplicated in more recent experiments (W. G. Eberhard, unpublished).

The Molting Process

An experienced arachnologist can usually predict when a spider is getting ready to molt. The animal withdraws into its retreat for several days and stops feeding. A closer examination of the spider's body reveals a darkening of the legs caused by the new hair sensilla shining through the old cuticle. Another sign is the movement of the abdomen away from the prosoma so that the pedicel becomes visible from above (Fig. 160). The definite signal for the imminent molting process of most spiders is their suspension on a molting thread. "Tarantulas" do not use molting threads, but simply lie on their backs while they molt (Melchers, 1964; Minch, 1977). In all spiders, however, three successive phases of the molting process can be distinguished: (1) lifting of the carapace, (2) liberation of the abdomen, and (3) extraction of the extremities.

(1) *Lifting of the carapace.* At the beginning of the molting process the heart rate increases and more hemolymph is pumped into the prosoma. The weight of the cephalothorax increases by 80%, while the abdomen shrinks and loses about 30% of its weight. The normal hemolymph pressure of 150 mm Hg (about 17.5 psi) doubles because of the increased frequency of the heartbeat and the

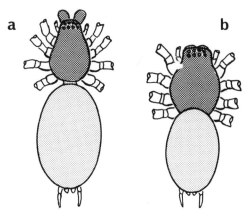

Fig. 160. Two young *Tegenaria agrestis* (*a*) immediately before and (*b*) after molting. Notice the change in the volumes of the prosoma and opisthosoma. (After Homann, 1949.)

concomitantly higher stroke volume. Under normal conditions the cuticle can withstand pressures of 600–750 mm Hg before it will split. Shortly before molting, however, the cuticle loses about two-thirds of its rigidity, because at this time most of the endocuticle has been dissolved from the inside (see below). It has been shown experimentally that at this stage a pressure of 200–300 mm Hg is sufficient to rupture the cuticle of the cephalothorax (Homann, 1949).

The first tearing occurs along the frontal or lateral parts of the prosoma. The chelicerae, which normally point slightly forward, are moved back and forth, producing additional tension near the clypeus. Most likely the first rent develops in this region and then extends laterally above the coxae until the entire carapace lifts off like the lid of a tin can (Fig. 161).

(2) *Liberation of the abdomen.* The two tears running along both sides of the prosoma soon spread to the opisthosoma. The old abdominal cuticle appears wrinkled because the volume of the abdomen has decreased, owing to the shift of the hemolymph anteriorly. Wavelike contractions of the abdominal musculature finally cause the abdomen to separate completely from the old skin (the exuvium). Just before the abdomen frees itself, the spinnerets attach a thread to the inside of the shed skin, and the spider descends a bit farther on this thread (Fischel, 1929).

(3) *Extraction of the extremities.* About the same time that the abdomen becomes free, the extremities are pulled out of their old cast. This is by far the most difficult part of the molting process, and consequently most complications arise during this phase. For instance, it may happen that a spider cannot extract all of its extremities from the old skin, a situation that is often fatal. Usually, however, the new cuticle is soft and sufficiently pliable that even rather bulky parts (like the bulb of the male palp) can be pulled through the narrow lumen of the old skin.

The increase in hemolymph pressure causes the folded leg cuticle to stretch somewhat, and by this action the leg coxae are pushed out of the exuvium. The many hairs and spines arising from the new leg cuticle are actually advantageous, since they point distally and thus prevent the leg from slipping back into the old cast. However, the increase in hemolymph pressure is only partly responsible for the extraction of the legs. When the femora are halfway free, the cephalothoracic muscles become active. Several legs remain fixed in their positions and act as braces for those legs that are pulled out. This is usually done in a certain sequence; for example, legs 1 and 4 on one side stay in a fixed position while

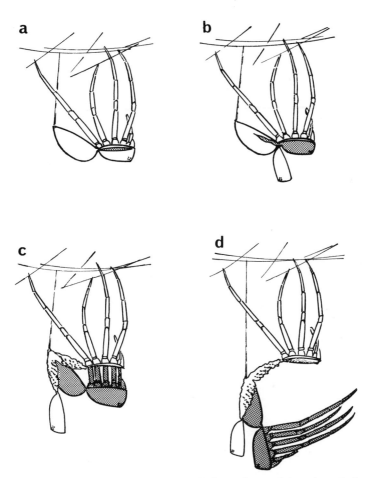

Fig. 161. Molting. (*a*) Spider suspended on the molting thread; lateral tearing of the cephalothorax. (*b*) Lifting off of the carapace and lateral fission of the abdominal cuticle. (*c*) Freeing of legs and abdomen. (*d*) Complete liberation from the exuvium. (After Bonnet, 1930.)

legs 2 and 3 are partially extracted on the other side. When the "new" legs are exposed down to the patellae, muscles of the legs themselves, the flexors, are activated. This leads to a shortening and, subsequently, to a jerky withdrawal of the legs from the old cuticle. Again, the hairs and spines of the legs help in this process, since they allow the legs to be moved only toward the body. As soon as the first legs are completely free, they aid in pulling out the remaining ones. Immediately after molting the legs usually hang down in a completely stretched fashion, but they are then bent abruptly. A period of "gymnastics" follows during which all extremities are flexed repeatedly. Presumably this helps to maintain elasticity of the joints while the cuticle begins to harden.

The largest force needed for extracting a leg, about 0.5 pond, must be exerted at the beginning of the liberation process, because friction is greatest when the entire leg is still encased in the exuvium. Once the extraction is underway, the friction diminishes rapidly (Homann, 1949). The suspended position that most spiders assume during molting is not absolutely necessary but is physiologically very economical. Often the freshly molted legs would still be too limp to support the weight of the spider. Perhaps this also explains why some wandering spiders lie on their backs while they molt.

The entire molting procedure lasts only 10–15 minutes for small spiders but may take several hours for large "tarantulas." Some spiders start to groom themselves extensively after molting, pulling all their extremities through the chelicerae and mouth parts.

Physiology of Molting

In a strict sense molting comprises two different processes: (1) *apolysis*, the separation of the old cuticle from the hypodermal cells, and (2) *ecdysis*, the shedding of the entire old skin (exuvium), which corresponds to what most people think of as molting. Apolysis precedes ecdysis by about one week.

Cellular events. The epidermal cells secrete certain enzymes (chitinases and proteases) into the gap that develops between the epithelium and the cuticle, the exuvial space. These enzymes gradually dissolve the endocuticle but attack neither the exocuticle nor the nerve fibers associated with the sensory hairs. The dissolved components of the endocuticle are largely resorbed, which means that very little material is actually lost in the molting process (Fig. 162). For a large "tarantula" weighing 80 grams, the dry weight of the shed skin was found to be 2 grams (Melchers, 1964).

About 4–5 days before the spider molts, the hypodermal cells secrete the first new layer of the cuticle (the *cuticulin*). The enzymes circulating in the exuvial fluid probably become activated only after the cuticulin layer has been deposited, that is, after the surface of the hypodermal cells is protected. Ecdysis begins when the endocuticle has largely been digested. That the prosoma tears first along the pleural areas (Fig. 161a) becomes quite understand-

Fig. 162. (*a*) Exuvium of a young tarantula. Ch = chelicerae, Cp = carapace with the cuticular lenses of the eyes (arrow), P = pedipalp, Sp = spinnerets. About natural size; weight of exuvium: 0.2 g. (*b*) Cross section of a leg of *Hypochilus* shortly before molting. The old cuticle (old C) is separated from the hypodermis (Hy) by a large exuvial space (EX). The hypodermis cells have already produced a thin corrugated cuticle (C) as well as new hair sensilla (HS). H = hemocyte, N = leg nerves, Sl = slit sensillum. 1,200×.

able when one remembers that exocuticle is lacking in the joint regions and thus only the thin epicuticle remains there after apolysis.

The following sequence of events, which is very similar to that observed in insects, occurs when spiders molt:

1. Activation of the hypodermal cells (cell division and cell growth)
2. Secretion of the exuvial fluid and apolysis
3. Secretion of the first new cuticle (cuticulin)
4. Activation of the enzymes in the exuvial fluid (dissolving of the endocuticle)
5. Absorption of the dissolved substances from the old cuticle
6. Secretion of the new cuticle
7. Ecdysis—the shedding of the old skin
8. Stretching of the wrinkled new cuticle
9. Sclerotization of the new exocuticle.

Subsequently, as further endocuticle is deposited during the weeks following the molt, the exoskeleton will increase considerably in thickness.

It seems particularly interesting that the sensory hairs remain functional during most of the molting process. The reason is that the innervation of the old sensilla is maintained while the new hairs develop on the surface of the hypodermis (Figs. 162, 163).

The long dendrites innervating each "old" hair sensillum lie freely in the exuvial space and become wrapped by a sheath cell (cell 2 in Fig. 163). This cell starts to secrete cuticle on its outside, thus producing the new hair shaft. Another sheath cell (cell 3 in Fig. 163) is responsible for the formation of the socket in which the hair shaft is articulated. About 24 hours before ecdysis all new hair sensilla are completely developed, and only then is the continuity between the old and the new sensory hair broken. When the exuvium is cast off, only the tips of the dendrites are lost, and the new hair sensilla are thus functional immediately after molting (Harris, 1977).

Hormonal control. For spiders, molting is triggered and controlled by hormones, as it is for insects and crustaceans. An increase of the molting hormone ecdysone is found in the spider's hemolymph a few days before ecdysis (Eckert, 1967; Bonaric and de Reggi, 1977). By injecting β-ecdysone it is possible to shorten the intermolt periods, or even to induce ecdysis (Krishnakumaran and Schneiderman, 1968; Bonaric, 1976).

Fig. 163. Formation of new tactile hairs before ecydsis. The old cuticle (C′, EC) is separated from the hypodermis by the exuvial space (Ex). The endocuticle has been largely dissolved. The dendritic connection between old and new hair sensillum is still continuous. C = new cuticle, D = dendrite, Hs = hair shaft, Htip = hair tip, So = socket, T = dendritic terminals, 1–4 = sheath cells. (After Harris, 1977.)

Various experiments have demonstrated that ecdysone does not act in a species-specific way. For instance, when pieces of integument from a young *Tegenaria* are transplanted into a nymph of *Coelotes*, they molt synchronously with the host. Even when adult integument is used, ecdysis can be induced (Eckert, 1967). Very little is known about the production site of the molting hormone. A type of endocrine tissue that is diffusely distributed in the prosoma and that has been termed the "prosomal gland" (Legendre, 1958) might be responsible for producing ecdysone. This seems plausible, since the molting hormone in insects originates from an analogous gland, the prothoracic gland. Other endocrine tissues, such as the neurosecretory cells of the CNS or Schneider's organs, are also most likely involved in the control of molting.

It has been known for a long time that besides the hypodermis the hemolymph is also affected by the molting process (Browning,

1942). Shortly before molting, special blood cells, the leberidiocytes, which are characterized by a large fluid-filled vacuole, appear in the hemolymph. Presumably these cells participate in regulating the amount of water in the spider's body by absorbing
water from the hemolymph (Seitz, 1976).

Autotomy and Regeneration

As a last resort in perilous situations, most spiders can "amputate"
one of their own legs. This voluntary separation of an extremity
following a dangerous stimulus is widespread among arthropods
and is called *autotomy*. Luckily, though, lost legs can be replaced,
at least as long as the animal still has to go through another molt.
Regeneration of autotomized legs is thus restricted to juvenile spiders—except for those cases where molting continues in the adult
stage.

Autotomy

One can easily induce a spider to autotomize a leg by pulling or
squeezing the femur of that leg. Tampering with the distal leg segments (the tarsus or metatarsus) does not usually lead to autotomy. It has been shown that anesthetized spiders cannot autotomize their limbs (Bonnet, 1930), so autotomy is indeed a voluntary
act.

The site where a leg is autotomized is always the same and lies
between coxa and trochanter. An externally applied pulling force
is not important for autotomy. More significant is the spider's own
sudden jerking upward of the coxa while the femur maintains its
position and acts as a brace. The trochanter tilts sharply, and the
high tension that develops between the coxa and the trochanter
causes the membrane of the joint to rupture dorsally (Fig. 164a).
Further separation poses no problem, because the site of amputation is traversed by only one muscle (m. gracilis), which readily de-
taches itself from the trochanter and then withdraws into the coxal
cavity. All other muscles insert on marginal thickenings, the
sclerites, of the joint membrane. These muscles aid in closing the
open coxa by pulling the sclerites toward each other—a closing
mechanism similar to that of certain garbage cans (Bauer, 1972).
Additionally, the hemolymph pressure forces the joint membrane
to bulge forward, which also helps to seal the wound.

Under natural conditions autotomy is used mostly as a defense

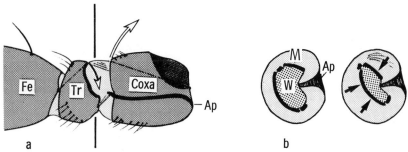

Fig. 164. (*a*) Site of autotomy in a spider leg (*Philodromus*), lateral view. A rapid jerk upwards (large arrow) causes a high tension in the joint membrane so that a tear (small arrow) develops dorsally near the edge of the trochanter (Tr). The articulation of the coxal apodeme (Ap) and the trochanter is shown already disrupted. Fe = femur. (After Bauer, 1972.) (*b*) Closing of the wound after autotomy; frontal view of coxa. Left: The wound opening (W) is bordered by sclerites (black) of the joint membrane (M). Right: The large wound is sealed by a closing movement of the sclerites. (After Bonnet, 1930, and Bauer, 1972.)

against an aggressor, often enough another spider, such as an attacking female. Another opportune use for autotomy may arise during molting, when an extremity cannot be freed from the old skin. Even if molting itself has been successful, injured or malformed legs can still be autotomized afterward. Such limbs are not discarded but are usually eaten by the spider (Bonnet, 1930).

Regeneration

When a juvenile spider looses a leg, it will often—but not always —be replaced at the next molt. Whether the leg is regenerated or not depends on the time of amputation: only if the leg has been severed within the first quarter of the intermolt phase will regeneration take place (Bonnet, 1930). If the leg is lost later, no regeneration occurs. Apparently, regeneration is an all-or-nothing process that is controlled hormonally.

Regeneration of an autotomized leg cannot be observed directly, because the leg grows inside the old coxa. The formation of the new leg is comparable to the differentiation seen during normal ontogeny. However, because of the limited space of the coxal cavity, the new leg will be highly folded (Fig. 165). After ecdysis the regenerated leg appears a bit shorter and thinner than the original leg, but all leg segments are present in the right proportions. Even

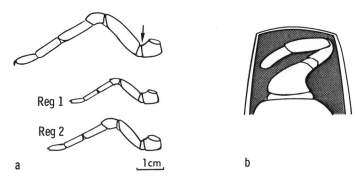

Reg 1

Reg 2

a   1cm   b

Fig. 165. Comparison of the legs of a tarantula before autotomy (above) and after regeneration (Reg 1, 2) in the subsequent two molts. The arrow indicates the site of autotomy. (Tracing of a photograph by Ruhland, 1976.) (*b*) The strongly folded regenerate developing inside the old coxa (After Bonnet, 1930.)

claws, spines, and sensory organs are regenerated, although the sensory organs are not always complete. The tarsal organ, for instance, is lacking in the first regenerate (Blumenthal, 1935), and the number of sensory hairs is usually less than normal. However, these are rather quickly supplemented in the course of further molts.

Whether a regenerated leg really replaces the original completely is a question that cannot fully be answered. Aside from the sensory organs, all the muscles and their innervation must be formed entirely anew. An analysis of regenerating "tarantula" legs has shown that the new legs do indeed have all 30 leg muscles — and all of them insert at the proper sites (Ruhland, 1976). However, the number of muscle fibers is less than normal. The pattern of innervation in the new leg muscles is also the same as it was in the original. Yet it is rather odd that newly regenerated legs are often stretched out and held away from the body and are not used for walking at all. If they are occasionally used for walking, their movements are not well coordinated with the other legs. This impaired function is presumably caused by undifferentiated neuromuscular contacts in the regenerated leg.

A spider's ability to regenerate a missing part is not restricted to legs; pedipalps, chelicerae, endites, the labium, and even the spinnerets can be regrown as well (Bonnet, 1930). If only the distal segments of these extremities are severed—and, of course, if the leg is not autotomized—the missing segments are regenerated directly at the site of injury.

The potential for regeneration in spiders is enormous. If several legs are amputated early in an intermolt phase, they will all regenerate by the time of the next molt. Indeed, in one drastic experiment, all eight legs were induced to autotomize, and all were nevertheless regenerated simultaneously (Bonnet, 1930). This was, however, possible only because the torso of the spider was fed artificially. If a regenerated leg is amputated again, it can also be replaced at the next molt (Bonnet, 1930; Ruhland, 1976). After the final molt a spider can still autotomize its legs, but no signs of regeneration will be detectable in the remaining coxa.

Life Cycle and Longevity

The exact course of the life of a spider has been investigated in only a few spiders. In the temperate zones of central Europe, the main reproductive period is in May (Tretzel, 1954), and the spiderlings hatch during summer. Some species may reach the adult stage in autumn, but most overwinter as nymphs. If the egg sac is constructed during late fall, as it is for most species of *Araneus*, the hatched spiderlings will remain inside the cocoon until spring.

Only females of the European spider *Tegenaria atrica* can be found in spring. They lay their eggs in April and the spiderlings hatch 21 days later. By the end of August most of the spiderlings have molted nine times and are then adults. In late summer there are thus two generations of females (a young and an old one), but only one generation of males (a young one). The reproductive period lasts from August to October, and shortly thereafter the males die. The young females overwinter; their ovaries start to grow as early as November (Collatz and Mommsen, 1974).

Most spiders of temperate regions do live only one year, but some may live for two. The "primitive" spiders are renowned for their longevity. The orthognath purse-web spider *Atypus* (Fig. 95) can survive seven years, large "tarantulas" over 20 (Berland, 1932). Another spider noted for its long life is the cribellate *Filistata*, which can get to be 10 years old. As a rule, only female spiders have a high life expectancy; most males die shortly after mating.

9

Ecology

THE interactions between spiders and their environment have been investigated systematically only within the past few decades. During this time, however, information about the ecology of spiders has burgeoned to such an extent that it is impossible to include all aspects in the scope of this book. A few selected examples must therefore suffice.

Occurrence and Distribution of Spiders

Spiders are found almost everywhere on earth, from arctic islands to dry desert regions. They are particularly abundant in areas of rich vegetation. (Shaking bushes over an opened umbrella or sweeping through low vegetation with a butterfly net are thus very efficient methods of collecting large quantities of spiders.) However, spiders are also found in rather barren environments such as sand dunes, tidal zones, or mountain tops. It is no exaggeration to say that spiders have conquered all possible ecological niches on land (Turnbull, 1973).

Such widespread distribution leads to the question of how spiders manage to populate very remote areas, such as islands, for instance. One explanation is based on the ability of many young spiders to float through the air on their own threads. This "ballooning," as it is called, is actively undertaken by the spider. The spiderling stands on "tiptoe," facing the wind, and inclines its abdomen upward while exuding a silk thread. This strand is caught by the slightest current, which can easily lift the spider. Usually the voyage ends after a rather short distance. Under favorable wind conditions, however, these aeronauts may attain quite remarkable heights and distances. Spiders, as a kind of "aerial plankton," have been caught from airplanes flying at altitudes of several thousand meters (Gertsch, 1949; Glick, 1939). In 1832 Darwin noted in his diary that innumerable small spiders had been blown into the rigging of the Beagle 100 km off the coast of South America. Yet, as Berland (1932) has rightly pointed out, spiders cannot really bridge large distances by aeronautical means. East Africa and Madagascar, for instance, are only 400 km apart, yet each has a quite different spider fauna. The problem of bridging large distances is even greater when one considers the Pacific islands, which are often thousands of kilometers from the mainland. Ancient land connections or driftwood are more likely routes for settlements of spiders there.

Formerly it was believed that only young spiders could fly on their own threads, but recently it has been found that many small spiders can do so as well (Richter, 1971; Blanke, 1973). In the linyphiids, adult males *and* females can take to the air—often thousands of them at a time (Bristowe, 1939; Van Wingerden and Vugts, 1974; Vugts and Van Wingerden, 1976). Whereas the gossamer threads of young spiderlings are seen in Indian summer, the mass flight of linyphiids occurs during fall and winter. A prerequisite for such aeronautical behavior is a sudden rise in temperature (Duffey, 1956). If the weather shifts to warm, sunny days after a long period of cold, the temperature on the ground will rise rapidly. This causes an updraft of air, and the spiders are easily lifted away. Of course, how far they will travel depends mainly on wind conditions. Only a few of the aeronauts will survive; many fall victim to birds (such as swallows), or they land on open water or in some other wholly unfit environment. However, since the number of spiders transported is so great, there are always a few that will survive to invade new habitats. It is certainly not merely by accident that the first spiders to colonize a newly emerged island near the volcano Krakatoa were found to be linyphiids (Bristowe, 1939).

The small spiderlings that usually live together during their first period of life gain two advantages by their aerial dispersal: (1) they become rapidly distributed over the available habitats so that overcrowding is minimized, and (2) they escape the gradually emerging cannibalistic behavior of their siblings (Tolbert, 1977).

Habitat

Most spiders live in strictly defined environments. The limitations are set by physical conditions, like temperature, humidity, wind, and light intensity, and also by biological factors such as the type of vegetation, the food supply, competitors, and enemies. Ecologically, vegetation can be classified into four vertical layers (Duffey, 1966): (1) a soil zone, consisting of leaf litter, stones, and low herbs up to 15 cm in height, (2) a field zone, consisting of vegetation from 15–180 cm, (3) a bush zone of shrubs and trees of 180–450 cm in height and (4) a wood zone of trees and treetops over 450 cm in height. Each zone has its characteristic microclimate, various niches for retreats, and a different spectrum of prey animals. Accordingly, we often find a corresponding "stratification" of different spider species.

Among wolf spiders, *Lycosa pullata* (now *Pardosa pullata*) lives in the lowest zone (0–5 cm), whereas *Lycosa nigriceps* is dominant in the lower field zone (20–30 cm; Duffey, 1966). Even within the same zone the microclimatic conditions can vary considerably, and these may cause an ecological separation of different species. For instance, *Pardosa pullata* and *Pirata piraticus* live together in bogs where sphagnum moss is found. However, *Pardosa* keeps almost exclusively to the surface of the moss, whereas *Pirata* prefers the more secluded stem region of the moss (Nørgaard, 1951). Continuous monitoring shows that the temperature fluctuates a great deal on the surface of the moss layer, but varies little inside (Fig. 166).

However, it cannot be stated as a general rule that only a single species will live in a given microhabitat. The American wolf spiders *Lycosa carolinensis* and *Lycosa timuqua* live in the same habitat, hunt the same type of prey, and are both active at night (Kuenzler, 1958). Other species, particularly among the jumping spiders, migrate back and forth between different vegetative zones (Luczak, 1966). Generally, however, small spiders usually stay close to the ground (Tretzel, 1955).

Many web-building spiders are also vertically distributed. The

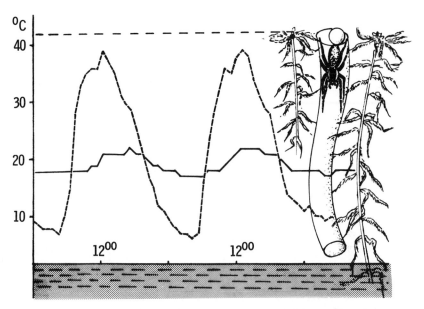

Fig. 166.   Temperature fluctuations in the habitat of the wolf spider *Pirata piraticus* during two summer days. On the surface of the sphagnum moss the temperature changes between 8 and 39°C (dashed line). In contrast, the temperature stays near 20°C inside the moss layer (solid line). During sunny periods the female exposes her egg sac to the sun at the entrance of her silken tube. (After Nørgaard, 1951.)

two orb weavers *Argiope aurantia* and *Argiope trifasciata* build their webs at different heights during the period from May to September (Fig. 167). Only during the adult stage do their habitats overlap (Enders, 1974, 1977). An explanation for this vertical stratification might be found in the distribution of prey animals. Spiders that build their webs higher up can also include larger flying insects among their prey.

In general, a specific spatial distribution of spider species would seem to be an adaptation to interspecies competition—that is, a strategy that aims to avoid such competition (Tretzel, 1955). Recent investigations of different species of wolf spiders showed, however, that the distribution pattern was determined more by environmental factors than by interspecific competition (Schaefer, 1972, 1974). Ecological separation may also be achieved by different reproductive periods, as is shown for certain species of *Lycosa* (now *Pardosa*) in Fig. 168. The same habitat may be used at different times of day by different species. Such differences in activity

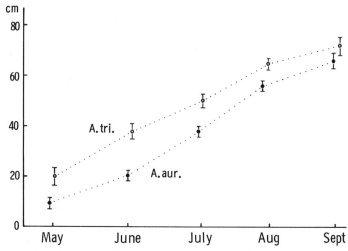

Fig. 167.   Vertical stratification of the orb webs of *Argiope aurantia* and *A. trifasciata*. Throughout the summer the height of the webs above the ground is different for both species. Only in September, when both species are adult, do the heights of their webs overlap. (After Enders, 1974.)

are known for many species of wandering spiders, but also for some web spiders, which exhibit different daily periods of web building.

The habitats of web spiders not only require specific microclimates but also must meet certain spatial demands. The environment must provide plenty of attachment sites for the scaffolding of the web. In addition, sufficient open space must be available, either vertically (for orb webs) or horizontally (for sheet webs). Web spiders are thus not distributed at random in their environment, and their population density is necessarily limited. It is likely that the space that a web spider occupies is about as large as is necessary to provide for the animal's minimal energy requirements (Riechert, 1974).

Web spiders are sit-and-wait predators, and they probably expend less energy for prey capture than do wandering spiders. In addition, web spiders often catch several prey items in their webs at once and thus can maintain a cache of food. In general, web spiders also kill larger prey than errant spiders do. Apparently, catching prey with a web is more efficient than direct attack (Enders, 1975). This view, however, has been challenged recently following the demonstration that several species of wandering spiders can also overpower rather large prey (Rovner, 1980c).

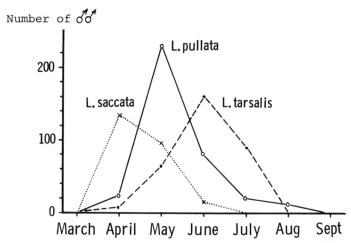

Number of ♂♂

Fig. 168.   Seasonal separation of the reproductive period in different *Ly-cosa* (now *Pardosa*) species. (After Tretzel, 1955.)

The web itself can be considered the spider's territory, since it is usually defended against invaders. Sometimes the web is con-quered by a conspecific, or even an unrelated spider. Such web robbery may be committed by conspecific males, who normally do not build webs of their own after their final molt (Eberhard, Bar-reto, and Pfizenmaier, 1978). In all other cases web robbery can be interpreted as a competition for the same habitat, because such in-cidents happen more often during periods of high population den-sity. Wandering spiders rarely show any territorial behavior. Only for the wolf spider *Pardosa* has a "mobile territory" been de-scribed: an area of 10 cm in diameter in the immediate vicinity of the spider is defended against invaders (Vogel, 1971, 1972).

A special type of web invasion is found in the pirate spiders (Mi-metidae) and in *Argyrodes* (synonym *Conopistha*, Theridiidae). For instance, *Ero*, a member of the Mimetidae, sneaks into the web of another spider, lures the owner by carefully plucking the threads (see chapter 6), and then applies a quick, fatal bite (Brach, 1977). The small *Argyrodes* parasitizes the webs of other spiders by cau-tiously removing their previously caught and wrapped prey (Kull-mann, 1959; Vollrath, 1979; Wiehle, 1928). The host spiders are aware of the thief but are apparently incapable of fending him off. Often one can even find several different species of *Argyrodes* in the same web; in this case, an interspecific competition is largely reduced, because some species are predominantly active during daytime, whereas others are mainly nocturnal (Vollrath, 1976).

Several interesting ecological investigations have focused on the question of whether spiders occupy a certain habitat more or less by chance, or whether they select it specifically. The funnel-web spider *Agelenopsis* has been shown to build sheet webs not only at sites where the microclimate is favorable, but also where prey is rather abundant (Riechert, 1974, 1976). For instance, if the spider constructs its web in bushes that are in bloom, it will have a better chance of catching insects there. Some spiders (like *Achaearanea tepidariorum*) have been observed to change the sites of their webs if they do not catch enough prey (Turnbull, 1964). On the other hand, the abundance of prey seems to have no effect on orb-web spiders in their selections of web sites (Enders, 1976).

Prey Animals

Insects are by far the largest part of the diet of a spider. Other arthropods, such as sowbugs or millipedes, are also on the list—as are spiders themselves! It is rather unusual to find vertebrates among a spider's prey, although tadpoles or small fish may fall victim to certain lycosids or pisaurids. Reports that claim that large "tarantulas" have been feeding on birds, lizards, or snakes are rarely scientifically verifiable.

Among the insects, flies and the wingless Collembola contribute to the bulk of the spider's diet. Because Collembola occur in huge numbers they are very important to many small spiders (Bristowe, 1941). Beetles, grasshoppers, and butterflies are another abundant source of prey. However, certain insects, such as stinkbugs, ants, and wasps, as well as certain beetles, moths, and caterpillars are generally avoided by most spiders. Either these insects actively use chemicals to defend themselves (as do ladybugs) or they may taste bad to the spider.

Most spiders are not fussy about what type of prey they feed on. Such spiders are called *polyphagous*, that is, they are generalists with respect to their prey. A good example is *Linyphia triangularis*, which, in one experiment, accepted 150 of 153 offered species of prey (Turnbull, 1960). Quite in contrast are *stenophagous* spiders, which are specialized for feeding on only a very few species of prey, such as ants (*Zodarium, Callilepis*) or other spiders (*Ero*).

The webs themselves can be regarded as selective filters for the potential prey. Insects with well developed flying abilities and acute eyesite (like the hoverflies, the Syrphidae) can apparently avoid spider webs. Pollinating insects (bees, wasps, certain flies, and beetles) are rather rarely found trapped in the space webs of theridiids and linyphiids, but plant-sucking insects (Aphidae, Homoptera, and Thysanoptera) are caught extremely often, that is to say, selectively (Nentwig, 1980).

One would expect that predation by spiders would severely limit insect populations. Indeed, we have impressive hypothetical calculations (Turnbull, 1973) based on an estimate of the population density of spiders ($130/m^2$) and on an assumption that each spider consumes 0.1 g of prey daily. The conclusion is that all the spiders living on one hectare of land would devour $1.3 \times 10^6 \times 0.1 \times 365 = 4.75 \times 10^7$ g, or 47,500 kg, of prey per year. Although 0.1g/spider/day is certainly an inflated estimate, even half that amount would be astounding. Bristowe (1958) gave a less quantitative yet less abstract estimate when he stated that "the weight of insects consumed annually in Britain exceeds that of the human inhabitants."

Even if such claims were realistic, it would be wrong to assume that spiders play a major role in the control of insect pests. As we have seen, most spiders are generalists with respect to their diet, but for efficient pest control spiders would need to "specialize" in eating such pests. Furthermore, spiders generally do not form social colonies, so their populations cannot really become very dense. Accordingly, we must discount their ability to control pests, although together with birds and insectivorous mammals, they are certainly among the main foes of insects (Bristowe, 1958).

Many spiders can adjust to the available food supply by eating more prey when it is abundant. This maximal energy uptake allows the spider not only to grow but also to mature more quickly (Miyashita, 1968). If a long period of food deprivation then follows, such well-fed spiders have better chances of surviving it. (A similar strategy of an "optimal food uptake" is also found in a completely different group of animals, the snakes). Of course, small spiders take in much less "biomass" than large spiders do. The small wolf spider *Pardosa* eats about 3.5 mg of insects daily, equivalent to 12% of its body weight (Edgar, 1970). Comparable values were found for the larger wolf spider *Trochosa* (3–12%; Breymeyer, 1967) and the sheet-web weaver *Linyphia* (10–25%; Turnbull, 1962).

The astonishing ability of spiders to survive several months without food is primarily due to their low rate of metabolism (Fig. 169; Anderson, 1970). Under conditions of starvation, metabolism is reduced drastically—in extreme situations by more than 80% (Collatz and Mommsen, 1975). Wolf spiders, which have a life ex-

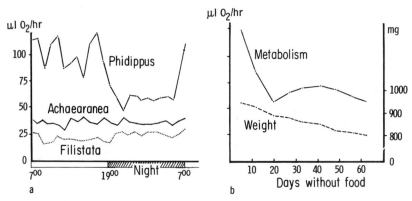

Fig. 169. (a) Oxygen consumption in three spider species in the course of 24 hours. Note the much higher metabolism of the day-active jumping spider (*Phidippus*) as compared to the sedentary theridiid *Achaearanea* and to the tube-dwelling *Filistata*. (After Anderson, 1970.) (b) Decrease in body weight and metabolism in *Lycosa lenta* during starvation. (After Anderson, 1974.)

pectancy of only 300 days, can survive up to 200 days without food (Anderson, 1974). Although such experiments were conducted in the laboratory, long periods of starvation no doubt occur naturally, for example, while the spider overwinters. In autumn the house spider *Tegenaria* deposits mainly fat, but also some carbohydrates and proteins, in its body; this "fuel" is then metabolized during the winter, when no sources of food are available. After 50 days of starvation, 60% of the stored carbohydrates, 47% of the fatty acids, and 9% of the original proteins have already been metabolized (Collatz and Mommsen, 1974).

Some spiders produce relatively more eggs when the food supply is abundant (Blanke, 1974; Kessler, 1973a; Wise, 1975). In general, however, the number of eggs is mainly a function of the spider's size: the larger the spider, the more eggs she will lay (Petersen, 1950; Kessler, 1971a). On the other hand, the number of eggs decreases with an increased level of brood care.

Enemies

Even the most skilled predators can fall victim to other hunters—and this applies likewise to spiders and their many foes. The main enemies of spiders are spiders themselves (Fig. 170). Many wandering spiders will attack each other, and web spiders, while defending their territories, often duel successfully with invaders. The pirate spiders (Mimetidae), which feed exclusively on other spiders, have already been discussed (see chapter 6). Another unusual example of a spider that prefers to attack other spiders is the cryptic jumping spider *Portia* (Fig. 170b); it can even capture other salticids and tackles large orb weavers in their webs (Bristowe, 1941; Jackson and Blest, 1981a, b). Other arachnids, such as mites, pseudoscorpions, and harvestmen, prey only occasionally on spiders.

Not all enemies of spiders threaten the life of the spider directly. Some steal only their prey, as do the "kleptoparasitic" spiders of the genus *Argyrodes*. Another, and rather extreme, example of such parasitic behavior is the symphytognathid spider *Curimagua bayano*, which shares in the prey of the rightful web owner (Vollrath, 1978). This tiny spider (1–2 mm body length) rides on its host, a large (40 mm) *Diplura*, in a way reminiscent of young wolf spiders' sitting atop their mother. When *Diplura* is feeding on its prey, *Curimagua* climbs down the large chelicerae of its host and imbibes the liquefied prey tissue. In fact, *Curimagua* seems unable to capture any sort of food on its own. Some insects also rob

Fig. 170.   Spiders as spider enemies. (*a*) The pholcid *Holocnemus pluchii* attacks the araneid *Cyrtophora citricola*, which has just caught prey. (From *Blanke*, 1972.) (*b*) The salticid *Portia fimbriata*, having delivered a fatal bite to a large theridiid.

Fig. 171. Wasps as spider enemies. (*a*) The pompilid *Episyron funerarius* stings a *Cyrtophora citricola* in the abdomen. (From *Blanke,* 1972.) (*b*) The araneid *Cyclosa conica* with a larva (L) of an ichneumonid wasp attached to its carapace. (Photo: Blanke.)

spiders of their prey. The scorpion fly *Panorpa* invades spider webs in order to steal prey (Nyffeler and Benz, 1980); sometimes *Panorpa* gets stuck in the web, but it can free itself by vomiting digestive juice, which quickly dissolves the silk threads (Thornhill, 1975).

Among the insects, certain types of wasps are the arch enemies of spiders (Fig. 171). The spider wasps (Pompilidae) hunt spiders exclusively, whereas the mud daubers (Sphecidae) pursue insects as well as spiders. The fate of the spider is always the same: it is paralyzed by the wasp's sting and an egg is laid on its abdomen. When the wasp larva hatches, it feeds on the living tissue of the paralyzed spider until the spider succumbs.

Different species of pompilid wasps use different strategies (Rathmayer, 1966). Some species paralyze the spider only temporarily, deposit an egg on it, and fly away. Other species first dig a hole into which they drag the paralyzed spider. When the spider recovers after a few hours, it finds itself locked inside a narrow tube where it cannot move. Most pompilids, however, paralyze the spider permanently, or at least for several weeks, and enclose their victim in an underground chamber. The wasp's poison acts very rapidly (in less than 1 second), via the hemolymph, on the motor system of the spider. Apparently neuromuscular transmission is blocked rather than the muscles themselves (Rathmayer, 1978).

In general, pompilids do not hunt one particular species of spider, although they may have a preference for certain species. The wasp *Episyron rufipes*, for instance, goes mostly after araneids, whereas *Pompilus cinctellus* searches for salticids. Some spider wasps (for example, *Pseudagenia*) do not dig holes in the ground but build tiny cells of clay into which they carry the paralyzed spiders. Some other wasp species (such as those of the genus *Anoplius*) do not even bother to hunt their own spiders; instead they attack other pompilids and take paralyzed spiders away from them.

It is very curious that spiders scarcely defend themselves when they are attacked by pompilid wasps. As soon as the wasp appears, the spider seems to be absolutely frightened and tries to escape (Bristowe, 1941). The spider's panic flight is probably caused by a scent that the excited wasp exudes (Petrunkevitch, 1926). Some wolf spiders (such as *Geolycosa*), however, do make some attempts to defend themselves, either by pushing the wasp away or by maintaining a plug of sand between itself and the wasp (McQueen, 1979; Gwynne, 1979). One spider, the cribellate *Amaurobius*, pays no heed to pompilid wasps. If a pompilid gets ensnared in the hackle band of the catching threads, *Amaurobius* simply overpowers it and eats it (Bristowe, 1941).

Even large "tarantulas" frequently fall victim to pompilids, and only rarely do they counterattack. A famous example is the huge wasp *Pepsis*, with a body length of 8 cm and a wingspan of 10 cm. It persecutes tropical "tarantulas" and does not even hesitate to follow them into their burrows. In its choice of prey, *Pepsis*, incidentally, is strictly species-specific. If it is put in a cage with the "wrong" species of "tarantula," it does not attack and, in fact, may get killed by the spider. In order to determine the "right" species, the wasp crawls over the entire spider, with its antennae vibrating. Only after a thorough olfactory inspection and positive identification of the spider does *Pepsis* set its stinger into the soft pleural areas near the spider's coxae (Petrunkevitch, 1952).

Mud daubers (Sphecidae) construct multichambered clay nests into which they deposit several paralyzed spiders. They sting mainly web spiders, which they either drag along the ground or, if these are light enough, carry off in flight. Even the very poisonous black widow spider is not safe from wasp attacks: *Chalybion cyaneum* regularly preys upon black widows (Irving and Hinman, 1935). A single sphecid wasp may have a considerable effect on a spider population, as one female catches 100–300 spiders in the course of one summer (Bristowe, 1941). It should be stressed that the spiders serve as a food source only for the developing larvae but not for the adult wasps, which feed mostly on plant juices. Thus, we are dealing here with a typical case of brood parasitism and not with food parasitism.

Members of the wasp family Ichneumonidae also plague spiders. They attach their eggs to the spider's body or deposit them in the spider's egg sacs. *Polysphincta* raids orb weavers and fastens its eggs to their abdomens (Fig. 171b). The larva lives as an ectoparasite on the spider's body, ingesting its body fluid (Nielsen, 1923, 1932). The hatched larvae of other ichneumonids, *Gelis*, for example, feed on spider eggs inside the cocoon (see Fig. 147d; Horstmann, 1970; Kessler and Fokkinga, 1973). Certain dipteran flies are also known to act as cocoon, or egg, parasites. Well-known examples are members of the families Chloropidae, Sarcophagidae, and Asilidae. It is quite astonishing that these flies manage to deposit their eggs in the spider cocoons, since the cocoon wall is usually tough and is often well camouflaged.

Finally, vertebrates are also enemies of spiders. Many fish, particularly trout, eat spiders that happen to fall onto the surface of the water. Among amphibians, toads are considered to feed most often on spiders; spiders constitute about 5% of a toad's diet (Bristowe, 1941). Lizards and geckos occasionally eat spiders, but in general reptiles have hardly any measurable effect on the spider population. The influence of birds as a factor controlling spider populations is generally overestimated. It is true that starlings and titmice catch quite a few spiders when raising their young, but the adult birds themselves feed on spiders only rarely. Spiders are relatively poorly perceived, and hence little harassed, by birds for several reasons: (1) many spiders hide in retreats, (2) most web spiders sit motionless in their webs, (3) many species are camouflaged, and (4) most spiders are active at night. Birds, in contrast, are visually oriented and usually active during the day. Thus, it is no surprise that the spiders found in the stomachs of birds were always rather conspicuous species, whereas cryptic forms, such as *Cyclosa*, were absent. Only a few spider enemies are found among the mammals. Spiders make up 1–2% of the diet of shrews (Soricidae; Bristowe, 1941). Monkeys feed on all kinds of arthropods and apparently do not spare spiders. The South American woolly monkeys *Lagothrix* have been observed to eat the poisonous brown recluse spider, *Loxosceles* (Fig. 38c), without ado (Macedo, personal communication, 1980).

Adaptations

Some spiders can tolerate a certain fluctuation in environmental factors and are referred to as *euryecious*. In contrast, *stenecious* species are less flexible to changing conditions. The distribution and population density of spiders in their habitat are therefore not accidental but are functions of a whole range of graded factors within a given biotope. These factors are not merely of a physical nature (like temperature, humidity, or wind conditions), but are more related to the type of vegetation present in the spider's habitat. Quite often, certain spiders associate with certain plant species. For instance, in tussocks of broom sedge (*Andropogon virginicus*) live five typical spider genera: *Phidippus*, *Oxyopes*, *Eustala*, *Clubiona*, and *Mangora*; the population density of these spiders is about the same in all tussocks, independent of the biotope in which this grass may grow (Barnes and Barnes, 1955). Of the many specific adaptations of spiders to their environment I shall select only those which show how well spiders can cope with rather extreme environmental conditions.

Thermoregulation

The ambient temperature is certainly important for determining the activity of a spider. Many web spiders, for instance, cease building their webs when the temperature drops below a critical point. Although spiders belong to the poikilothermic animals, it would be incorrect to believe that their body temperature simply follows the ambient air temperature. Spiders can adjust their behavior to keep their body temperature at a higher or lower level than that of the environment. Such thermoregulation is well known in lizards, yet a comparable ability in spiders has only recently been observed.

For example, the Australian wolf spider *Geolycosa godeffroyi* lives in a burrow in the soil but often comes up to the surface to warm its body in the sun (Humphreys, 1974, 1975). Its body temperature can then climb quickly to 40°C, although the ambient air temperature may be only between 15 and 25°C (Fig. 172). The spider avoids overheating by returning to its cool burrow; this situation is reversed at night, when the burrow provides insulation from the cold outside. In winter the spider has been found to maintain its body temperature at + 1.8°C inside the burrow while the outside temperature was − 2.5°C. Throughout the year, the spider maintains a body temperature that is, on average, 4 to 5°C above the ambient air temperature. An even larger temperature difference has been noted inside the egg sacs of *Geolycosa*, which the spider periodically exposes to the sun at the entrance of its burrow (see Fig. 166).

Behavioral thermoregulation has also been observed in various

Fig. 172.   Changes in the air temperature and body temperature of the wolf spider *Geolycosa* in a 24-hour period. Early in the morning (6^{00}), when the spider is still inside the burrow, its body temperature is 8°C higher than the ambient air temperature. Exposure to the sun results in a rapid increase in body temperature (first peak). The following fluctuations in body temperature result from the spider's shuttling between the warm outside and the cool burrow. (After Humphreys, 1974.)

web spiders. Some araneids (*Nephila, Cyrtophora*) of tropical and subtropical regions are often exposed to extreme solar radiation when they sit in the center of their webs. The spider reacts by adjusting the axis of its body to make it parallel to the incident sun rays, thus keeping the exposed body area to a minimum (Krakauer, 1972; Robinson and Robinson, 1974). The light-reflecting guanine crystals of the abdomen may also play a role in preventing overheating. If the body temperature increases to above 40°C, the spider withdraws into the shade (Blanke, 1972); such high temperatures cause an anesthesia-like state in the spider, and such stupors can easily be induced experimentally.

Some web spiders can also adjust their body temperatures to cold conditions. In Florida, for instance, *Nephila* may experience rather low temperatures during winter. In response, these spiders orient their webs in an east-west direction; the spider's body thus becomes fully exposed to the sun's rays and can reach 7°C above the ambient air temperature (Carrel, 1978).

Behaviorally mediated thermoregulation entails one disadvantage for spiders: a higher body temperature also means a higher transpiration rate and a correspondingly greater loss of water. If a spider loses more than 20% of its body weight because of transpiration, it will die (Cloudsley-Thompson, 1957). It seems, however, that most spiders can take up water from moist soil, provided that the humidity of the substrate is more than 12%. Normally, early morning dew is quite sufficient for that purpose.

Overwintering

In the temperate zones, poikilothermic animals have to adjust to the harsh cycles of the seasons. Spiders have developed several adaptations to survive such adverse conditions as cold, dampness, flooding—and naturally, lack of food. Spiders meet these challenges by colonizing the appropriate microhabitats, by increasing their resistance to cold, and by reducing their metabolic rate. They are thus well prepared for overwintering, and as a consequence, mortality during the cold winter months is surprisingly low.

About 85% of the spider fauna overwinters in the soil, mainly in leaf litter, which is a good insulator against the cold. During that time most spiders assume a rigid posture, with the legs drawn close to the body so that the exposed body surface is kept to a minimum. The microhabitat of the leaf litter zone protects not only from extreme temperature fluctuations but also from desiccation (Edgar and Loenen, 1974). Even heavy snow cover is by no means lethal for spiders. On the contrary, the insulating properties of a layer of snow ensure a rather steady temperature of about 0°C (Buche, 1966). Thus, ambient air temperatures of −40°C, which have been recorded, for example, in Canada, have little effect on the spiders beneath the snow (Aitchison, 1978, 1980).

Spiders of the temperate zones can be put into one of five groups, based on their annual cycles or periods of maturation (Schaefer, 1976, 1977): (1) *eurychronous* species, which take a long time to mature and overwinter in various developmental stages (these spiders constitute 23% of the species investigated); (2) *stenochronous* species whose reproductive period lasts from spring until summer and which overwinter as nymphs (45%); (3) *stenochronous* species whose period of reproduction is during the fall and whose young spiderlings remain inside the egg case during winter (7%); (4) *diplochronous* species, having two separate reproductive periods (spring and fall) and overwintering in the adult stage (4–13%); and (5) *stenochronous* species with their reproduction period in winter, the winter-active spiders (9%).

The winter-active spiders of the temperate zones belong mostly to the family Linyphiidae. They are not particularly resistant to cold but simply most active at rather low temperatures. Below −4°C they become as rigid as other spiders do, and below −7°C they die. Those spiders that overwinter passively are much more cold resistant. Most garden spiders (*Araneus* species) can withstand temperatures of −20°C, even in unprotected locations

(Kirchner, 1973). It is not quite clear how these spiders achieve their remarkable resistance to cold. It is known that the spider's hemolymph contains glycerol, which acts as an antifreezing agent, and that the glycerol content is markedly higher in winter than in summer. Nevertheless, it seems unlikely that the glycerol alone can account for such resistance to cold, since it has been found that this chemical lowers the freezing point of the spider's hemolymph by only 1°C (Kirchner and Kestler, 1969). On the other hand, a liny-phiid (*Bolyphantes*) spider's body fluid would normally freeze at − 1°C, yet antifreezing agents, perhaps proteinaceous, prevent the formation of ice crystals down to − 7°C (Husby and Zachariassen, 1980). At present we can state only that cold-resistant spiders are able to become extremely undercooled before their hemolymph freezes (Kirchner and Kullmann, 1975); the exact mechanism of this "supercooling" still needs to be clarified.

Special Adaptations: Camouflage and Mimicry

More impressive than the physiological adaptations of spiders toward the changing physical conditions of their environments are adaptations that protect spiders from their enemies. These protective measures range from simple camouflaging colors to complex behavior, including mimicry. Most spiders are rather drab and are not very noticeable within their environment. Even such conspicuously green species as *Micrommata virescens* or *Araniella cucurbitina* are difficult to detect in nature, because they live mostly on leaves. More interesting, however, are those spiders which can actively change their coloration to match the substrate they live on: the crab spiders *Misumena vatia* and *Thomisius onustus*, for example, change the color of their white or yellow abdomens to correspond to the white or yellow blossom on which they are sitting. This process usually takes a few days (Weigel, 1941). The advantage of this color adaptation is twofold: first, insects visiting the blossoms do not perceive the camouflaged spider and can be taken by surprise, and second, the spider is not recognized by its enemies (Bristowe, 1958). Some web spiders can also change their coloration gradually. If *Cyrtophora citricola* is kept in the dark for several weeks, its abdomen becomes markedly darker (Fig. 173; Blanke, 1972).

Aside from this slow color change, a rapid color change, as a kind of startle response, can also occur in some spiders. The tropical araneid *Cyrtophora cicatrosa* drops immediately out of its web when disturbed; at the same time, the color pattern of its abdomen changes rapidly so that the animal blends with its background (Blanke, 1975). This rapid color change probably results from a quick reduction of the light areas (that is, the guanine deposits) in the abdomen. The return to normal coloration takes only a few minutes.

Startle reactions among spiders, such as dropping suddenly on a thread, are quite common. When the spider falls to the ground, it often pulls its legs close to its body and "plays dead," a behavior that is termed *catalepsy*. Some web spiders, *Argiope*, for instance, react by violently shaking their webs if they are disturbed by sudden vibrations or by shadows passing overhead. The most striking response occurs in daddy-longleg spiders (Pholcidae), which can tremble so rapidly in their webs that they become too blurred to be seen. Many wandering spiders quickly assume defensive postures when threatened. The front legs are jerked upward, the chelicerae are widely spread, and the whole prosoma is lifted up (Tretzel, 1959). "Tarantulas" may remain in such threatening postures for several minutes.

Perhaps the most impressive adaptations are the various kinds

Fig. 173.   Slow darkening of the abdomen in *Cyrtophora citricola. (a)* Appearance under normal conditions, and (*b*) after 4 weeks in a dark room. (From Blanke, 1972.)

Fig. 174.   Ant mimicry. (*a*) The "model," the tropical ant *Ectatomma rui-dum.* (*b*) The "copy," the clubionid *Mazax pax*, which lives in the same habitat. Note the close resemblance in body size, shape, and coloration. (Photos, Reiskind.)

of mimicry. Spiders are renowned for their ant mimicry: several hundred species copy the shapes and body colors of ants and also move in a way that is very similar to that of ants. Striking examples are found in certain salticids and clubionids, whose short and sturdy forelegs look like the antennae of ants. This optical illusion is even more convincing when one watches a spider in motion: the forelegs are rarely used for walking but instead are raised above the body, quivering in an antlike fashion. The other legs are thin, and the prosoma (or opisthosoma) may be constricted so that the typical shape of an ant's body is achieved (Fig. 174). Of course, morphological and behavioral adaptations vary considerably among different spider species. Some species are only superficially antlike and still walk with all eight legs, whereas others are detailed copies of a specific ant species (Reiskind, 1977). The Central American *Castianeira rica* (Clubionidae) has one of the most interesting types of mimicry because it exhibits *multiple* mimicry (Reiskind, 1970). Females of this species look like a rather generalized version of the ant subfamily Ponerinae, but the bright orange males resemble ants of the genera *Atta* and *Odontomachus.* In contrast, the second and third nymphal stages of *C. rica* are black and shiny like ants of the subfamily Myrmicinae, while the fourth and fifth nymphs are yellow-orange, mimicking leaf-cutter ants (*Atta*).

The crucial question of ant mimicry, namely, whether the spider derives any advantage from its resemblance to ants, has been discussed quite often (Berland, 1932); certainly, there is little experimental evidence that would demonstrate a biological meaning for this mimicry. It has been proved, however, that birds cannot distinguish at least one ant mimic (*Synageles venator*, Salticidae) from the actual ant (Engelhardt, 1971). Furthermore, it is known that birds usually avoid eating ants, presumably because they are distasteful. In one experiment, when a *Synageles* was fed to a bird by hand, it was readily accepted; however, when *Synageles* was offered in a dish together with ants (*Lasius niger*), the bird ate neither. This speaks clearly in favor of protective mimicry (Batesian mimicry), for which a prerequisite is that the model and the mimic occur in the same habitat. This is indeed true for most cases of ant mimicry in spiders. Other, if more indirect, evidence, that ant mimicry is self-protective for spiders is provided by the ant-mimicking salticids *Synageles venator* and *Peckhamia picata*, which lay only three or four eggs: the low number of offspring must have a relatively good chance for survival; in other words, the species is little endangered by enemies.

Communication

As I mentioned in chapters 4 and 7, spiders have developed various means to communicate with each other. Especially during courtship, mechanical, chemical, or visual signals may play important roles in communication. The exchange of chemical signals was probably the first type of communication in spiders to evolve (Weygoldt, 1977), because contact chemoreceptors permit mutual identification of the sexual partners. Also important are receptors that perceive various mechanical signals, especially the vibrations transmitted by a web (Barth, 1982). It is quite likely that the vibrational signals emitted by web spiders during courtship are species-specific and thus also serve to identify potential mates (see Fig. 139). Wandering spiders also generate vibratory signals during courtship; the vibrations may be transmitted by a solid substrate (such as the ground or leaves) or through the air as sound. I restrict the following discussion of communication in spiders to the exchange of acoustical signals, because the other modes of communication have been described in chapter 7.

Like certain insects, several species of spiders produce sounds. They can use three methods: (1) *drumming* with parts of the body (palps, legs, or abdomen) against the substrate, (2) *stridulation*, that is, generating a sound on the spider's body by moving a "scraper" over a "file," and (3) *vibration* of legs (Rovner, 1980a). Drumming is seen in many male wolf spiders during courtship (see chapter 7). Since females react to it, the communicative function of drumming is clear. The situation is somewhat more complex for

Fig. 175. Stridulatory organs. (*a*) The kleptoparasite *Argyrodes* (Theridiidae) has strong cutilucar spines (S) on its opisthosoma (Op). The spines are scraped across the rippled area on the prosoma (Pro). The hair sensilla projecting from the opisthosoma may function as proprioreceptors. 400×, Photo: Vollrath and Foelix.) (*b*, and *c*) The male wolf spider *Pardosa fulvipes* has spiny bristles on the coxae of legs 4. These are rubbed over the rills on the cover of the book lungs. *b*, 70×; *c*, 1,250×. (Photos: Kronestedt.)

stridulation. Many types of stridulatory organs have been well described structurally, yet any communicative function ascribed to them has been met with skepticism (Berland, 1932; Legendre, 1963). However, investigations of the cobweb spider *Steatoda bipunctata* have now shown that stridulation is indeed involved both in courtship and in agonistic encounters (Gwinner-Hanke, 1970).

In *Steatoda bipunctata* only the adult male possesses stridulatory organs. These consist of ridged areas (1 mm²) on the prosoma that are apposed to strong cuticular spurs on the opisthosoma (see Fig. 175a). When the spider vibrates its abdomen vertically, the organs produce a faintly audible sound, as does a fingernail run along the teeth of a comb. The main frequency of the sound is around 1,000 Hz, or, as a music connoisseur would say, a C^{III}. The male stridulates only in the presence of a female or if a competing male is nearby. Proof that the stridulatory organs have a communicative function is seen from the female's reactions: she waves her forelegs, plucks the threads of her web, vibrates her entire body, and makes searching movements.

The male's direct contact with the female's web is not necessary, and this is evidence that the stridulatory signals are transmitted through the air as sound. When the stridulatory organs are put out of action by covering them with glue, the males do not start courtship at all. Courtship is probably elicited by chemical substances that adhere to the female's threads. These threads alone suffice to trigger the male's courtship; they fail to do so after the substances have been washed off with ether. In the related theridiid *Steatoda grossa*, however, it is not yet clear whether a communicative function can be assigned to the stridulatory organs, since the females do not show any definite reactions toward stridulating males (Gwinner-Hanke, 1970).

Morphologically, the stridulatory organs are always paired "files" that lie close to cuticular teeth on an adjacent body part. Eight types of stridulatory organs, occurring in over 100 species of 23 families, have been described (Legendre, 1963, 1970). In addition to the type described for *Steatoda* (opisthosoma-prosoma), stridulatory organs may lie between the chelicerae and the pedipalps (as they do in *Scytodes*) or between the opisthosoma and the fourth legs (Fig. 175b, c; Hinton and Wilson, 1970; Kronestedt, 1973). Many of the large "tarantulas" have stridulatory organs in both sexes, not just in males. When one of these spiders is threatened, it emits a hissing noise that is quite like the defensive hissing of a snake. In general, then, stridulatory organs may serve a defensive purpose when present in both sexes and are used for identification when restricted to the male of the species (Meyer, 1928).

Stridulation is quite common among crustaceans (in fiddler crabs, for example) and in insects. Crickets, grasshoppers, and cicadas use stridulation mainly to identify their own species. Many beetles, roaches, bugs, and butterflies also possess stridulatory organs, which in many cases serve to startle predators. In leaf-cutter ants stridulation functions as an alarm system: if an ant is in trouble, buried under sand or caught in a spider's web, it will stridulate vigorously; this attracts other ants in the vicinity which quickly come to the aid of the victim (Markl, 1967).

Social Spiders

Anyone who has collected live spiders knows that one has to keep them apart, or otherwise they are likely to kill each other. The reputation spiders have of being solitary and intolerant certainly has a lot of truth to it. And yet among the 30,000 different species of spiders about 20 species are known to live together in peaceful colonies; these are the social spiders.

Three preconditions are necessary for sociality (Kullmann, 1972b): (1) *tolerance*, that is, lack of aggression toward other members of the same species; (2) *interattraction*, a tendency to aggregate which is not simply caused by external factors; and (3) *cooperation*, the collaboration of individuals when hunting prey and when caring for offspring. About four species are known to fulfill all three requirements: *Agelena consociata* (Agelenidae) and *Stegodyphus sarasinorum* (Eresidae) in the Old World and *Anelosimus eximius* (Theridiidae) and *Mallos gregalis* (Dictynidae) in the New World. These species have not quite reached the eusocial level of ants, termites, bees, or wasps, because they have never developed a caste system; yet it still seems permissible to call them social, or at least quasi-social (for definitions of sociality see E. O. Wilson, 1971).

The most extensively studied social spider is the African funnelweb spider *Agelena consociata* (Fig. 176). Several hundred, or even a thousand, individuals may live together in one web without showing any animosity toward each other. This tolerance must no doubt be based on mutual recognition, because social spiders are just as aggressive toward their prey as are their solitary relatives. Most likely, a spider is recognized as a member of the same species by the typical vibrations it generates in its web. When a spider is made to vibrate artificially, its conspecifics attack it immediately. However, they quickly release it after they briefly touch it with their first tarsi. Sometimes they will also use their pedipalps for a closer inspection, but a spider of their own species will never be bitten. Probably, certain chemical substances (pheromones) help the spiders recognize a conspecific, since spiders washed with a mixture of ether and alcohol do get bitten (Krafft, 1971).

The chemical signals are apparently not very specific, because it is possible to exchange spiders from different web communities and even of different species without eliciting any aggressive reactions. For example, the solitary *Agelena labyrinthica* can be peacefully introduced into the web of the social *Agelena consociata* (Krafft, 1975). The social spiders thus differ remarkably from the "closed" societies of certain ants, where members of the same species from different nests often fight each other; the open societies of social spiders are more comparable to the anonymous schools of fish or flocks of birds. However, some kind of hierarchical system seems evident in *Agelena consociata* — at least, for example, when one of the spiders is to carry prey from the web to the retreat.

Even more impressive than the mutual tolerance of social spiders is their cooperation. Web building, prey catching, feeding, and brood care are often performed communally. Of course, cooperative web building is not particularly coordinated and is dic-

Fig. 176. Sociality in the African funnel-web spider *Agelena consociata.* (*a*) Two adult females in close contact on the communal sheet web. (*b*) During prey capture, several adults attack, while the young spiders wait at a distance. (Photos: Krafft.)

tated mainly by necessity. Several animals of different age classes spin largely independently of each other when repairing or extending the existent web structure.

Prey catching in *Agelena consociata* is also communal (Darchen, 1965; Krafft, 1971). When prey falls on the sheet web, its movements attract the attention of all spiders in the vicinity. If the prey is small (less than 1 cm), only a single adult spider rushes in, grasps the victim, bites it, and carries it off to the common retreat. There the actual feeding begins and as many other spiders participate as can find a place on the prey. If a larger prey animal has blundered into the web, several, mostly adult spiders attack it. Some hold fast to the legs or wings while others climb on the victim's back to inflict the poisonous bite. Nevertheless, only one spider carries off the prey to the retreat. The spiderlings do not participate in hunting but wait until food is brought to them by an adult spider. During the entire course of hunting and feeding, aggression is never displayed between conspecifics.

This social mode of life gives a species an important advantage. A group of cooperative spiders can overpower prey larger than a single spider could. In addition, sociality has other advantageous effects (group effects) that cannot be explained solely on the grounds of better nutrition: (1) a higher rate of metabolism and a more rapid growth, (2) a higher life expectancy, (3) a lower rate of mortality, and (4) a smaller number of eggs.

The fact that social spiders produce fewer eggs than their solitary relatives (*Agelena consociata*, 12; *Agelena labyrinthica*, 50–100) seems paradoxical at first. However, it is a general trend that a higher level of sociality correlates with a lower number of eggs laid. As in other animals, a relatively small number of offspring will suffice to continue the species if brood care is highly developed. The longer life of a spider within a group has been demonstrated in experiments where social spiders were kept singly and their life spans were compared to those of their grouped siblings (Darchen, 1965). Similar observations of social insects are well known: bees kept in isolation survive only for a few days, although inside the hive they live longer than a month.

Origin of Sociality

Social spiders have been found in quite different families, such as Amaurobiidae, Dictynidae, Eresidae, Oecobiidae, and Uloboridae among the cribellate spiders, and Agelenidae, Araneidae, Dipluridae, and Theridiidae among the ecribellates. Since these families

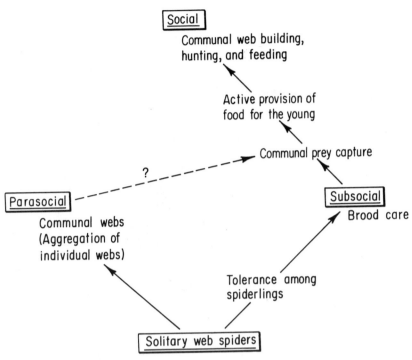

Fig. 177. Hypothetical origin of sociality in spiders. (After Shear, 1970.)

are hardly related, sociality in spiders must have evolved independently several times. How did this sociality originate?

Only a few of the approximately 20 species of social spiders have members that live together on a permanent basis, while all the other species are only "periodically social"; that is, their individuals congregate only temporarily (Kullmann, 1972b). Furthermore, although some species (some of the Araneidae and the Uloboridae, for example) form web colonies, each member retains its individual snare (Buskirk, 1975). One might refer to such loosely organized web colonies, which lack any cooperation, as *parasocial*. Those species in which the temporary social bond is closely linked with brood care may be termed *subsocial*. It is now generally assumed that evolution from a solitary to a permanently social mode of life has proceeded through various subsocial stages (Fig. 177). Quite likely, any higher form of sociality originated from a mother-offspring relationship (Markl, 1971). This relationship seems to be

Fig. 178. (*a*) Communal hunting in the theridiid *Anelosimus eximius.* Several females fling sticky threads over a fly that got entangled in the mesh of the cobweb. (*b*) Young spiderlings gather around a female to be fed mouth-to-mouth (left) or they may feed communally on the prey killed by the adults (right).

the basis of social systems of insects and spiders as well as of the highly organized social systems of certain mammals.

The evolutionary origins of sociality in spiders must be sought among the solitary *web* spiders, since their threads certainly play a central role in communication between individual spiders. Among the freely roaming wandering spiders we do not find any social species, probably because the "connecting wire" is lacking. Within some spider families (such as Eresidae and Theridiidae) we can find several different "periodically social" stages that ultimately may have led to permanent sociality (Kullmann, 1972b). Among theridiid species one can observe gradually improved methods of brood care, starting with mere guarding of the egg case, followed by passive provision of the brood with food (that is, the dead mother may serve as their nourishment), and finally, actively supplying food for the spiderlings. Examples for the latter are regurgitative feeding, carrying prey to the young, and communal prey hunting and feeding. Each increase in the complexity of brood care denotes a higher level of sociality.

A comparison between the two social theridiids *Anelosimus eximius* and *Anelosimus studiosus* is enlightening in this regard (Brach, 1975, 1977). *A. eximius* can be regarded as a typical social spider, since these spiders demonstrate tolerance, interattraction, and cooperation (Fig. 178) almost as well as *Agelena consociata*. In *A. studiosus*, however, tolerance is not permanent among the members of a colony. After the death of the colony founder, the mother, the colony remains together peacefully only until one sibling female has reached maturity. This female then tolerates only juvenile spiders and adult males, but chases any other adult females away. This aggression toward conspecific females precludes the formation of large colonies in this species. In contrast, up to 1,000 individuals may live together peacefully in one web of the consistently placid *A. eximius*.

10

Phylogeny and Systematics

Now a book on biology is hardly the place to insert a chapter on classification.

W. S. Bristowe, 1938

DESPITE Bristowe's warning it seems necessary to cover briefly the descent and classification of spiders. I must admit, however, that our real knowledge of the phylogeny of spiders is very scanty, and hence to present any reliable pedigree is quite impossible.

Fossils

Fossils of spiders are rare and have been found only from widely separate geological eras. Although several fossils of spiders (*Arthrolycosa, Protolycosa*) have been preserved from the Carboniferous period of the Paleozoic era 300 million years ago, none have remained from the entire Mesozoic era. Only from the early Tertiary period, the Oligocene epoch, 30 million years ago, do we know of fossils of spiders again, mostly in the form of well-preserved amber spiders. These spiders from the Tertiary period, however, resemble recent spider families so closely that they provide hardly any clues as to their phylogeny.

The first spiders probably appeared during the Devonian period, almost 400 million years ago. The arachnids were quite likely at their peak during the Paleozoic era, since 4 of the 16 known arachnid orders were already extinct by the Carboniferous period (Petrunkevitch, 1955). During that time the evolution of insects was still in its infancy, and flying was just about to be "invented" (Bristowe, 1958). The ancient spiders (Araneae) of the Carboniferous period were all segmented, quite similar to the Mesothelae (Liphistiidae) that still live today. It is for this reason that the liphistiids are considered the most primitive of all living spiders and are often referred to as "living fossils." The Paleozoic spiders *Arthrolycosa* (Fig. 179a) and *Protolycosa* were certainly closely related to the liphistiids of today (Petrunkevitch, 1955). Yet probably even during the Carboniferous period there were other spiders with segmented abdomens not closely related to the liphistiids (such as the Archaeometidae). Remnants of abdominal segmentation are still clearly present in some recent spider families, for example, in the cribellate Hypochilidae as well as in several orthognath spiders of the Antrodiaetidae family.

Evolutionary Trends

Because our paleontological record of fossilized spiders is so skimpy, we must apply indirect methods to elucidate—at least partly—their phylogeny. Comparative studies of the spider's closest living relatives, the whip spiders (order Amblypygi), and of spider embryology are particularly suited for that purpose. A reconstruction of the Paleozoic archetype of a spider would exhibit the following characteristics (Fig. 177b; Bristowe, 1958; Savory, 1971):

6 prosomal and 12 abdominal segments consisting of tergites and
   sternites
Body segment 8 bearing the genital opening
Body segments 8 and 9 with respiratory organs
Body segments 10 and 11 carrying spinnerets
Prosoma and opisthosoma initially broadly joined together, later
   constricted at the pedicel
Prosoma consisting initially of 6 segments, later of a single plate
   (carapace)
Chelicerae of two or three segments, formerly chelate (pincers)
Palps resembling legs

During the course of their evolution arachnids acquired several new characteristics that can be explained primarily as adaptations

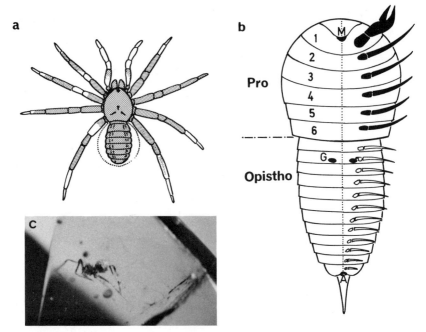

Fig. 179. (a) The fossil spider *Arthrolycosa antiqua* from the Carboniferous period of North America. Preserved body parts are stippled. (After Petrunkevitch, 1955.) (b) Hypothetical archetype of a chelicerate from which
the various arachnid orders may be derived. M = mouth opening, G =
genital opening, A = anus, 1–6 = prosomal segments. (After Størmer,
1955.) (c) Small amber spider (1 mm body length, a linyphiid?) that became fossilized in a drop of resin about 40 million years ago (found in the
Dominican Republic).

to a terrestrial mode of life (Grasshoff, 1978). For instance, preoral
digestion, typical of arachnids, is possible only on land. Concomitantly more efficient mouth parts were needed, and apparently the
palpal coxae were best suited, and thus were preadapted, for that
purpose. Also, the chelicerae may have proved to be more efficient
tools than pincers, once their terminal segment was modified into
a movable claw and the basal segment became mainly a site of
muscle attachment. Further improvements were certainly the development of cheliceral poison glands and a second, postcerebral
pump (the sucking stomach), within the intestinal tract. Other
changes involved: (1) a general reduction of body segmentation, (2)
a constriction of the 7th segment, which led to the formation of the
typical pedicel, (3) the hydraulic extension of some leg joints, (4) a

direct transfer of sperm with modified palps instead of deposited spermatophores, and finally, (5) a development and refinement of spinning apparatus for use in prey catching. In general, spiders probably became gradually smaller and lived shorter lives, while their entire behavioral repertoire became more complex.

Classification

A "natural system" of animal classification should mirror the relationships among different species. Since direct kinships of spiders can not be proved, because of the lack of any continuous fossil records, spider systematics is based almost entirely on comparative morphology. The procedure commonly used is to regard certain characters as primitive (*plesiomorphic*) and others as derived (*apomorphic*). For instance, the orthognath position of the chelicerae is considered plesiomorphic, whereas the labidognath position represents an apomorphic state. If within two different groups the same (homologous) character has been changed in the same way, it is referred to as *synapomorphic*, and a direct interrelationship between the groups ("sister groups") is deduced. This mode of classification implies that the direction, or polarity, of the evolutionary pathway is known.

In practice, however, it is not always simple to decide whether a certain character state is primitive or derived. One possible method of deciding is to assume that a character is apomorphic if it represents an adaptive improvement of a basic construction. Since evolution is probably directed toward an improvement of efficiency, any changes of a phylogenetic character may be thought of as a part of a continuous process of adaptation. Thus the polarity of a character transformation can be determined, and—at least hypothetically—the evolutionary pathway can be reconstructed (Grasshoff, 1975). To date, all spider systems are based on similarities, and depending on which and how many characters are being considered—and how they are appraised—taxonomists arrive at widely different classifications. Therefore it comes as no surprise that "spider classification at the present is in chaos," as H. W. Levi has said (1978).

Suborders

Most of the present classifications of spiders are derived from the system of the French arachnologist Eugène Simon, and an abbreviated form of that system has been presented in chapter 1. Systematicists are already in disagreement over the various suborders, especially over the position of the Mesothelae (Liphistiidae). Although some authors (Millot, 1949; Glatz, 1973) group them with the "tarantulas" into one suborder Orthognatha, others assign the Mesothelae a much more isolated position (Platnick and Gertsch, 1976): they are thought to be a sister group of all other recent spiders, which are then classified as the suborder Opisthothelae. Similarities that no doubt exist between Liphistiidae and some orthognath families (such as an abdominal segmentation in the Antrodiaetidae) are not considered synapomorphic but symplesiomorphic and thus do not indicate direct relationships. In most current systems of classification, the order Araneae (Araneida) is divided into three suborders of equal rank, namely, the Mesothelae, the Orthognatha (Mygalomorphae), and the Labidognatha (Araneomorphae).

The Cribellate Problem. The common subdivision of labidognath spiders into two groups, the Cribellatae and the Ecribellatae, according to the presence or absence of a cribellum, has been questioned repeatedly (see Lehtinen, 1967). In general, cribellate forms are considered primitive (plesiomorphic), because the cribellum corresponds to the anterior median spinnerets of the Mesothelae. The ecribellate forms lack both a cribellum and anterior median spinnerets; instead they may possess a vestigial structure with no apparent function, the colulus. Based on embryological studies, however, anterior median spinnerets, cribellum, and colulus are believed to be homologous structures.

Now, what relationships exist between the Cribellatae and the Ecribellatae? Did they evolve independently from a common ancestral group? Or is one derived from the other? Is there any fundamental difference at all between cribellate and ecribellate spiders?

Most arachnologists agree that cribellate spiders are monophyletic, that is, that they are all descendants of a common ancestor. It is argued to be highly improbable that a complex character combination like the cribellum-calamistrum could have evolved independently several times. However, many ecribellate spiders hardly differ from some cribellate forms except that they lack such a cribellum-calamistrum complex. One could deduce then that ecribellates may have evolved from cribellates by having lost their cribellum and calamistrum. To put it pointedly: ecribellates are in fact cribellate spiders which have simply lost their cribellum during their evolution. But have *all* ecribellate spiders passed through a cribellate stage? If so, such a transition would have taken place more than 30 times, independent of each other, during the spider's phylogeny. An alternative explanation would assume that, through convergent evolution, similar spider families developed among the cribellates and the ecribellates—comparable to the parallel evolution of marsupials and the other mammals.

Both interpretations may be valid. Transformations from a cribellate to an ecribellate form probably occurred between the Oecobiidae and the Urocteidae (Kullmann and Zimmermann, 1976), or from the Psechridae to the Lycosidae (Homann, 1971). In contrast, the similarities between the ecribellate orb weavers Araneidae and the cribellate Uloboridae are more likely the result of convergence. Superficially, the orb webs of both are strikingly similar, but a closer investigation reveals distinctly different catching threads (araneids use glue, while uloborids use cribellate wool) that originate from different, nonhomologous silk glands. It is thus difficult to imagine that the araneid orb web evolved from a uloborid orb; more likely both webs are merely analogous snares (Kullmann, Nawabi, and Zimmermann, 1971/72).

Subdividing the Ecribellatae. The grouping of ecribellate spiders into Haplogynae and Entelegynae is nowadays considered largely artificial, especially with respect to the heterogeneous group of Haplogynae (Cooke, 1970; Brignoli, 1975; Lehtinen, 1975). A further subdivision of the Entelegynae into Dionycha (spiders with two claws) and Trionycha (those with three claws) can also no longer be maintained, since even within a single family there may be genera with two or three claws; furthermore, even within the same species (such as those of *Ctenus* and *Phoneutria*) adults may have two claws while their nymphs have three (Homann, 1971). Probably the third, median claw has been reduced repeatedly as spiders converted from a life inside a web to free hunting. The third claw thus is not a useful taxonomic character, although it can be quite convenient for identification.

Family Relationships

The number, position, relative size, and internal structure of the eyes are very important characters for classifying spider families. In ancient spiders all eight eyes were probably the same size but then developed differently during their phylogeny. The lateral eyes, which can be separated into three groups according to the type of tapetum present, are systematically quite useful, since their synapomorphies can be established rather well (Homann, 1971).

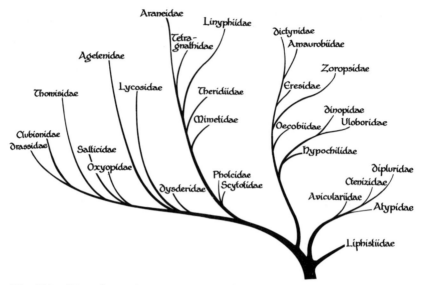

Fig. 180.   Hypothetical pedigree of the major spider families. (After Bristowe, 1938, 1958.)

Probably all complex lateral eyes with a grated tapetum are of monophyletic origin; at the same time they represent an apomorphic character. This means that all spiders with a grated tapetum are related to one another, for example, the Psechridae, Zoropsidae, Lycosidae, Oxyopidae, and Senoculidae. It seems noteworthy that these families contain both cribellate and ecribellate forms. As I have already pointed out, the Lycosidae are presumably derived from the Psechridae by loss of the cribellum. Like the reduction of the third claw, the loss of the cribellum may be correlated with the transition from life within a web (Psechridae) to free hunting (Lycosidae).

Whereas genital structures are used mainly for the separation of species, the classification of families relies on the structure of the spinnerets, chelicerae, tarsal claws, and the labium. The "chaos" of the present systems of spider classification is caused less by the different opinions of systematicists about the facts than by their interpretation of them. At present many "classical" families are radically rearranged and may even group cribellate and ecribellate forms within the same genus (Lehtinen, 1967; Forster and Wilton, 1973).

A "classical" family tree of spiders concludes this chapter (Fig.

180). I do not mean to denigrate modern cladograms (which define sister groups but not direct ancestor-descendant relationships), but the lay reader, unfamiliar with the esoterics of spider classification, should be given a basic scheme so that he or she can see how the many different spider families may be related to each other. Nobody is more aware of the hypothetical and subjective nature of such a pedigree than Bristowe himself when he cites Sir James Frazer: "Now as always I hold all my theories very lightly, and am ever ready to modify or abandon them in the light of new evidence."

References

Aitchison, C. W.: Spiders active under snow in southern Canada. Symp. Zool. Soc. Lond. 42 (1978) 139

Aitchison, C. W.: A preliminary study of the phenology of winter-active spiders. Proc. 8th Int. Congr. Arachnol. (Vienna, 1980), p. 61

Anderson, J. F.: Metabolic rates of spiders. Comp. Biochem. Physiol. 33 (1970) 51

Anderson, J. F.: Responses to starvation in the spiders *Lycosa lenta* Hentz and *Filistata hibernalis* (Hentz). Ecology 55 (1974) 576

Anderson, J. F., K. N. Prestwich: The fluid pressure pumps of spiders (Chelicerata, Araneae). Z. Morph. Tiere 81 (1975) 257

André, J., C. Rouiller: The ultrastructure of the vitelline body in the oocyte of the spider *Tegenaria parietina*. J. Biophys. Biochem. Cytol. 3 (1957) 977

Angersbach, D.: Oxygen pressures in haemolymph and various tissues of the tarantula *Eurypelma helluo*. J. Comp. Physiol. 98 (1975) 133

Aspey, W. P.: Agonistic behaviour and dominance-subordinance relationships in the wolf spider *Schizocosa crassipes*. Proc. 6th Int. Arachnol. Congr. (Amsterdam, 1975), p. 102

Babu, K. S.: Anatomy of the central nervous system of arachnids. Zool. Jb. Anat. 82 (1965) 1

Babu, K. S.: Certain histological and anatomical features of the central nervous system of a large Indian spider, *Poecilotheria*. Amer. Zool. 9 (1969) 113

Babu, K. S.: Histology of the neurosecretory system and neurohaemal organs of the spider *Argiope aurantia* (Lucas). J. Morphol. 141 (1973) 77

Babu, K. S.: Post embryonic development of the central nervous system of the spider *Argiope aurantia* (Lucas). J. Morphol. 146 (1975) 325

Baccetti, B., R. Dallai, F. Rosati: The spermatozoon of arthropoda. VIII. The 9+3 flagellum of spider sperm cells. J. Cell Biol. 44 (1970) 681

Bachmann, M.: Das Gift der orthognathen Spinne *Pterinochilus* spec. Isolierung und teilweise biochemische und biologische Charakterisierung eines Neurotoxins und einer Hyaluronidase. Doct. thesis, University of Basel, 1976

Baerg, W. J.: The life cycle and mating habits of the male tarantula. Quart. Rev. Biol. 3 (1928) 109

Balogh, J. I.: Vorläufige Mitteilung über radnetzbauende Pachygnathen. Fol. Zool. Hydrobiol. 6 (1934) 94

Baltzer, F.: Über die Orientierung der Trichterspinne *Agelena labyrinthica* (Cl.) nach der Spannung des Netzes. Rev. Suisse Zool. 37 (1930) 363

Barnes, R. D., B. M. Barnes: The spider population of the abstract broomsedge community of the southeastern Piedmont. Ecology 36 (1955) 658

Barrows, W. M.: The reactions of an orb-weaving spider, *Epeira sclopetaria* Clerck, to rhythmic vibrations of its web. Biol. Bull. 29 (1915) 316

Bartels, M.: Sinnesphysiologische und psychologische Untersuchungen an der Trichterspinne *Agelena labyrinthica* (Cl.). Z. vergl. Physiol. 10 (1929) 527

Bartels, M.: Über den Fressmechanismus und chemischen Sinn einiger Netzspinnen. Rev. Suisse Zool. 37 (1930) 1

Bartels, M., F. Baltzer: Über Orientierung und Gedächtnis der Netzspinne *Agelena labyrinthica*. Rev. Suisse Zool. 35 (1928) 247

Barth, F. G.: Ein einzelnes Spaltsinnesorgan auf dem Spinnentarsus: Seine Erregung in Abhängigkeit von den Parametern des Luftschallreizes. Z. vergl. Physiol. 55 (1967) 407

Barth, F. G.: Die Feinstruktur des Spinneninteguments. I. Die Cuticula des Laufbeins adulter häutungsferner Tiere (*Cupiennius salei* Keys.). Z. Zellforsch. 97 (1969) 137

Barth, F. G.: Die Feinstruktur des Spinneninteguments. II. Die räumliche Anordnung der Mikrofasern in der lamellierten Cuticula und ihre Beziehung zur Gestalt der Porenkanäle (*Cupiennius salei* Keys., adult, häutungsfern, Tarsus). Z. Zellforsch. 104 (1970) 87

Barth, F. G.: Der sensorische Apparat der Spaltsinnesorgane (*Cupiennius salei* Keys., Araneae). Z. Zellforsch. 112 (1971) 212

Barth, F. G.: Die Physiologie der Spaltsinnesorgane. I. Modellversuche zur Rolle des cuticularen Spaltes beim Reiztransport. J. Comp. Physiol. 78 (1972a) 315

Barth, F. G.: Die Physiologie der Spaltsinnesorgane. II. Funktionelle Morphologie eines Mechanoreceptors. J. Comp. Physiol. 81 (1972b) 159

Barth, F. G.: Microfiber reinforcement of an arthropod cuticule. Laminated composite material in biology. Z. Zellforsch. 144 (1973a) 409

Barth, F. G.: Bauprinzipien und adäquater Reiz bei einem Mechanoreceptor. Verh. dtsch. zool. Ges. 66 (1973b) 25

Barth, F. G.: Sensory information from strains in the exoskeleton. In *The Insect Integument*, edited by H. R. Hepburn (Amsterdam: Elsevier, 1976), p. 445

Barth, F. G.: Spiders and vibratory signals. Sensory reception and behavioral significance. In *Communication in Spiders*, edited by J. Rovner and P. Witt (Princeton: Princeton University Press, 1982), in press

Barth, F. G., W. Libera: Ein Atlas der Spaltsinnesorgane von *Cupiennius salei* Keys. Chelicerata (Araneae). Z. Morph. Tiere 68 (1970) 343

Barth, F. G., P. Pickelmann: Lyriform slit sense organs. Modelling an arthropod mechanoreceptor. J. Comp. Physiol. 103 (1975) 39

Baschwitz, G. G.: Sobre la ultraestructura del endosternito de *Araneus diadematus* Clerck. Rev. Fac. Cienc. Oviedo 14 (1973) 37

Baschwitz, G. G.: Sobre las conexiones musculares de los aracnidos. Rev. Fac. Cienc. Oviedo 15 (1974) 43

Bauer, K.-H.: Funktionsmechanismus der Autotomie bei Spinnen (Araneae) und seine morphologischen Voraussetzungen. Z. Morph. Tiere 72 (1972) 173

Bays, S. M.: A study on the training possibilities of *Araneus diadematus* Cl. Experientia (Basel) 18 (1962) 423

Bell, A. L., D. B. Peakall: Changes in the fine structure during silk protein production in the ampullate gland of the spider *Araneus sericatus*. J. Cell Biol. 42 (1969) 284

Berland, L.: Les Arachnides. In *Encyclopédie entomologique* (Paris: Lechevalier, 1932), p. 79

Bertkau, P.: Über den Verdauungsapparat der Spinnen. Arch. mikr. Anat. 24 (1885) 398

Blanke, R.: Untersuchungen zur Ökophysiologie und Ökethologie von *Cyrtophora citricola* Forskal (Araneae, Araneidae) in Andalusien. Forma et functio 5 (1972) 125

Blanke, R.: Neue Ergebnisse zum Sexualverhalten von *Araneus cucurbitinus* Cl. (Araneae, Araneidae). Forma et functio 6 (1973a) 279

Blanke, R.: Nachweis von Pheromonen bei Netzspinnen. Naturwissenschaften 10 (1973b) 481

Blanke, R.: Rolle der Beute beim Kopulationsverhalten von *Meta segmentata* (Cl.) (Araneae, Araneidae). Forma et functio 7 (1974a) 83

Blanke, R.: Der Zusammenhang zwischen Beuteangebot und Reproduktionsrate bei *Cyrtophora citricola* Forskal (Araneae, Araneidae). Beitr. naturk. Forsch. Südw.-Dtl. 33 (1974b) 223

Blanke, R.: Die Bedeutung der Guanocyten für den physiologischen Farbwechsel bei *Cyrtophora cicatrosa* (Arachnida: Araneidae). Ent. Germ. 2 (1975a) 1

Blanke, R.: Untersuchungen zum Sexualverhalten von *Cyrtophora cicatrosa* (Stoliczka) (Araneae, Araneidae). Z. Tierpsychol. 37 (1975b) 62

Blest, A. D., M. F. Land: The physiological optics of *Dinopis subrufus* L. Koch: a fish-lens in a spider. Proc. Roy. Soc. B 196 (1977) 197

Blumenthal, H.: Untersuchungen über das "Tarsalorgan" der Spinnen. Z. Morph. Ökol. Tiere 29 (1935) 667

Boissin, L.: Etude ultrastructurale de la spermiogenèse de *Meta bourneti* Simon (Arachnides, Aranéides, Metinae). 2ième Réun. Arachnol. Langue Franç. (Montpellier, 1973), p. 7

Bonaric, J. C.: Effects of ecdysterone on the molting mechanisms and duration of the intermolt period in *Pisaura mirabilis*. Gen. Comp. Endocr. 30 (1976) 267

Bonaric, J. C., M. de Reggi: Changes in ecdysone levels in the spider *Pisaura mirabilis* nymphs (Araneae, Pisauridae). Experientia 33 (1977) 1664

Bonnet, P.: La mue, l'autotomie et la régénération chez les Araignées, avec une étudè des Dolomèdes d'Europe. Bull. Soc. Hist. Nat. Toulouse 59 (1930) 237

Bösenberg, H.: Beiträge zur Kenntnis der Spermatogenese bei den Arachnoiden. Zool. Jb. Anat. 21 (1905) 505

Boys, C. V.: The influence of a tuning fork on the garden spider. Nature (London) 23 (1881) 149

Brach, V.: The biology of the social spider *Anelosimus eximius* (Araneae: Theridiidae). Bull. Southern Calif. Acad. Sci. 74 (1975) 37

Brach, V.: *Anelosimus studiosus* (Araneae: Theridiidae) and the evolution of quasisociality in theridiid spiders. Evolution 31 (1977) 154

Braun, F.: Beiträge zur Biologie und Atmungsphysiologie der *Argyroneta aquatica* Cl. Zool. Jb. Syst. 62 (1931) 175

Braunitzer, G., D. Wolff: Vergleichende chemische Untersuchungen über die Fibroine von *Bombyx mori* und *Nephila madagascariensis*. Z. Naturforsch. 10b (1955) 404

Brenner, H. R.: Evidence for peripheral inhibition in an arachnid muscle. J. Comp. Physiol. 80 (1972) 227

Breymeyer, A.: Preliminary data estimating the biological production of wandering spiders, edited by K. Petrusewicz (Warsaw, 1967), p. 821

Breymeyer, A., J. Jóźwik: Consumption of wandering spiders (Lycosidae, Araneae) estimated in laboratory conditions. Bull. Acad. Polon. Sci. Sér. Sci. Biol. 23 (1975) 93

Brignoli, P. M.: Über die Gruppe der Haplogynae (Araneae). Proc. 6th Int. Arachnol. Congr. 1974. (Amsterdam, 1975) p. 33

Bristowe, W. S.: The mating habits of spiders, with special reference to the problems surrounding sex dimorphism. Proc. Zool. Soc. (London) 100 (1929) 309

Bristowe, W. S.: The liphistiid spiders. With an appendix on their internal anatomy by J. Millot. Proc. Zool. Soc. (London) 103 (1932) 1015

Bristowe, W. S.: The classification of spiders. Proc. Zool. Soc. (London) 108 (1938) 285

Bristowe, W. S.: The Comity of Spiders. Ray Soc. No. 126, London 1939

Bristowe, W. S.: The Comity of Spiders. Ray Soc. No. 128, London 1941

Bristowe, W. S.: *The World of Spiders.* London: Collins, 1958

Bristowe, W. S.: Notes on rare spiders and courtship as a clue to relationships. Proc. Southern London Entomol. Nat. Hist. Soc. (1962) 184

Bristowe, W. S.: Eine Familie lebender Fossilien. Endeavour 34 (1975) 115

Bristowe, W. S., G. H. Locket: The courtship of British lycosid spiders and its probable significance. Proc. Zool. Soc. (London) (1926) 317

Bristowe, W. S., J. Millot: The Liphistiid spiders. Proc. Zool. Soc. (London) 103 (1933) 1015

Browning, H. C.: The integument and moult cycle of *Tegenaria atrica* (Araneae). Proc. Roy. Soc. B 131 (1942) 65

Buche, W.: Beiträge zur Ökologie und Biologie winterreifer Kleinspinnen mit besonderer Berücksichtigung der Linyphiidae *Macrargus rufus rufus* (Wider), *Macrargus rufus carpenteri* (Cambridge) und *Centromerus silvaticus* (Blackwall). Z. Morph. Ökol. Tiere 57 (1966) 329

Bücherl, W.: Novo processo de obtençao de veneno sèco, puro, de *Phoneutria nigriventer* (Keyserling 1891) e titulaçao da LD_{50} em camundongos. Mem. Inst. Butantan 25 (1953) 153

Bücherl, W.: Südamerikanische Spinnen und ihre Gifte. Arzneimittel-Forsch. 6 (1956) 293

Buchli, H. R.: Hunting behaviour in the Ctenizidae. Amer. Zool. 9 (1969) 175

Burch, T. L.: The importance of communal experience to survival for spiderlings of *Araneus diadematus* (Araneae: Araneidae). J. Arachnol. 7 (1979) 1

Buskirk, R. E.: Coloniality, activity patterns and feeding in a tropical orb-weaving spider. Ecology 56 (1975) 1314

Buxton, B. H.: Coxal glands of the arachnids. Zool. Jb. Anat. 37 (1913) 231

Carrel, J. E.: Behavioral thermoregulation during winter in an orb-weaving spider. Symp. Zool. Soc. Lond. 42 (1978) 41

Carrel, J. E., R. D. Heathcote: Heart rate in spiders: Influence of body size and foraging energetics. Science 193 (1976) 148

Ceccarelli, B., F. Grohovatz, W. P., Hurlbut, N. Jezzi: Freeze-fracture studies of frog neuromuscular junctions during intense release of neurotransmitter. I. Effects of black widow spider venom and Ca^{2+}-free solutions on the structure of the active zone. J. Cell. Biol. 81 (1979) 163

Christian, U.: Zur Feinstruktur der Trichobothrien der Winkelspinne *Tegenaria derhami* (Scopoli), (Agelenidae, Araneae). Cytobiologie 4 (1971) 172

Christian, U. H.: Trichobothrien, ein Mechanorezeptor bei der Winkelspinne *Tegenaria derhami* (Scopoli) (Agelenidae, Araneae). Verh. dtsch. zool. Ges. 66 (1973) 31

Clark, A. W., W. P. Hurlbut, A. Mauro: Changes in the fine structure of the neuromuscular junction of the frog caused by Black Widow spider venom. J. Cell Biol. 52 (1972) 1

Cloudsley-Thompson, J. L.: Studies in diurnal rhythms. V. Nocturnal ecology and water-relations of the British cribellate spiders of the genus *Ciniflo* Bl. J. Linn. Soc. Zool. 43 (1957) 134

Cloudsley-Thompson, J. L.: The water-relations of scorpions and tarantulas from the Sonoran desert. Entomol. Mon. Mag. 103 (1968) 217

Cloudsley-Thompson, J. L.: Biological clocks in Arachnida. Bull. Brit. Arachnol. Soc. 4 (1978) 184

Collatz, K.-G., T. Mommsen: Lebensweise und jahreszyklische Veränderungen des Stoffbestandes der Spinne *Tegenaria atrica* C. L. Koch (Agelenidae). J. Comp. Physiol. 91 (1974) 91

Collatz, K.-G., T. Mommsen: Veränderung der Körperzusammensetzung und der Stoffwechselintensität der Spinne *Tegenaria atrica* C. L. Koch (Agelenidae) nach kurzem und langem Hunger. J. Comp. Physiol. 98 (1975) 205

Cooke, J. A. L.: Synopsis of the structure and function of the genitalia in *Dysdera crocata* (Araneae, Dysderidae). Senck. Biol. 47 (1966) 35

Cooke, J. A. L.: Spider genitalia and phylogeny. Bull. Mus. Nat. Hist. Natur. 41 (1970) 142

Cooke, J. A. L., V. D. Roth, F. H. Miller: The urticating hairs of theraphosid spiders. Amer. Mus. Novitates 2498 (1972) 1

Cooke, J. A. L., F. H. Miller, R. W. Grover, J. L. Duffy: Urticaria caused by tarantula hairs. Amer. J. Trop. Med. Hyg. 22 (1973) 130

Crane, J.: Comparative biology of salticid spiders at Rancho Grande, Venezuela. IV. An analysis of display. Zoologica 34 (1949) 159

Crome, W.: Die Respirations- und Circulationsorgane der *Argyroneta aquatica* Cl. (Araneae). Wiss. Z. Humboldt Univ. Berlin 2, Math.-naturwiss. Reihe 3/4 (1953) 53

Crome, W.: Kokonbau und Eiablage einiger Kreuzspinnenarten des Genus *Araneus* (Araneae, Araneidae). Dtsch. Ent. Z. (N. F.) 3 (1956a) 28

Crome, W.: Taranteln, Skorpione und Schwarze Witwen. Die Neue Brehm Bücherei. (Wittenberg Lutherstadt: Ziemsen, 1956b), p. 4

Crome, W.: Arachnida-Spinnentiere. In *Exkursionsfauna von Deutschland*, vol. I: Wirbellose, edited by E. Stresemann (Berlin: VEB Volk und Wissen, 1957), p. 289

Crome, W.: Embryonalentwicklung ohne ,Umrollung' (= Reversion) bei Vogelspinnen (Araneae: Orthognatha). Dtsch. Ent. Z. (N. F.) 10 (1963) 83

Crome, W., I. Crome: "Wachstum ohne Häutung" und Entwicklungsvorgänge bei den Weibchen von *Argyope bruennichi* (Scopoli) (Araneae: Araneidae). Dtsch. Ent. Z. (N. F.) 8 (1961) 443

Cutler, B., A. G. Richards: On the absence of chitin in the endosternite of chelicerata. Experientia (Basel) 30 (1974) 1393

Czajka, M.: Unknown facts of the biology of the spider *Ero furcata* (Villers). Pol. Pismo Entomol. 33 (1963) 229

Dabelow, S.: Zur Biologie der Leimschleuderspinne *Scytodes thoracica*. Zool. Jb. Syst. 86 (1958) 85

Dahl, F.: Über die Hörhaare bei Arachnoideen. Zool. Anz. 6 (1883) 276

Darchen, R.: Ethologie d'une araignée sociale, *Agelena consociata* Denis. Biol. Gabonica 1 (1965) 117

Dawydoff, C.: Développement embryonnaire des Arachnides. In *Traité de Zoologie*, vol. VI, edited by P.-P Grassé (Paris: Masson, 1949), p. 320.

Deevey, G. B.: The blood cells of the Haitian tarantula and their relation to the moulting cycle. J. Morph. 68 (1941) 457

Den Otter, C. J.: Setiform sensilla and prey detection in the Bird-Spider *Sericopelma rubronitens* Ausserer (Araneae, Theraphosidae). Neth. J. Zool. 24 (1974) 219

De Voe, R. D.: Ultraviolet and green receptors in principal eyes of jumping spiders. J. Gen. Physiol. 66 (1975) 193

Dijkstra, H.: Comparative research of the courtship behaviour in the genus Pardosa (Arachn., Araneae) III. Agonistic behaviour in *Pardosa amentata*. Bull. Mus. Natl. Hist. Natur. 41 (1970) 91

Dijkstra, H.: Searching behaviour and tactochemical orientation in males of the wolfspider *Pardosa amentata* (Cl.) (Araneae, Lycosidae). Proc. kon. ned. Akad. Wet. Ser. C 79 (1976) 235

Dillon, L. S.: The myology of the araneid leg. J. Morph. 90 (1952) 467

Dondale, C. D., B. M. Hegdekar: The contact sex pheromone of *Pardosa lapidicina* Emerton (Araneida: Lycosidae). Can. J. Zool. 51 (1973) 400

Dornfeldt, K.: Die Bedeutung der Haupt- und Nebenaugen für das Heimfindevermögen der Trichterspinne *Aglena labyrinthica* (Clerck) mit Hilfe einer Lichtquelle. Diss., Berlin, 1972

Dornfeldt, K.: Die Bedeutung der Haupt- und Nebenaugen für die photomenotaktische Orientierung der Trichterspinne *Agelena labyrinthica* (Cl.) Z. Tierpsychol. 38 (1975) 113

Drees, O.: Untersuchungen über die angeborenen Verhaltensweisen bei Springspinnen (Salticidae). Z. Tierpsychol. 9 (1952) 169

Drewes, C. D., R. A. Bernard: Electrophysiological responses of chemosensitive sensilla in the wolf spider. J. Exp. Zool. 198 (1976) 423

Duffey, E.: Aerial dispersal in a known spider population. J. Anim. Ecol. 25 (1956) 85

Duffey, E.: Spider ecology and habitat structure (Arach., Araneae). Senck. Biol. 47 (1966) 45

Dumpert, K.: Spider odor receptor: Electrophysiological proof. Experientia (Basel) 34 (1978) 754

Eakin, R. M., J. L. Brandenburger: Fine structure of the eyes of jumping spiders. J. Ultrastruct. Res. 37 (1971) 618

Eberhard, W.: Attack behaviour of diguetid spiders and the origin of prey wrapping in spiders. Psyche 74 (1967) 173

Eberhard, W. G.: The spider *Uloborus diversus* (Marx) (Uloboridae) and its web. Diss., Harvard University, 1969

Eberhard, W. G.: The web of *Uloborus diversus* (Araneae, Uloboridae). J. Zool. (London) 166 (1972) 417

Eberhard, W. G.: The "inverted ladder" orb web of *Scoloderus* sp. and the intermediate orb of *Eustala* (?) *sp*. Araneae: Araneidae. J. Nat. Hist. 9 (1975) 93

Eberhard, W. G.: Physical properties of sticky spirals and their connections: Sliding connections in orb webs. J. Nat. Hist. 10 (1976a) 481

Eberhard, W. G.: Photography of orb webs in the field. Bull. Brit. Arachnol. Soc. 3 (1976b) 200

Eberhard, W. G.: The webs of newly emerged *Uloborus diversus* and of a male *Uloborus* sp. (Araneae: Uloboridae). J. Arachnol. 4 (1977a) 201

Eberhard, W. G.: Aggressive chemical mimicry by a Bolas spider. Science 198 (1977b) 1173

Eberhard, W. G., M. Barreto, W. Pfizenmaier: Web robbery by mature male orb-weaving spiders. Bull. Brit. Arachnol. Soc. 4 (1978) 228

Eckert, M.: Experimentelle Untersuchungen zur Häutungsphysiologie bei Spinnen. Zool. Jb. Physiol. 73 (1967) 49

Edgar, W. E.: Prey and feeding behaviour of adult females of the wolf spider *Pardosa amentata* (Clerck). Neth. J. Zool. 20 (1970) 487

Edgar, W. E., M. Loenen: Aspects of the overwintering habitat of the wolf spider *Pardosa lugubris*. J. Zool. (London) 172 (1974) 383

Edwards, G. B., J. F. Carroll, W. H. Whitcomb: *Stoidis aurata* (Araneae: Salticidae), a spider predator of ants. Florida Entomol. 57 (1974) 337

Ehlers, M.: Untersuchungen über Formen aktiver Lokomotion bei Spinnen. Zool. Jb. Syst. 72 (1939) 373

Eisner, T., J. Dean: Ploy and counterploy in predator-prey interactions: Orb-weaving spiders versus bombardier beetles. Proc. Nat. Acad. Sci. (Washington, D.C.) 73 (1976) 1365

Eisner, T., R. Alsop, G. Ettershank: Adhesiveness of spider silk. Science 146 (1964) 1058

Ellis, C. H.: The mechanism of extension in the legs of spiders. Biol. Bull. 86 (1944) 41

Emerit, M.: Contribution à l'étude des Gasteracanthes (Aranéides, Argiopides) de Madagascar et des îles voisines. Diss., Montpellier Univ., 1969

Emerit, M., J. C. Bonaric: Contribution à l'étude du développement de l'appareil mechanorécepteur des Araignées: la trichobothriotaxie de *Pisaura mirabilis* Cl. (Araneae-Pisauridae). Zool. Jb. Anat. 94 (1975) 358

Enders, F.: Vertical stratification in orb-web spiders and a consideration of other methods of coexistence. Ecology 55 (1974) 317

Enders, F.: The influence of hunting manner on prey size, particularly in spiders with long attack distances (Araneidae, Linyphiidae, and Salticidae). Amer. Natur. 109 (1975) 737

Enders, F.: Effects of prey capture, web destruction and habitat physiognomy on web-site tenacity of *Argiope* spiders (Araneidae). J. Arachnol. 3 (1976) 75

Enders, F.: Web-site selection by orb-web spiders, particularly *Argiope aurantia* Lucas. Anim. Behav. 25 (1977) 694

Engelhardt, W.: Die mitteleuropäischen Arten der Gattung *Trochosa* C. L. Koch 1848 (Araneae, Lycosidae). Morphologie, Chemotaxonomie, Biologie, Autökologie. Z. Morph. Ökol. Tiere 54 (1964) 219

Engelhardt, W.: Gestalt und Lebensweise der "Ameisenspinne" *Synageles venator* (Lucas). Zugleich ein Beitrag zur Ameisenmimikryforschung. Zool. Anz. 185 (1971) 21

Fahrenbach, W. H.: The cyanoblast: Hemocyanin formation in *Limulus polyphemus*. J. Cell Biol. 44 (1970) 445

Fischel, W.: Wachstum und Häutung der Spinnen. I. Mitt.: Studien an retitelen Spinnen. Z. wiss. Zool. 133 (1929) 441

Foelix, R. F.: Structure and function of tarsal sensilla in the spider *Araneus diadematus*. J. exp. Zool. 175 (1970a) 99

Foelix, R. F.: Chemosensitive hairs in spiders. J. Morph. 132 (1970b) 313

Foelix, R. F., A. Choms: Fine structure of a spider joint-receptor and associated synapses. Europ. J. Cell Biol. 13 (1979) 149

Foelix, R. F., I.-W. Chu-Wang: The morphology of spider sensilla. I. Mechanoreceptors. Tissue and Cell 5 (1973a) 451

Foelix, R. F., I.-W. Chu-Wang: The morphology of spider sensilla. II. Chemoreceptors. Tissue and Cell 5 (1973b) 461

Foelix, R. F., I.-W. Chu-Wang: The structure of scopula hairs in spiders. Proc. 6th Int. Arachnol. Congr. 1974 (Amsterdam, 1975), p. 156

Foelix, R. F., H. Jung: Some anatomical aspects of *Hypochilus thorelli* with special reference to the calamistrum and cribellum. Symp. Zool. Soc. Lond. 42 (1978) 417

Foelix, R. F., G. Müller-Vorholt, H. Jung: Organisation of sensory leg nerves in the spider *Zygiella x-notata* (Clerck) (Araneae, Araneidae). Bull. Brit. Arachnol. Soc. 5 (1980) 20

Ford, M. J.: Locomotory activity and the predation strategy of the wolf-spider *Pardosa amentata* (Clerck) (Lycosidae). Anim. Behav. 26 (1978) 31

Forster, R. R.: Evolution of the tarsal organ, the respiratory system and the female genitalia in spiders. Proc. 8th Int. Congr. Arachnol. (Vienna, 1980), p. 269

Forster, R. R., L. M. Forster: *New Zealand Spiders*. Auckland: Collins, 1973

Forster, R. R., C. L. Wilton: The Spiders of New Zealand. Part IV. Otago Museum Bull. No. 4, Dunedin, 1973

Fourtner, C. R.: Chelicerate skeletal neuromuscular systems. Amer. Zool. 13 (1973) 271

Frank, H.: Untersuchungen zur funktionellen Anatomie der lokomotorischen Extremitäten von *Zygiella x-notata*, einer Radnetzspinne. Zool. Jb. Anat. 76 (1957) 423

Franz, V.: Über die Struktur des Herzens und die Entstehung von Blutzellen bei Spinnen. Zool. Anz. 27 (1904) 192

Friedrich, V. L., R. M. Langer: Fine structure of cribellate spider silk. Amer. Zool 9 (1969) 91 von Frisch, K.: *The Dance Language and Orientation of Bees.* Cambridge, Mass.: Harvard University Press, 1967

Gabe, M.: Données histologiques sur la neurosécrétion chez les Arachnides. Arch. Anat. Micr. Morph. Exp. 44 (1955) 351

Gerhardt, U.: Studien über die Copulation einheimischer Epeiriden. Zool. Jb. Syst. 31 (1911) 643

Gerhardt, U.: Neue Studien zur Sexualbiologie und zur Bedeutung des sexuellen Grössendimorphismus der Spinnen. Z. Morph. Okol. Tiere 1 (1924) 507

Gerhardt, U.: Weitere Untersuchungen zur Biologie der Spinnen. Z. Morph. Ökol. Tiere 6 (1926) 1

Gerhardt, U.: Neue biologische Untersuchungen an einheimischen und ausländischen Spinnen. Z. Morph. Ökol. Tiere 8 (1927) 96

Gerhardt, U.: Biologische Studien an griechischen, corsischen und deutschen Spinnen. Z. Morph. Ökol. Tiere 10 (1928) 576

Gerhardt, U.: Zur vergleichenden Sexualbiologie primitiver Spinnen, insbesondere der Tetrapneumonen. Z. Morph. Ökol. Tiere 14 (1929) 699

Gerhardt, U.: Biologische Untersuchungen an südfranzösischen Spinnen. Z. Morph. Ökol. Tiere 19 (1930) 184

Gerhardt, U.: Neue Untersuchungen zur Sexualbiologie der Spinnen, insbesondere an Arten der Mittelmeerländer und der Tropen. Z. Morph. Ökol. Tiere 27 (1933) 1

Gerhardt, U., A. Kaestner: 8. Ordnung der Arachnida: Araneae = Echte Spinnen = Webspinnen. In *Handbuch der Zoologie*, edited by W. Kükenthal, and T. Krumbach (Berlin: de Gruyter, 1938), p. 394

Gertsch, W. J.: *American Spiders.* New York: Van Nostrand 1949

Gettmann, W. W.: Beutefang bei Wolfspinnen der Gattung *Pirata* (Araneae: Lycosidae). Ent. Germ. 3 (1976) 93

Gettmann, W. W.: Untersuchungen zum Nahrungsspektrum von Wolfsspinnen (Lycosidae) der Gattung *Pirata*. Mitt. dtsch. Ges. allg. angew. Ent. 1 (1978) 63

Glatz, L.: Der Spinnapparat haplogyner Spinnen. Z. Morph. Tiere 72 (1972) 1

Glatz, L.: Der Spinnapparat der Orthognatha (Arachnida, Araneae). Z. Morph. Tiere 75 (1973) 1

Glick, P. A.: The distribution of insects, spiders and mites in the air. USDA Tech. Bull. No. 673, Dept. Agricult. Washington, D.C., 1939

Gonzalez-Fernandez, F., R. G. Sherman: Cardioregulatory nerves in a spider. Neurosci. Abstr. 5 (1979) 246

Görner, P.: Die optische und kinästhetische Orientierung der Trichterspinne *Agelena labyrinthica* (Cl.). Z. vergl. Physiol. 41 (1958) 111

Görner, P.: Orientierung der Trichterspinne nach polarisiertem Licht. Z. vergl. Physiol. 45 (1962) 307

Görner, P.: Mehrfach innervierte Mechanorezeptoren bei Spinnen. Naturwissenschaften 52 (1965) 437

Görner, P.: Über die Koppelung der optischen und kinaesthetischen Orientierung der Trichterspinne *Agelena labyrinthica* (Clerck) und *Agelena gracilens* C. L. Koch. Z. vergl. Physiol. 53 (1966) 253

Görner, P.: Resultant positioning between optical and kinesthetic orientation in the spider *Agelena labyrinthica* Clerck. In *Information Processing in the Visual Systems of Arthropods*, edited by R. Wehner (Berlin: Springer, 1972), p. 269

Görner, P.: Beispiele einer Orientierung ohne richtende Aussenreize. Fortschr. Zool. 21 (1973) 20

Görner, P., P. Andrews: Trichobothrien, ein Ferntastsinnesorgan bei Webespinnen (Araneen). Z. vergl. Physiol. 64 (1969) 301

Görner, P., C. Zeppenfeld: The runs of *Pardosa amentata* (Araneae, Lycosidae) after removing its cocoon. Proc. 8th Int. Congr. Arachnol. (Vienna, 1980), p. 243

Grasshoff, M.: Die Kreuzspinne *Araneus pallidus*—ihr Netzbau und ihre Paarungsbiologie. Natur und Museum 94 (1964) 305

Grasshoff, M.: Morphologische Kriterien als Ausdruck von Artgrenzen bei Radnetzspinnen der Subfamilie Araneinae (Arachnida: Araneae: Araneidae). Abh. Senckenberg, naturforsch. Ges. 516 (1968) 1

Grasshoff, M.: Konstruktions- und Funktionsanalyse an Kopulationsorganen einiger Radnetzspinnen. Aufs. u. Red. Senckenberg naturforsch. Ges. 24 (1973) 129

Grasshoff, M.: Reconstruction of an evolutionary transformation—the copulatory organs of *Mangora* (Arachnida, Araneae, Araneidae). Proc. 6th Int. Arachnol. Congr. (Amsterdam, 1975), p. 12

Grasshoff, M.: A model of the evolution of the main chelicerate groups. Symp. Zool. Soc. (Lond.) 42 (1978) 273

Gray, M. R.: Silk, spinnerets and snares. Aust. Nat. Hist. 19 (1978) 228

Greenquist, E. A., J. S. Rovner: Lycosid spiders on artificial foliage: stratum choice, orientation preferences, and prey-wrapping. Psyche 83 (1976) 196

Grégoire, C.: Sur la coagulation du sang des Araignées. Arch. Int. Physiol. 60 (1952) 100

Griffiths, D. J. G., T. Smyth, Jr.: Action of Black Widow spider venom at insect neuromuscular junctions. Toxicon 11 (1973) 369

Grünbaum, A. A.: Über das Verhalten der Spinne (*Epeira diademata*), besonders gegenüber vibratorischen Reizen. Psychol. Forschg. 9 (1927) 275

Gwinner-Hanke, H.: Zum Verhalten zweier stridulierender Spinnen *Steatoda bipunctata* Linné und *Teutana grossa* Koch (Theridiidae, Araneae) unter besonderer Berücksichtigung des Fortpflanzungsverhaltens. Z. Tierpsychol. 27 (1970) 649

Gwynne, D. T.: Nesting biology of the spider wasps (Hymenoptera: Pompilidae) which prey on burrowing wolf spiders (Araneae: Lycosidae, Geolycosa). J. Nat. Hist. 13 (1979) 681

Habermehl, G.: Vergiftungen durch die Dornfingerspinne. Naturwissenschaften 61 (1974) 368

Habermehl, G.: Die biologische Bedeutung tierischer Gifte. Naturwissenschaften 62 (1975) 15

Hackmann, W.: Chromosomenstudien an Araneen mit besonderer Berücksichtigung der Geschlechtschromosomen. Acta. Zool. Fenn 54. (1948) 1

Hanström, B.: Über die Histologie und vergleichende Anatomie der Sehganglien und Globuli der Araneen. Kungl. Sv. Vet. Akad. Handlingar 61 (1921) 2

Hanström, B.: *Vergleichende Anatomie des Nervensystems der wirbellosen Tiere*. Berlin, 1928

Hanström, B.: Fortgesetzte Untersuchungen über das Araneengehirn. Zool. Jb. Anat. 59 (1935) 455

Harkness, R., R. Wehner: Cataglyphis. Endeavour (n. s.) 1 (1977) 115

Harm, M.: Beiträge zur Kenntnis des Baues, der Funktion und der Entwicklung des akzessorischen Kopulationsorgans von *Segestria bavarica* C. L. Koch. Z. Morph. Ökol. Tiere 22 (1931) 629

Harris, D. J.: Personal communication (1974)

Harris, D. J.: Hair regeneration during moulting in the spider *Ciniflo similis* (Araneae, Dictynidae). Zoomorphologie 88 (1977) 37

Harris, D. J., P. J. Mill: The ultrastructure of chemoreceptor sensilla in *Ciniflo* (Araneida, Arachnida) Tissue and Cell 5 (1973) 679

Harris, D. J., P. J. Mill: Observations on the leg receptors of *Ciniflo* (Araneida: Dictynidae). I. External mechanoreceptors. J. Comp. Physiol. 119 (1977a) 37

Harris, D. J., P. J. Mill: Observations on the leg receptors of *Ciniflo* (Araneida: Dictynidae). II. Chemoreceptors. J. Comp. Physiol. 119 (1977b) 55

Heil, K. H.: Beiträge zur Physiologie und Psychologie der Springspinnen. Z. vergl. Physiol. 23 (1936) 1

Heller, G.: Zur Biologie der ameisenfressenden Spinne *Callilepis nocturna* L. 1758 (Aranea, Drassodidae). Diss., Mainz, 1974

Heller, G.: Zum Beutefangverhalten der ameisenfressenden Spinne *Callilepis nocturna* (Arachnida: Araneae: Drassodidae). Ent. Germ. 3 (1976) 100

von Helversen, O.: Gedanken zur Evolution der Paarungsstellungen bei den Spinnen (Arachnida: Araneae). Ent. Germ. 3 (1976) 13

Higashi, G. A., J. S. Rovner: Post-emergent behaviour of juvenile lycosid spiders. Bull. Brit. Arachnol. Soc. 3 (1975) 113

Hill, D. E.: The pretarsus of salticid spiders. Zool. J. Linn. Soc. 60 (1977a) 319

Hill, D. E.: Some observations on the physiology of living *Lyssomanes viridis* which should apply to the Araneae in general. Peckhamia 1 (1977b) 41

Hill, D. E.: Orientation by jumping spiders of the genus *Phidippus* (Araneae: Salticidae) during the pursuit of prey. Behav. Ecol. Sociobiol. 5 (1979) 301

Hiller, U.: Untersuchungen zum Feinbau und zur Funktion der Haftborsten von Reptilien. Z. Morph. Tiere 62 (1968) 307

Hingston, R. W. G.: *A Naturalist in Himalaya*. London: Willoby, 1920

Hinton, H. E., R. S. Wilson: Stridulatory organs in spiny orb-weaver spiders. J. Zool. (London) 162 (1970) 481

Hirschberg, D.: Beiträge zur Biologie, insbesondere zur Brutpflege einiger Theridiiden. Z. wiss. Zool. 179 (1969) 189

Holm, A.: Studien über die Entwicklung und Entwicklungsbiologie der Spinnen. Zool. Bidr. (Uppsala) 19 (1940) 1

Holm, A.: Experimentelle Untersuchungen über die Entwicklung und Entwicklungsphysiologie der Spinnenembryos. Zool. Bidr. (Uppsala) 29 (1952)

Holzapfel, M.: Die Bedeutung der Netzstarrheit für die Orientierung der Trichterspinne *Agelena labyrinthica* (Cl.). Rev. Suisse Zool. 40 (1933) 247

Holzapfel, M.: Die nicht-optische Orientierung der Trichterspinne *Agelena labyrinthica* (Cl.). Z. vergl. Physiol. 20 (1934) 55

Homann, H.: Beiträge zur Physiologie der Spinnenaugen. I. Untersuchungsmethoden. II. Das Sehvermögen. Z. vergl. Physiol. 7 (1928) 201

Homann, H.: Beiträge zur Physiologie der Spinnenaugen. III. Das Sehvermögen der Lycosiden. Z. vergl. Physiol. 14 (1931) 40

Homann, H.: Beiträge zur Physiologie der Spinnenaugen. IV. Das Sehvermögen der Thomisiden. Z. vergl. Physiol. 20 (1934) 420

Homann, H.: Die Funktion des männlichen Spinnentasters im Versuch. Zool. Anz. 109 (1935) 73

Homann, H.: Beiträge zur Physiologie der Spinnenaugen. V. Der Lichtsinn von *Aranea sexpunctata* (Argiopidae). Biol. Zbl. 66 (1947) 251

Homann, H.: Über das Wachstum und die mechanischen Vorgänge bei der Häutung von *Tegenaria agrestis* (Araneae). Z. vergl. Physiol. 31 (1949) 413

Homann, H.: Die Nebenaugen der Araneen. Zool. Jb. Anat. 71 (1950) 1

Homann, H.: Die Nebenaugen der Araneen. Zool. Jb. Anat. 72 (1952) 345

Homann, H.: Haften Spinnen an einer Wasserhaut? Naturwissenschaften 44 (1957) 318

Homann, H.: Die Augen der Araneae. Anatomie, Ontogenie und Bedeutung für die Systematik (Chelicerata, Arachnida). Z. Morph. Tiere 69 (1971) 201

Homann, H.: Die Stellung der Thomisidae und der Philodromidae im System der Araneae (Chelicerata, Arachnida). Z. Morph. Tiere 80 (1975) 181

Horstmann, K.: Ökologische Untersuchungen über die Ichneumoniden (Hymenoptera) der Nordseeküste Schleswig-Holsteins. Oecologia 4 (1970) 29

Humphreys, W. F.: Behavioral thermoregulation in a wolf spider. Nature (London) 251 (1974) 502

Humphreys, W. F.: The influence of burrowing and thermoregulatory behaviour on the water relations of *Geolycosa godeffroyi* (Araneae: Lycosidae), an Australian wolf spider. Oecologia 21 (1975) 291

Husby, J. A., K. E. Zachariassen: Antifreeze agents in the body fluid of winter active insects and spiders. Experientia 36 (1980) 963

Irving, W. G., E. H. Hinman: The blue mud-dauber as a predator of the Black Widow spider. Science 82 (1935) 395

Jackson, R. R.: Fine structure of the thread connections in the orb web of Araneus diadematus. Psyche 78 (1971) 12

Jackson, R. R.: Courtship versatility in the jumping spider *Phidippus johnsoni* (Araneae: Salticidae). Anim. Behav. 25 (1977a) 953

Jackson, R. R.: Prey of the jumping spider *Phidippus johnsoni* (Araneae, Salticidae) J. Arachnol. 5 (1977b) 145

Jackson, R. R.: Analysis of alternative mating tactics of the jumping spider *Phidippus johnsoni* (Araneae, Salticidae). J. Arachnol. 5 (1978) 185

Jackson, R. R.: Nests of *Phidippus johnsoni* (Araneae, Salticidae): Characteristics, pattern of occupation, and function. J. Arachnol. 7 (1979) 47

Jackson, R. R., A. D. Blest: The biology of *Portia fimbriata* (Doleschall), a primitive web-building jumping spider from Queensland (Araneae, Salticidae). (In review.) (1981a)

Jackson, R. R., A. D. Blest: The predatory versatility of *Portia fimbriata* (Doleschall), a primitive web-building jumping spider from Queensland (Araneae, Salticidae). (In review.) (1981b)

Jacobi-Kleemann, M.: Über die Lokomotion der Kreuzspinne *Aranea diadema* beim Netzbau (nach Filmanalysen). Z. vergl. Physiol. 34 (1953) 606

Järlsfors, U., D. S. Smith, F. E. Russell: Innervation of the venom-secreting cells in the Black Widow Spider (*Latrodectus mactans*). In *Toxins of Animal and Plant Origin*, vol. I, edited by A. De Vries and E. Kochva (London: Gordon and Breach, 1971), p. 159

Kaestner, A.: Bau und Funktion der Fächertracheen einiger Spinnen. Z. Morph. Ökol. Tiere 13 (1929) 463

Kaestner, A.: Reaktionen der Hüpfspinnen (Salticidae) auf unbewegte farblose und farbige Gesichtsreize. Zool. Beitr. 1 (1950) 12

Kaestner, A.: Die Mundwerkzeuge der Spinnen, ihr Bau, ihre Funktion und ihre Bedeutung für das System. 1. Teil. Orthognatha, Palaeocribellata. Zool. Jb. Anat. 72 (1952) 101

Kaestner, A.: *Lehrbuch der Speziellen Zoologie*, 3rd ed., vol. 1: Wirbellose. Stuttgart: Fischer, 1969

Kaiser, E., W. Raab: Collagenolytic activity of snake and spider venoms. Toxicon 4 (1967) 251

Kaston, B. J.: The senses involved in the courtship of some vagabond spiders. Ent. Amer. 16 (1936) 97

Kaston, B. J.: The evolution of spider webs. Amer. Zool. 4 (1964) 191

Kaston, B. J.: Comparative biology of American Black Widow spiders. Transact. San Diego Soc. Nat. Hist. 16 (1970) 33

Kaston, B. J.: *How to Know the Spiders*. Dubuque, Iowa: Browne, 1972

Kavanagh, E. J., E. K. Tillinghast: Fibrous and adhesive components of the orb webs of *Araneus trifolium* and *Argiope trifasciata*. J. Morphol. 160 (1979) 17

Kessler, A.: Relation between egg production and food consumption in species of the genus Pardosa (Lycosidae, Araneae) under experimental conditions of food-abundance and food-shortage. Oecologia 8 (1971a) 93

Kessler, A.: Hymenopterous egg parasites in Pardosa cocoons. 5th Int. Archnol. Congr. (Brno, 1971b), p. 145

Kessler, A.: A comparative study of the production of eggs in eight Pardosa species in the field (Araneae, Lycosidae). Tijdschr. Entomol. 116 (1973) 23

Kessler, A., A. Fokkinga: Hymenopterous parasites in egg sacs of spiders of the genus Pardosa (Araneida, Lycosidae). Tijdschr. Entomol. 116 (1973) 43

Kirchner, W.: Ecological aspects of cold resistance in spiders (A comparative study). In *Effects of Temperature on Ectothermic Organisms*, edited by W. Wieser (Berlin: Springer, 1973), p. 271

Kirchner, W., P. Kestler: Untersuchungen zur Kälteresistenz der Schilfradspinne *Araneus cornutus* (Araneidae). J. Insect Physiol. 15 (1969) 41

Kirchner, W., E. Kullmann: Überwinterung und Kälteresistenz der Haubennetzspinnenarten *Theridion impressum* (L. Koch) und *Theridion sisyphium* (Clerck) (Araneae, Theridiidae). Decheniana 127 (1975) 241

Klingel, H.: Beobachtungen an *Lipistius batuensis* Abr. (Araneae, Mesothelae). Verh. dtsch. zool. Ges. (Göttingen) Suppl. 30 (1966) 246

Knost, S. J., J. S. Rovner: Scavenging by wolf spiders (Araneae: Lycosidae). Amer. Midl. Natur. 93 (1975) 239

Kovoor, J.: Etude histochimique et cytologique des glandes séricigènes de quelques Argiopidae. Ann. Sci. Nat. Zool. 14 (1972) 1

Kovoor, J., L. Zylberberg: Histologie et infrastructure de la glande chélicérienne de *Scytodes delicatula* Sim. (Araneidae, Scytodidae). Ann. Sci. Nat. Zool. 14 (1972) 333

Kovoor, J., Zylberberg: Fine structural aspects of silk secretion in a spider (*Araneus diadematus*). I. Elaboration in the pyriform glands. Tissue and Cell 12 (1980) 547

Krafft, B.: La société d'*Agelena consociata* Denis, araignée sociale du Gabon. 96 Congr. Nat. Soc. Savantes, Toulouse, 1971

Krafft, B.: La tolérance réciproque chez l'araignée sociale *Agelena consociata* Denis. Proc. 6th Int. Arachnol. Congr. 1974 (Amsterdam, 1975), p. 107

Krafft, B.: The recording of vibratory signals performed by spiders during courtship. Symp. Zool. Soc. Lond. 42 (1978) 59

Krakauer, T.: Thermal responses of the orb-weaving spider *Nephila clavipes* (Araneae: Argiopidae). Amer. Midl. Natur. 88 (1972) 245

Krishnakumaran, A., H. A. Schneiderman: Chemical control of moulting in arthropods. Nature (London) 220 (1968) 601

Kronestedt, T.: Study of a stridulatory apparatus in *Pardosa fulvipes* (Collett) (Araneae, Lycosidae) by scanning electron microscopy. Zool. Scripta 2 (1973) 43

Kuenzler, E. J.: Niche relations of three species of lycosid spiders. Ecology 39 (1958) 494

Kühne, H.: Die neurosekretorischen Zellen und der retrocerebrale neuroendokrine Komplex von Spinnen (Araneae, Labidognatha) unter Berücksichtigung einiger histologisch erkennbarer Veränderungen während des postembryonalen Lebens. Zool. Jb. Anat. 77 (1959) 527

Kullmann, E.: Beobachtungen und Betrachtungen zum Verhalten der Theridiide *Conopista argyrodes* Walckenaer (Araneae). Mitt. Zool. Mus. 35 (1959) 275

Kullmann, E.: Der Eierkokonbau von *Cyrtophora citricola* Forskal (Araneae, Araneidae). Zool. Jb. Syst. 89 (1961) 369

Kullmann, E.: Spinnorgan mit 40 000 "Düsen". Umschau Wiss. Techn. 3 (1969) 82

Kullmann, E. J.: The convergent development of orb-webs in cribellate and ecribellate spiders. Amer. Zool. 12 (1972a) 395

Kullmann, E.: Evolution of social behaviour in spiders (Araneae; Eresidae and Theridiidae). Amer. Zool. 12 (1972b) 419

Kullmann, E.: *Theridion impressum* (Theridiidae) Brutfürsorge und periodisch-soziales Verhalten. Encycl. Cinemat. E 1864, Göttingen 1974

Kullmann, E., W. Kloft: Traceruntersuchungen zur Regurgitationsfütterung bei Spinnen (Araneae, Theridiidae). Zool. Anz., Supp. 32 (1969) 487

Kullmann, E., W. Zimmermann: Ein neuer Beitrag zum Cribellaten-Ecribellaten-Problem: Beschreibung von *Uroecobius ecribellatus* n. gen. n. spec. und Diskussion seiner phylogenetischen Stellung (Arachnida: Araneae: Oecobiidae). Ent. Germ. 3 (1976) 29

Kullmann, E., St. Nawabi, W. Zimmermann: Neue Ergebnisse zur Brutbiologie cribellater Spinnen aus Afghanistan und der Serengeti. Z. d. Kölner Zoo 14 (1971/72) 87

Kullmann, E., H. Sittertz, W. Zimmermann: Erster Nachweis von Regurgitationsfütterungen bei einer cribellaten Spinne (*Stegodyphus lineatus* Latreille, 1817, Eresidae). Bonn. Zool. Beitr. 22 (1971) 175

Lamy, E.: Recherches anatomiques sur les trachées des Araignées. Ann. Sci. Nat. Zool. 15 (1902) 149

Land, M. F.: Structure of the retinae of the principal eyes of jumping spiders (Salticidae: Dendryphantinae) in relation to visual optics. J. Exp. Biol. 51 (1969a) 443

Land, M. F.: Movements of the retinae of jumping spiders (Salticidae: Dendryphantinae) in response to visual stimuli. J. Exp. Biol. 51 (1969b) 471

Land, M. F.: Orientation by jumping spiders in the absence of visual feedback. J. Exp. Biol. 54 (1971) 119

Land, M. F.: Stepping movements made by jumping spiders during turns mediated by the lateral eyes. J. Exp. Biol. 57 (1972a) 15

Land, M. F.: Mechanism of orientation and pattern recognition by jumping spiders. In *Information Processing in the Visual Systems of Arthropods*, edited by R. Wehner (Berlin, Springer, 1972b), p. 231

Le Berre, M.: Modifications temporelles de l'activité chez de jeunes Argiopidés. Rev. Arachnol. 2 (1979) 193

Legendre, R.: Localisation d'un organe olfactif non encore décrit chez les Aranéides. Comptes Rendus Acad. Sci. (Paris) 243 (1956) 1237

Legendre, R.: Contributions à l'étude du système nerveux des Aranéides. Ann. Biol. 34 (1958) 13

Legendre, R.: Le méchanism de la prise de nourriture chez les Araignées. Comptes Rendus Acad. Sci. (Paris) 252 (1961a) 321

Legendre, R.: Sur deux particularités du système nerveux central de la mygale *Scodra calceata* Fabr. Ann. Sci. Nat. Zool. 3 (1961b) 767

Legendre, R.: L'audition et l'émission de sons chez les aranéides. Ann. Biol. 2 (1963) 371

Legendre, R.: Morphologie et développement des chélicérates. Embryologie, développement et anatomie des aranéides. Fortschr. Zool. 17 (1965) 237

Legendre, R.: Sur la présence d'un nerf cardiaque chez les Araignées orthognathes. Comptes Rendus Acad. Sci. (Paris) 267 (1968) 84

Legendre, R.: Un organ stridulent nouveau chez les Archaeidae (Araneida). Bull. Soc. Zool. France 95 (1970) 1

Legendre, R.: Les Arachnides de Madagascar. In *Biogeography and Ecology in Madagascar*, edited by R. Battistini and G. Richard-Vindard (The Hague: Junk, 1972), p. 427

LeGuelte, L.: Learning in spiders. Amer. Zool. 9 (1969) 145

Lehmensick, R., E. Kullmann: Über den Feinbau der Fäden einiger Spinnen. (Vergleich des Aufbaues der Fangfäden cribellater und ecribellater Spinnen). Zool. Anz. 19, Suppl. (1956) 123

Lehtinen, P. T.: Classification of the cribellate spiders and some allied families. Ann. Zool. Fennica 4 (1967) 199

Lehtinen, P. T.: Notes on the phylogenetic classification of Araneae. Proc. 6th Int. Arachnol. Congr. 1974 (Amsterdam, 1975), p. 26

Lehtinen, P. T.: Trichobothrial patterns in high-level taxonomy of spiders. Proc. 8th Int. Congr. Arachnol. (Vienna, 1980), p. 466

Levi, H. W.: Adaptations of respiratory systems of spiders. Evolution 21 (1967) 571

Levi, H. W.: Personal communication, 1978

Levi, H. W.: Orb-webs: primitive or specialized. Proc. 8th Int. Congr. Arachnol. (Vienna, 1980), p. 367

Liesenfeld, F.: Über Leistung und Sitz des Erschütterungssinnes von Netzspinnen. Biol. Zbl. 80 (1961) 465

Linzen, B., P. Gallowitz: Enzyme activity pattern in muscles of the lycosid spider, *Cupiennius salei*. J. Comp. Physiol. 96 (1975) 101

Loewe, R., B. Linzen, W. v. Stackelberg: Die gelösten Stoffe in der Haemolymphe einer Spinne, *Cupiennius salei* Keyserling. Z. vergl. Physiol. 66 (1970) 27

Lubin, Y. D.: Web structure and function: the non-adhesive orb-web of *Cyrtophora moluccensis* (Doleschall) (Araneae: Araneidae). Forma et functio 6 (1973) 337

Lubin, Y. D., W. G. Eberhard, G. G. Montgomery: Webs of *Miagrammopes* (Araneae: Uloboridae) in the neotropics. Psyche 85 (1978) 1

Lucas, F.: Spiders and their silks. Discovery 25 (1964) 1

Luczak, J.: The distribution of wandering spiders in different layers of the environment as a result of interspecies competition. Ekol. Polska A 14 (1966) 233

Lüters, H.: Der Lebenszyklus von *Agroeca brunnea* Blackwall (Araneae, Clubionidae) unter besonderer Berücksichtigung des Kokonbau- und des Häutungsverhaltens. Diss., Göttingen, 1966

McCrone, J. D., R. J. Hatla: Isolation and characterization of a lethal compound from the venom of *Latrodectus mactans mactans*. In *Animal Toxins*, edited by F. E. Russel and P. R. Saunders (New York: Pergamon, 1967), p. 29

McCrone, J. D., M. L. Netzloff: An immunological and electrophoretical comparison of the venoms of the North American *Latrodectus* spiders. Toxicon 3 (1965) 107

McQueen, D. J.: Interactions between the pompilid wasp *Anoplius relativus* (Fox) and the burrowing wolf spider *Geolycosa domifex* (Hancock). Can. J. Zool. 57 (1979) 542

Magni, F.: Analysis of polarised light in wolf spiders. In *The Functional Organisation of the Compound Eye*, edited by C. G. Bernhard (Oxford: Pergamon Press, 1966), p. 201

Maretić, Z.: Toxicity of "nonvenomous" spiders. Proc. 5th Int. Arachnol. Congr. (Brno, 1971), p. 201

Maretić, Z.: European Araneism. Bull. Brit. Arachnol. Soc. 3 (1975) 126

Markl, H.: Die Verständigung durch Stridulationssignale bei Blattschneiderameisen. I. Die biologische Bedeutung der Stridulation. Z. vergl. Physiol. 57 (1967) 299

Markl, H.: Vom Eigennutz des Uneigennützigen. Die Evolution hochentwickelter Sozialsysteme im Tierreich. Naturw. Rdsch. 24 (1971) 281

Maroli, M., S. Bettini, B. Panfili: Toxicity of *Latrodectus mactans tredecimguttatus* venom on frogs and birds. Toxicon 11 (1973) 203

Marples, B. J.: The spinnerets and epiandrous glands of spiders. J. Linn. Soc. (Zool.) 46 (1967) 209

Martin, A. W.: Circulation in invertebrates. Ann. Rev. Physiol. 36 (1974) 171

Martin, D.: Zum Radnetzbau der Gattung *Pachygnatha* Sund. (Araneae: Tetragnathidae). Mitt. Zool. Mus. Berlin 54 (1978) 83

Meier, F.: Beiträge zur Kenntnis der postembryonalen Entwicklung der Spinnen *Araneida, Labidognatha*, unter besonderer Berücksichtigung der Histogenese des Zentralnervensystems. Rev. Suisse Zool. 74 (1967) 127

Melchers, M.: Zur Biologie und zum Verhalten von *Cupiennius salei* (Keyserling), einer amerikanischen Ctenide. Zool. Jb. Syst. 91 (1963) 1

Melchers, M.: Zur Biologie der Vogelspinnen (Fam. Aviculariidae). Z. Morph. Ökol. Tiere 53 (1964) 517

Melchers, M.: Der Beutefang von *Cupiennius salei* (Keyserling) (Ctenidae). Z. Morph. Ökol. Tiere 58 (1967) 321

Meyer, E.: Neue sinnesbiologische Beobachtungen an Spinnen. Z. Morph. Ökol. Tiere 12 (1928) 1

Midttun, B.: Ultrastructure of cardiac muscle of *Trochosa terricola* Thor., *Pardosa amentata* Clerck, P. pullata Cl., and *Pisaura mirabilis* Cl. (Araneae: Lycosidae, Pisauridae). Cell Tiss. Res. 181 (1977) 299

Mill, P. J., D. J. Harris: Observations on the leg receptors of *Ciniflo* (Araneida: Dictynidae). III. Proprioreceptors. J. Comp. Physiol. 119 (1977) 63

Millot, J.: Contribution à l'histophysiologie des Aranéides. Bull. Biol. Franç. Belg., Suppl. 8 (1926) 1

Millot, J.: Glandes venimeuses et glandes séricigènes chez les Sicariides. Bull. Soc. Zool. Franç. 55 (1930) 150

Millot, J.: Le sens du goût chez les Araignées. Bull. Soc. Zool. Franç. 61 (1936) 27

Millot, J.: Sens chimiques et sens visuel chez les Araignées. Ann. Biol. 22 (1946) 1

Millot, J.: Ordre des Aranéides (Araneae). In *Traité de Zoologie*, vol. 6, edited by P.-P. Grassé (Paris: Masson, 1949), p. 589

Minch, E. W.: The molting sequence in *Aphonopelma chalcodes* (Araneae: Theraposidae). J. Arachnol. 5 (1977) 133

Minch, E. W.: Daily activity patterns in the tarantula *Aphonopelma chalcodes* Chamberlin. Bull. Brit. Arachnol. Soc. 4 (1978) 231

Mittal, O. P.: Karyological studies on the Indian spiders. II. An analysis of the chromosomes during spermatogenesis in five species belonging to the family Salticidae. Res. Bull. Panjab Univ. (n. s.) 15 (1964) p. 315

Mittal, O. P.: Sex mechanism in spiders. Proc. 53rd Ind. Sci. Congr. 1966 (abstract), p. 320

Miyashita, K.: Growth and development of *Lycosa T-insignata* Boes. et Str. (Araneae: Lycosidae) under different feeding conditions. Appl. Entomol. Zool. 3 (1968) 81

Moller, P.: Die systematischen Abweichungen bei der optischen Richtungsorientierung der Trichterspinne *Agelena labyrinthica*. Z. Vergl. Physiol. 66 (1970) 78

Monterosso, B.: Note araneologiche.—Su la biologia degli Scitotidi e la ghiandola glutinifera di essi. Arch. Zool. Ital. 12 (1928) 63

Montgomery, T. H.: On the maturation, mitosis and fertilization of the egg of *Theridium*. Zool. Jb. Anat. 25 (1908) 237

Mullen, G. R.: Morphology and histology of the silk glands in *Araneus sericatus* Cl. Trans. Amer. Microsc. Soc. 88 (1969) 232

Nawabi, S.: Histologische Untersuchungen an der Mitteldarmdrüse von *Stegodyphus pacificus* (Pocock 1900) (Araneae, Eresidae). Diss., Bonn, 1974

Nemenz, H.: Der Wasserhaushalt einiger Spinnen. Öst. Zool. Z. 5 (1954) 123

Nemenz, H.: Über den Bau der Kutikula und dessen Einfluss auf die Wasserabgabe bei Spinnen. S.-B. Öst. Akad. Wiss., math.-naturw. Kl., Abt. I, 164 (1955) 65

Nentwig, W.: The selective prey of linyphiid-like spiders and of their webs. Oecologia (Berlin) 45 (1980) 236

Nielsen, E.: Contributions to the life history of pimpline spider parasites. Ent. Med. 14 (1923) 137

Nielsen, E.: *The Biology of Spiders: With Especial Reference to the Danish Fauna.* (Copenhagen: Lewin and Munksgaard, 1932) p. 218

Nørgaard, E.: On the ecology of two Lycosid spiders (*Pirata piraticus* and *Lycosa pullata*) from a Danish sphagnum bog. Oikos 3 (1951) 1

Nørgaard, E.: Environment and behaviour of *Theridion saxatile*. Oikos 7 (1956) 159

Nyffeler, M., G. Benz: Kleptoparasitismus von juvenilen Kreuzspinnen und Skorpionsfliegen in den Netzen adulter Spinnen. Rev. Suisse Zool. 87 (1980) 907

Osaki, H.: Electron microscope study on the spermatozoon of the Liphistiid spider *Heptathela*. Acta Arachnol. 22 (1969) 1

Osaki, H.: Electron microscope studies on developing oocytes of the spider *Plexippus paykulli*. Annot. Zool. Jap. 45 (1972) 187

Painter, T. S.: Spermatogenesis in spiders. Zool. Jb. Anat. 38 (1914) 509

Palmgren, P.: On the muscular anatomy of spiders. Acta Zool. Fenn. 155 (1978) 1

Papi, F.: Astronomische Orientierung bei der Wolfspinne *Arctosa perita* (Latr.). Z. vergl. Physiol. 37 (1955) 230

Parry, D. A.: The small leg-nerve of spiders and a probable mechanoreceptor. Quart. J. Micr. Sci. 101 (1960) 1

Parry, D. A., R. H. J. Brown: The hydraulic mechanism of the spider leg. J. Exp. Biol. 36 (1959a) 423

Parry, D. A., R. H. J. Brown: The jumping mechanism of salticid spiders. J. Exp. Biol. 36 (1959b) 654

Peakall, D. B.: Synthesis of silk, mechanism and location. Amer. Zool. 9 (1969) 71

Peakall, D. B.: Conservation of web proteins in the spider *Araneus diadematus*. J. Exp. Zool. 176 (1971) 257

Peters, H.: Die Fanghandlung der Kreuzspinne (*Epeira diademata* L.). Experimentelle Analysen des Verhaltens. Z. vergl. Physiol. 15 (1931) 693

Peters, H.: Experimente über die Orientierung der Kreuzspinne *Epeira diademata* Cl. im Netz. Zool. Jb. Zool. 51 (1932) 239

Peters, H.: Weitere Untersuchungen über die Fanghandlung der Kreuzspinne (*Epeira diademata* Cl.). Z. vergl. Physiol. 19 (1933) 47

Peters, H.: Über das Kreuzspinnennetz und seine Probleme. Naturwissenschaften 47 (1939a) 777

Peters, H.: Probleme des Kreuzspinnennetzes. Z. Morph. Ökol. Tiere 36 (1939b) 179

Peters, H.: Orientierungsvermögen und Gedächtnis der Kreuzspinne (*Aranea diadema*). Erläuterung zum Hochschulfilm C 595/1950, Institut f. Film und Bild in Wissenschaft und Unterricht. Göttingen, 1951

Peters, H.: Über den Spinnapparat von *Nephila madagascariensis*. Z. Naturforsch. 10b (1955) 395

Peters, H. M.: Maturing and coordination of web-building activity. Amer. Zool. 9 (1969) 223

Peters, P. J.: Orb-web construction: Interaction of spider (*Araneus diadematus* Cl.) and thread configuration. Behaviour 18 (1970) 478

Peters, R.: Vergleichende Untersuchungen über Bau und Funktion der Spinnwarzen und Spinnwarzenmuskulatur einiger Araneen. Zool. Beitr. 13 (1967) 29

Petersen, B.: The relation between size of mother and number of eggs and young in some spiders and its significance for the evolution of size. Experientia (Basel) 6 (1950) 96

Petrunkevitch, A.: Contributions to our knowledge of the anatomy and relationships of spiders. Ann. Ent. Soc. Amer. 2 (1909) 11

Petrunkevitch, A.: Über die Circulationsorgane von *Lycosa carolinensis*. Zool. Jb. Anat. 31 (1910) 161

Petrunkevitch, A.: Tarantula versus tarantulahawk: A study in instinct. J. Exp. Zool. 45 (1926) 367

Petrunkevitch, A.: An inquiry into the natural classification of spiders, based on a study of their internal anatomy. Trans. Conn. Acad. Arts and Sci. 31 (1933) 299

Petrunkevitch, A.: The spider and the wasp. Sci. Amer. 187 (1952) 20

Petrunkevitch, A.: Arachnida. In *Treatise on Invertebrate Paleontology; Arthropoda 2*, edited by R. C. Moore (Lawrence, Kan.: University of Kansas Press, 1955), p. 42

Pinkston, K. N., J. H. Frick: Determinations of osmolarity on the fresh unfixed hemolymph of four species of spiders. Ann. Ent. Soc. Amer. 66 (1973) 696

Plateau, F.: Recherches sur la structure de l'appareil digestif et sur les phénomènes de la digestion chez les aranéides dipneumones. Bull. Acad. Roy. Belg. 44 (1877) 129

Platnick, N.: The evolution of courtship behaviour in spiders. Bull. Brit. Arachnol. Soc. 2 (1971) 40

Platnick, N. I.: On the validity of Haplogynae as a taxonomic grouping in spiders. Proc. 6th Int. Arachnol. Congr. 1974 (Amsterdam, 1975), p. 30

Platnick, N. I.: The hypochiloid spiders: A cladistic analysis, with notes on the Atypoidea (Arachnida, Araneae). Amer. Mus. Novitates, No. 2627 (1977) 1

Platnick, N. I., W. J. Gertsch: The suborders of spiders: A cladistic analysis (Arachnida, Araneae). Amer. Mus. Novitates, No. 2607 (1976) 1

Pötzsch, J.: *Von der Brutfürsorge heimischer Spinnen.* Neue Brehm-Bücherei. Wittenberg Lutherstadt: Ziemsen, 1963

Purcell, E. F.: Development and origin of the respiratory organs of Araneae. Quart. J. Micr. Sci. 54 (1909) 1

Purcell, W. F.: The phylogeny of trachea in Araneae. Quart. J. Micr. Sci. 54 (1910) 519

Ramousse, R.: Organisation temporelle du comportement constructeur chez huit espèces d'Argiopidées. Comptes Rendus 5ᵉ Colloque Arach. IX (Barcelone, 1980), p. 203

Ramousse, R., F. Davis: Web-building time in a spider: Preliminary application of ultrasonic detection. Physiol. Behav. 17 (1976) 997

Ramousse, R., L. LeGuelte: Relations spatio-temporelles dans le comportement constructeur d'*Araneus diadematus* Rev. Arachnol. 2 (1979) 183

Rathmayer, W.: Die Innervation der Beinmuskeln einer Spinne, *Eurypelma hentzi* Chamb. (Orthognatha, Aviculariidae). Verh. dtsch. zool. Ges. (Jena) (1965a) 505

Rathmayer, W.: Polyneurale Innervation bei Spinnen. Naturwissenschaften 52 (1965b) 114

Rathmayer, W.: Neuromuscular transmission in a spider and the effect of calcium. Comp. Biochem. Physiol. 14 (1965c) 673

Rathmayer, W.: The effect of the poison of spiders and diggerwasps on their prey (Hymenoptera: Pompilidae, Sphecidae). Mem. Inst. Butantan. Simp. Internac. 33 (1966) 651

Rathmayer, W.: Elektrophysiologische Untersuchungen an Propriorezeptoren im Bein einer Vogelspinne (*Eurypelma hentzi* Chamb.). Z. vergl. Physiol. 54 (1967) 438

Rathmayer, W.: Venoms of Sphecidae, Pompilidae, Mutillidae and Bethylidae. In *Handbook of Experimental Pharmacology*, vol. XLVIII, edited by S. Bettini (Berlin: Springer, 1978), p. 661

Rathmayer, W., J. Koopmann: Die Verteilung der Propriorezeptoren im Spinnenbein. Z. Morph. Tiere 66 (1970) 212

Reed, C. F., P. N. Witt, R. L. Jones: The measuring function of the first legs of *Araneus diadematus* Cl. Behaviour 25 (1965) 98

Reed, C. F., P. N. Witt, M. B. Scarboro, D. B. Peakall: Experience and the orb web. Devel. Psychobiol. 3 (1970) 251

Reger, J. F.: Spermiogenesis in the spider, *Pisaurina* sp.: A fine structure study. J. Morph. 130 (1970) 421

Reiskind, J.: Multiple mimetic forms in an ant-mimicking clubionid spider. Science 169 (1970) 587

Reiskind, J.: Ant-mimicry in Panamian clubionid and salticid spiders (Araneae: Clubionidae, Salticidae). Biotropica 9 (1977) 1

Richardson, C. E. W.: Specificity of the spider web pattern and its efficiency in trapping prey. Amer. Zool. 13 (1973) 59

Richter, C. J. J.: Morphology and function of the spinning apparatus of the wolf spider *Pardosa amentata* (Cl.) (Araneae, Lycosidae). Z. Morph. Tiere 68 (1970) 37

Richter, C. J. J.: Some aspects of the serial dispersal in different populations of wolf spiders, with particular reference to *Pardosa amentata* (Araneae, Lycosidae). Misc. Pap. Landb. Hogesch. Wageningen 8 (1971) 77

Riechert, S. E.: Thoughts on the ecological significance of spiders. Biol. Sci. 24 (1974) 352

Riechert, S. E.: Web-site selection in the desert spider *Agelenopsis aperta*. Oikos 27 (1976) 311

Robinson, B. C., M. H. Robinson: The biology of some *Argiope* species from New Guinea: Predatory behaviour and stabilimentum construction (Araneae: Araneidae). Zool. J. Linn. Soc. 54 (1974) 145

Robinson, M. H.: The evolution of predatory behaviour in araneid spiders. In *Function and Evolution in Behaviour*, edited by G. Baerends, C. Beer, and A. Manning (Oxford: Clarendon Press, 1975), p. 292

Robinson, M. H.: Ecology and behaviour of tropical spiders. Proc. 8th Int. Arachnol. Congr. (Vienna, 1980), p. 13

Robinson, M. H., H. Mirick: The predatory behaviour of the golden-web spider *Nephila clavipes* (Araneae: Araneidae) Psyche 78 (1971) 123

Robinson, M. H., B. Robinson: The predatory behaviour of the ogre-faced spider *Dinopis longipes* F. Cambridge. Amer. Midl. Natur. 85 (1971) 85

Robinson, M. H., B. Robinson: The structure, possible function and origin of the remarkable ladder-web built by a New Guinea orb-web spider. J. Nat. Hist. 6 (1972) 687

Robinson, M. H., B. Robinson: The stabilimenta of *Nephila clavipes* and the origins of stabilimentum-building in Araneids. Psyche 80 (1973) 277

Robinson, M. H., B. Robinson: Adaptive complexity: The thermoregulatory postures of the Golden-web spider, *Nephila clavipes*, at low latitudes. Amer. Midl. Natur. 92 (1974) 368

Robinson, M. H., B. Robinson: Evolution beyond the orb web: The web of the araneid spider *Pasilobus* sp., its structure, operation and construction. Zool. J. Linn. Soc. 56 (1975) 301

Robinson, M. H., B. Robinson: The evolution of courtship systems in tropical araneid spiders. Symp. Zool. Soc. Lond. 42 (1978) 17

Robinson, M. H., B. Robinson: Comparative studies of the courtship and mating behaviour of tropical araneid spiders. Pacific Insects Monogr. 36 (1980) 1

Rovner, J. S.: Courtship in spiders without prior sperm induction. Science 152 (1966) 543

Rovner, J. S.: Copulation and sperm induction by normal and palpless male Linyphiid spiders. Science 157 (1967) 835

Rovner, J. S.: An analysis of display in the lycosid spider *Lycosa rabida* Walckenaer. Anim. Behav. 16 (1968a) 358

Rovner, J. S.: Territoriality in the sheet-web spider *Linyphia triangularis* (Clerck) (Araneae, Linyphiidae). Z. Tierpsychol. 25 (1968b) 232

Rovner, J. S.: Sound production by nearctic wolf spiders: A substratum-coupled stridulatory mechanism. Science 190 (1975) 1309

Rovner, J. S.: Detritus stabilimenta on the webs of *Cyclosa turbinata* (Araneae, Araneidae). J. Arachnol. 4 (1976) 215

Rovner, J. S.: Adhesive hairs in spiders: Behavioral functions and hydraulically mediated movement. Symp. Zool. Soc. Lond. 42 (1978) 99

Rovner, J. S.: Vibration in *Heteropoda venatoria* (Sparassidae): A third method of sound production in spiders. J. Arachnol. 8 (1980a) 193

Rovner, J. S.: Adaptations for prey capture in oxyopid spiders: Phylogenetic implications. Proc. 8th Int. Congr. Arachnol. (Vienna, 1980b), p. 233

Rovner, J. S.: Morphological and ethological adaptations for prey capture in wolf spiders (Araneae, Lycosidae). J. Arachnol. 8 (1980c) 201

Rovner, J. S., S. J. Knost: Post-immobilization wrapping of prey by lycosid spiders of the herbaceous stratum. Psyche 81 (1974) 398

Rovner, J. S., G. A. Higashi, R. F. Foelix: Maternal behaviour in wolf spiders: The role of abdominal hairs. Science 182 (1973) 1153

Ruhland, M.: Die neuromuskuläre Organisation normaler und regenerierter Laufbeine einer Vogelspinne (*Dugesiella hentzi* Ch., Orthognatha, Aviculariidae). Diss., Konstanz, 1976

Ruhland, M., W. Rathmayer: Die Beinmuskulatur und ihre Innervation bei der Vogelspinne *Dugesiella hentzi* (Ch.) (Araneae, Aviculariidae). Zoomorphologie 89 (1978) 33

Sadana, G. L.: A note on the entry of eggs into the oviduct of *Lycosa chaperi* Simon (Lycosidae: Araneida). Science and Culture 36 (1970) 111

Saint Rémy, G.: Contribution à l'étude du cerveau chez les arthropodes trachéates. Arch. Zool. Exp. 5, Suppl. (1887) 1

Savory, T. H.: *The Biology of Spiders*. London: Sidgwick and Jackson, 1928

Savory, T. H.: *The Spider's Web*. London: Warne, 1952

Savory, T. H.: Daddy longlegs. Sci. Amer. 207 (1962) 119

Savory, T. H.: *Evolution in the Arachnida*. Watford, England: Merrow, 1971

Schaefer, M.: Ökologische Isolation und die Bedeutung des Konkurrenzfaktors am Beispiel des Verteilungsmusters der Lycosiden einer Küstenlandschaft. Oecologia 9 (1972) 171

Schaefer, M.: Experimentelle Untersuchungen zur Bedeutung der interspezifischen Konkurrenz bei 3 Wolfspinnen-Arten (Araneida Lycosidae) einer Salzwiese. Zool. Jb. Syst. 101 (1974) 213

Schaefer, M.: Experimentelle Untersuchungen zum Jahreszyklus und zur Überwinterung von Spinnen (Araneida). Zool. Jb. Syst. 103 (1976) 127

Schaefer, M.: Winter ecology of spiders (Araneida). Z. ang. Ent. 83 (1977) 113

Schanbacher, F. L., C. K. Lee, J. E. Hall, I. D. Wilson, D. E. Howell, G. V.

Odell: Composition and properties of tarantula *Dugesiella hentzi* (Girard) venom. Toxicon 11 (1973) 21

Scheuring, L.: Die Augen der Arachnoideen. Zool. Jb. Anat. 37 (1914) 369

Schildknecht, H., P. Kunzelmann, D. Krauss, C. Kuhn: Über die Chemie der Spinnwebe, I. Arthropodenabwehrstoffe. LVII Naturwissenschaften 59 (1972) 98

Schimkewitsch, W.: Etude sur l'anatomie de l'Epeire. Ann. Sci. Nat. 17 (1884) 7

Schmidt, G.: Giftspinnen—auch ein Problem des Ferntourismus. Münch. med. Wschr. 115 (1973) 2237

Schröer, W.-D.: Zum Mechanismus der Analyse polarisierten Lichtes bei *Agelena gracilens* C. L. Koch (Araneae, Agelenidae). Z. Morph. Tiere 79 (1974) 215

Schröer, W.-D.: Polarisationsempfindlichkeit rhabdomerialer Systeme in den Hauptaugen der Trichterspinne *Agelena gracilens* (Arachnida: Araneae: Agelenidae). Ent. Germ. 3 (1976) 88

Schröer, W.-D.: Personal communication (1977)

Seitz, K.-A.: Normale Entwicklung des Arachniden-Embryos *Cupiennius salei* Keyserling und seine Regenerationsfähigkeit nach Röntgenbestrahlung. Zool. Jb. Anat. 83 (1966) 327

Seitz, K.-A.: Embryonale Defekt- und Doppelbildungen im Ei der Spinne *Cupiennius salei* (Ctenidae) als Folgen röntgeninduzierter Koagulationsarbeiten. Zool Jb. Anat. 87 (1970) 588

Seitz, K.-A.: Licht- und elektronenmikroskopische Untersuchungen zur Ovarentwicklung und Oogenese bei *Cupiennius salei* Keys. (Araneae, Ctenidae). Z. Morph. Tiere 69 (1971) 283

Seitz, K.-A.: Zur Histologie und Feinstruktur des Herzens und der Hämocyten von *Cupiennius salei* Keys. (Araneae, Ctenidae). I. Herzwandung, Bildung und Differenzierung der Hämocyten. Zool. Jb. Anat. 89 (1972a) 351

Seitz, K.-A.: Zur Histologie und Feinstruktur des Herzens und der Hämocyten von *Cupiennius salei* Keys (Araneae, Ctenidae). II. Zur Funktionsmorphologie der Phagocyten. Zool. Jb. Anat. 89 (1972b) 385

Seitz, K.-A.: Elektronenmikroskopische Untersuchungen an den Guaninspeicherzellen von *Araneus diadematus* Clerck (Araneae, Araneidae). Z. Morph. Tiere 72 (1972c) 245

Seitz, K.-A.: Licht- und elektronenmikroskopische Untersuchungen an den Malpighischen Gefässen der Spinne *Cupiennius salei* Keys. (Ctenidae, Araneae). Zool. Jb. Anat. 94 (1975) 413

Seitz, K.-A.: Zur Feinstruktur der Häutungshämocyten von *Cupiennius salei* Keys. (Araneae, Ctenidae). Zool. Jb. Anat. 96 (1976) 280

Seyfarth, E.-A.: Daily patterns of locomotor activity in a wandering spider. Physiol. Entomol. 5 (1980) 199

Seyfarth, E.-A., F. G. Barth: Compound slit sense organs on the spider leg: Mechanoreceptors involved in kinesthetic orientation. J. Comp. Physiol. 78 (1972) 176

Shear, W. A.: The evolution of social phenomena in spiders. Bull. Brit. Arachnol. Soc. 1 (1970) 65

Sherman, R. G.: Ultrastructural features of cardiac muscle cells in a tarantula spider. J. Morph. 140 (1973a) 215

Sherman, R. G.: Ultrastructurally different hemocytes in a spider. Can. J. Zool. 51 (1973b) 1155

Sherman, R. G., A. R. Luff: Structural features of the tarsal claw muscles of the spider *Eurypelma marxi* Simon. Can. J. Zool. 49 (1971) 1549

Sherman, R. G., R. A. Pax: The heartbeat of the spider *Geolycosa missouriensis*. Comp. Biochem. Physiol. 26 (1968) 529

Sherman, R. G., R. A. Pax: The spider heart. In *Experiments in Physiology and Biochemistry*, edited by F. A. Kerkut (London: Academic Press, 1970a), p. 351

Sherman, R. G., R. A. Pax: Spider cardiac physiology. II. Responses of a tarantula heart to cholinergic compounds. Comp. Gen. Pharmacol. 1 (1970b) 171

Sherman, R. G., R. A. Pax: Spider cardiac physiology. III. Responses of a tarantula heart to certain catecholamines, amino acids, and 5-hydroxytryptamine. Comp. Gen. Pharmacol. 1 (1970c) 185

Sherman, R. G., C. R. Bursey, C. R. Fourtner, R. A. Pax: Cardiac ganglia in spiders (Arachnida, Araneae). Experientia (Basel) 25 (1969) 438

Simon, E.: Histoire naturelle des Araignées, vol. 1, p. 1084; vol. 2, p. 1030 (Paris: Librairie Encyclopédique de Roret, 1892– 1903)

Smith, D. S., U. Järlfors, F. E. Russell: The fine structure of muscle attachments in a spider (*Latrodectus mactans*, Fabr.). Tissue and Cell 1 (1969) 673

Sotelo, J. R., O. Trujillo-Cenóz: Electron microscope study of the vitellin body of some spider oocytes. J. Biophys. Biochem. Cytol. 3 (1957) 301

Stewart, D. M., A. W. Martin: Blood and fluid balance of the common tarantula, *Dugesiella hentzi*. Z. vergl. Physiol. 70 (1970) 223

Stewart, D. M., A. W. Martin: Blood pressure in the tarantula, *Dugesiella hentzi*. J. Comp. Physiol. 88 (1974) 141

Størmer, L.: Chelicerata. In *Treatise on Invertebrate Paleontology, Arthropoda 2*, edited by R. C. Moore (Lawrence, Kan.: University of Kansas Press, 1955), p. 1

Stowe, M. K.: Observations of two nocturnal orb weavers that build specialized webs: *Scoloderus cordatus* and *Wixia ectypa* (Araneae: Araneidae). J. Arachnol. 6 (1978) 141

Streble, H.: Untersuchungen über das hormonale System der Spinnentiere (Chelicerata) unter besonderer Berücksichtigung des "endokrinen Gewebes" der Spinnen (Araneae). Zool. Jb. Physiol. 72 (1966) 157

Szlep, R.: Developmental changes in the web-spinning instinct of Uloboridae: Construction of the primary-type web. Behaviour 17 (1961) 60

Thornhill, R.: Scorpionflies as kleptoparasites of web-building spiders. Nature (London) 258 (1975) 709

Tietjen, W. J.: Dragline-following by male lycosid spiders. Psyche 84 (1977) 165

Tietjen, W. J.: Tests for olfactory communication in four species of wolf spiders (Araneae, Lycosidae). J. Arachnol. 6 (1979a) 197

Tietjen, W. J.: Is the sex pheromone of *Lycosa rabida* (Araneae, Lycosidae) deposited on a substratum? J. Arachnol. 6 (1979b) 207

Tietjen, W. J., J. S. Rovner: Trail-following behaviour in two species of wolf spiders: Sensory and etho-ecological concomitants. Anim. Behav. 28 (1980) 735

Tolbert, W. W.: Aerial dispersal behavior of two orb weaving spiders. Psyche 84 (1977) 13

Tretzel, E.: Reife- und Fortpflanzungszeit bei Spinnen. Z. Morph. Ökol. Tiere 42 (1954) 634

Tretzel, E.: Intragenerische Isolation und interspezifische Konkurrenz bei Spinnen. Z. Morph. Ökol. Tiere 44 (1955) 43

Tretzel, E.: Zum Begegnungsverhalten von Spinnen. Zool. Anz. 163 (1959) 194

Tretzel, E.: Biologie, Ökologie und Brutpflege von *Coelotes terrestries* (Wider) (Araneae, Agelenidae), Teil I: Biologie und Ökologie. Z. Morph. Ökol. Tiere 49 (1961a) 658

Tretzel, E.: Biologie, Ökologie und Brutpflege von *Coelotes terrestris* (Wider) (Araneae, Agelenidae), Teil II: Brutpflege. Z. Morph. Ökol. Tiere 50 (1961b) 375

Trujillo-Cenóz, O.: Some aspects of the structural organization of the arthropod eye. Cold Harbor Symp. Quant. Biol. 30 (1965) 371

Turnbull, A. L.: The prey of the spider *Linyphia triangularis* (Clerck) (Araneae, Linyphiidae). Can. J. Zool. 38 (1960) 859

Turnbull, A. L.: Quantitative studies of the food of *Linyphia triangularis* Clerck (Araneae: Linyphiidae). Can. Entomol. 94 (1962) 1233

Turnbull, A. L.: The search for prey by a web-building spider *Achaearanea tepidariorum* (C. L. Koch) (Araneae, Theridiidae). Can. Entomol. 96 (1964) 568

Turnbull, A. L.: Ecology of the true spiders (Araneomorphae). Ann. Rev. Entomol. 18 (1973) 305

Ude, J., K. Richter: The submicroscopic morphology of the heart ganglion of the spider *Tegenaria atrica* (C. L. Koch) and its neuroendocrine relations to the myocard. Comp. Biochem. Physiol. 48A (1974) 301

Vachon, M.: Contribution à l'étude du développement postembryonnaire des araigneés. Première note. Généralités et nomenclature des stades. Bull. Soc. Zool. France 82 (1957) 337

Van Wingerden, W. K. R. E., H. F. Vugts: Factors influencing aeronautic behaviour of spiders. Bull. Brit. Arachnol. Soc. 3 (1974) 6

Vogel, B. R.: Individual interactions of *Pardosa*. Armadillo Papers 5 (1971) 1

Vogel, B. R.: Apparent niche sharing of two *Pardosa* species (Araneidae, Lycosidae). Armadillo Papers 7 (1972) 1

Vollrath, F.: Konkurrenzvermeidung bei tropischen kleptoparasitischen Haubennetzspinnen der Gattung *Argyrodes* (Arachnida: Araneae: Theridiidae). Ent. Germ. 3 (1976) 104

Vollrath, F.: A close relationship between two spiders (Arachnida, Araneidae): *Curimagua bayano* synecious on a *Diplura* species. Psyche 85 (1978) 347

Vollrath, F.: Behaviour of the kleptoparasitic spider *Argyrodes elevatus* (Araneae, Theridiidae). Anim. Behav. 27 (1979b) 515

Vollrath, F.: Male body size and fitness in the web-building spider *Nephila clavipes*. Z. Tierpsychol. 53 (1980) 61

Vugts, H. F., W. K. R. E. van Wingerden: Meteorological aspects of aeronautic behaviour of spiders. Oikos 27 (1976) 433

Walcott, C., W. G. van der Kloot: The physiology of the spider vibration receptor. J. Exp. Zool. 141 (1959) 191

Wallstabe, P.: Beiträge zur Kenntnis der Entwicklungsgeschichte der Araneinen. Die Entwicklung der äusseren Form und Segmentierung. Zool. Jb. Anat. 26 (1908) 683

Wehner, R.: Polarized-light navigation by insects. Sci. Amer. 235 (1976) 106

Weigel, G.: Färbung und Farbwechsel der Krabbenspinne *Misumena vatia*. Z. vergl. Physiol. 29 (1941) 195

Weygoldt, P.: Communication in crustaceans and arachnids. In *How Animals Communicate*, edited by T. A. Sebeok (Bloomington, Ind.: Indiana University Press, 1977), p. 303

Whitehead, W. F., J. G. Rempel: A study of the musculature of the Black Widow spider, *Latrodectus mactans* (Fabr.). Can. J. Zool. 37 (1959) 831

Wiehle, H.: Beiträge zur Kenntnis des Radnetzbaues der Epeiriden, Tetragnathiden und Uloboriden. Z. Morph. Ökol. Tiere 8 (1927) 468

Wiehle, H.: Beiträge zur Biologie der Araneen, insbesondere zur Kenntnis des Radnetzbaues. Z. Morph. Ökol. Tiere 11 (1928) 115

Wiehle, H.: Weitere Beiträge zur Biologie der Araneen, insbesondere zur Kenntnis des Radnetzbaues. Z. Morph. Ökol. Tiere 15 (1929) 262

Wiehle, H.: Neue Beiträge zur Kenntnis des Fanggewebes der Spinnen aus den Familien Argiopidae, Uloboridae und Theridiidae. Z. Morph. Ökol. Tiere 22 (1931) 349

Wiehle, H.: *Vom Fanggewebe einheimischer Spinnen*. Neue Brehm-Bücherei. Akademische Verlagsgesellschaft (Leipzig: Geest and Portig, 1949)

Wiehle, H.: Der Embolus des männlichen Spinnentasters. Zool. Anz., Suppl. 24 (1961) 457

Wiehle, H.: Meta—eine semientelegyne Gattung der Araneae (Arach.). Senck. biol. 48 (1967) 183

Willem, V.: Observations sur la circulation sanguine et la respiration pulmonaire chez les araignées. Arch. néerl. sci. 1 (1918) 226

Wilson, D. M.: Stepping patterns in tarantula spiders. J. Exp. Biol. 47 (1967) 133

Wilson, E. O.: *The Insect Societies* (Cambridge, Mass.: Harvard University Press, 1971), p. 130

Wilson, R. S.: The structure of the dragline control valves in the garden spider. Quart. J. Micr. Sci. 103 (1962a) 549

Wilson, R. S.: The control of the dragline spinning in the garden spider. Quart. J. Micr. Sci. 104 (1962b) 557

Wilson, R. S.: The heartbeat of the spider *Heteropoda venatoria*. J. Insect Physiol. 13 (1967) 1309

Wilson, R. S.: Some comments on the hydrostatic system of spiders (Chelicerata, Araneae). Z. Morph. Tiere 68 (1970) 308

Wilson, R. S., J. Bullock: The hydraulic interaction between prosoma and opisthosoma in *Amaurobius ferox* (Chelicerata, Araneae). Z. Morph. Tiere 74 (1973) 221

Wise, D. L.: Food limitation of the spider *Linyphia marginata:* Experimental food studies. Ecology 56 (1975) 637

Witt, P. N.: *Die Wirkung von Substanzen auf den Netzbau der Spinne als biologischer Test.* Berlin: Springer, 1956

Witt, P. N.: Behavioral consequences of laser lesions in the central nervous system of *Araneus diadematus* Cl. Amer. Zool. 9 (1969) 121

Witt, P. N.: Drugs alter web-building of spiders: A review and evaluation. Behav. Sci. 16 (1971) 98

Witt, P. N.: The web as a means of communication. Biosci. Comm. 1 (1975) 7

Witt, P. N., C. F. Reed: Spider web building. Measurement of web geometry identifies components in a complex invertebrate behaviour pattern. Science 149 (1965) 1190

Witt, P. N., J. O. Rawlings, C. F. Reed: Ontogeny of web-building behaviour in two orb-weaving spiders. Amer. Zool. 12 (1972) 445

Witt, P. N., C. F. Reed, D. B. Peakall: *A spider's web.* Berlin: Springer, 1968

Witt, P. N., M. B. Scarboro, D. B. Peakall, R. Gause: Spider web-building in outer space: Evaluation of records from the Skylab spider experiment. Amer. J. Arachnol. 4 (1977) 115

von Wittich, G. H.: Observationes quaedam de Aranearum ex ovo evolutione. Inaug.-Diss., Halle, 1845

Yamashita, S., H. Tateda: Spectral sensitivities of jumping spider eyes. J. Comp. Physiol. 105 (1976) 29

Yoshikura, M.: Comparative embryology and phylogeny of Arachnida. J. Sci. Biol. 12 (1975) 71

Young, M. R., F. Wanless: Observations on fluorescence and function of spider's eyes. J. Zool. Proc. Zool. Soc. (Lond.) 151 (1967) 1

Zebe, E., W. Rathmayer: Elektronenmikroskopische Untersuchungen an Spinnenmuskeln. Z. Zellforsch. 92 (1968) 377

Zimmermann, E. W.: Untersuchungen über den Bau des Mundhöhlendaches der Gewebespinnen. Rev. Suisse Zool. 41 (1934) 149

Index